Not Guilty

Not Guilty

Are the Acquitted Innocent?

Daniel Givelber and Amy Farrell

NEW YORK UNIVERSITY PRESS

New York and London

NEW YORK UNIVERSITY PRESS
New York and London
www.nyupress.org

References to Internet websites (URLs) were accurate at the time of writing.
Neither the author nor New York University Press is responsible for URLs
that may have expired or changed since the manuscript was prepared.

Library of Congress Cataloging-in-Publication Data
Givelber, Daniel.
Not guilty : are the acquitted innocent? / Daniel Givelber and Amy Farrell.
p.   cm.
Includes bibliographical references and index.
ISBN 978-0-8147-3217-5 (cl : alk. paper) — ISBN 978-0-8147-2534-4 (ebook)
ISBN 978-0-8147-4440-6 (ebook)
1. Judicial error—United States. 2. Criminal procedure—United States.
3. Criminal justice, Administration of—United States. 4. Jury—United
States. 5. Judges—United States.   I. Farrell, Amy. II. Title.
KF9756.G59 2012
345.73'0122—dc23   2011052263

New York University Press books are printed on acid-free paper,
and their binding materials are chosen for strength and durability.
We strive to use environmentally responsible suppliers and materials
to the greatest extent possible in publishing our books.

Manufactured in the United States of America

10 9 8 7 6 5 4 3 2 1

Contents

Tables

Preface

      This book examines the question of whether those found "not guilty" are actually innocent of the crime charged. We return to a question supposedly resolved definitively a half-century ago when Harry Kalven and Hans Zeisel reported in their classic 1966 monograph *The American Jury* that judges believed that most jury acquittals were (a) inaccurate and (b) attributable to the jury's embrace of values. Our criminal justice system was doing its job. Jurors were convicting the guilty except when there was a good reason for them to ignore the formal demands of the law and acquit despite the law. In these cases, jurors were believed to be embracing the values of the community and guarding against the blind application of the law in situations where community sentiment dictated otherwise. This process was hardly benign in all of its manifestations—jurors could ignore the evidence and acquit those who murdered civil rights workers as readily as they could exonerate peace activists who crossed a police line to protest at the Pentagon. On the whole, though, the message was a comforting one—an acquitting jury was likely to have tempered the law with mercy and thus served one of its highest and best purposes.

    As a rationalization for the criminal justice system, this view covered "all the bases." If the acquitted were actually guilty, we did not need to blame the police for failing to correctly identify the suspect or amass the evidence. The acquittal of the guilty might suggest that the prosecutor did not perform admirably, but the more likely culprit in the eyes of the public was the Supreme Court's overly broad interpretation of the Constitution, which appeared to award criminal defendants unfair advantages both before and at trial. In the view of critics, liberal judges with no accountability to the electorate were freeing the guilty through an interpretation of the Constitution that shackled the police in their effort to suppress crime. Unless the police and prosecutors were punctilious in their observance of often obscure constitutional demands, evidence could and would be excluded and the obviously guilty would go free. The public and its elected representatives might well wonder whether courts and prosecutors were "too soft" on criminals, but there was no reason to be concerned that they were "too hard" on the innocent.

Long before the DNA revolution in the 1990s revealed that some *convictions* were erroneous, courts, legislatures, and sentencing authorities shared the view that *acquittals* were likely to be *factually inaccurate* even if legally appropriate. The defendant "did it" even if the prosecutor failed to persuade twelve jurors beyond a reasonable doubt. A jury may acquit because prosecution witnesses prove unconvincing or evasive or simply fail to appear. Jurors may be confused by the evidence or misled by the silver-tongued oratory of the defense counsel. Jurors may fall into error and credit the (false) testimony of the defendant and his witnesses. Those who administer and adjudicate know of these possibilities and often attempt to remedy the wrongs of jury acquittals in subsequent legal proceedings. Thus, acquittals represent a one-time failure by the prosecution to persuade a jury of guilt beyond a reasonable doubt rather than a positive indication that the defendant did not commit the crime. Should an acquitted defendant be prosecuted in a later unrelated case, the defendant can be treated as having committed the earlier crime for a variety of purposes. These range from the setting of bail to the impeachment (discrediting) of the defendant's testimony to the severity of the sentence he receives if convicted. These practices are justified legally by reference to the prosecution's burden of proof, which is to convince the jury of the defendant's guilt beyond a reasonable doubt. If the jury believes such a doubt exists, it should acquit even if it also believes that the defendant is *probably* guilty. Given this legal framework, many observers consider it but a short step to the conclusion that the difference between the convicted and the acquitted is not whether the defendant committed the crime (he did) but whether or not either the prosecution or the jury did its job poorly. There are no innocents.

Much has happened in the years since Kalven and Zeisel wrote *The American Jury* that suggests that we need to reexamine the view that, the jury's verdict notwithstanding, only the guilty stand trial. The work of the Innocence Project, in particular, has led to a sea change in our collective attitude toward this perception. That work—and the scholarly inquiry it has spawned—has properly commanded the attention of all interested in how our criminal justice system operates.[1] It has led to the creation of Innocence Projects in forty-four states.[2] It has demonstrated that, on occasion, we err when we convict even those whose guilt seems most apparent. What, then, of those whom the jury *acquits*? Have courts and legislatures been correct that they are simply beneficiaries of prosecutorial lapses or defense pyrotechnics? Or are the wrongfully convicted but the tip of the iceberg of those who are charged with crimes that they did not commit?

We suggest that there is much to commend the latter view—juries acquit because of the evidence, not in spite of it. Acquittals are evidence—not sentiment—based. Defendants go free because the state has failed to provide sufficient persuasive evidence of their guilt. What accounts for the state's failure to offer persuasive evidence? While there are many possible explanations, the most likely is that the defendant is not guilty of the crime and the state's effort to convict him or her reflects an attempt to establish a proposition that is simply false.

We do not (because we cannot) claim to have special knowledge as to whether a jury verdict of not guilty is correct or not. By definition, the acquittals we examine are not cases that involve dispositive forensic evidence—particularly DNA evidence. The cases we examine were tried at a time when DNA techniques were widely available, so it seems fair to conclude that these are not cases in which there was an obvious scientific test that might conceivably have persuaded all observers that the defendant either did or did not commit the crime in question. What we can do is empirically compare acquittals with other dispositions to determine whether they differ in ways that are consistent with innocence. If the answer to this question is in the affirmative

—and we will demonstrate that it is—we leave it to others to demonstrate why the simplest explanation for acquittals—innocence—may not be the correct one.

The conclusions drawn here are the product of collaboration between a law professor and a social scientist. Given our different disciplinary backgrounds, we came to the challenge of understanding acquittals from different perspectives. The law professor's perspective is that of someone long skeptical of the claim that criminal trials resulting in convictions reflect the objective truth about the defendant's behavior while those resulting in acquittals do not. In part, this skepticism flows from the experience, now many years in the past, of having been a prosecutor in more than twenty-five criminal jury trials. In part, it is triggered by the courts' "head I win, tails you lose" approach to the outcome of criminal trials. Convictions represent the truth, acquittals the failure of proof.

The judicial embrace of these practices finds support in Kalven and Zeisel's research presented in *The American Jury* and its comforting but empirically questionable finding that when judge and jury disagree about guilt, they do so because the judge evaluates the evidence objectively while the jury is moved by sentiment. It is unusual, if not downright weird, to determine how a group arrived at a decision by valorizing the explanation provided by an observer—even an experienced observer—who disagreed with the decision. If we are going to embrace the policy of treating acquitted individuals as though they were guilty, at the least we ought to try to understand the views of those who rendered the verdict—the jurors themselves. From a social science perspective, questions about the accuracy of acquittals in criminal trials should be addressed through empirical research. Since modern assumptions about the process by which juries arrive at acquittals are informed largely by research conducted over fifty years ago, it is timely to revisit questions of the meaning of acquittals through empirical research with more recent data and more sophisticated empirical techniques. Additionally, new sources of data allow us to address deficiencies in previous research, most notably the need to include the experiences and perceptions of jurors, who are the actual decision makers in criminal trials. Too long has our understanding of their actions, particularly our understanding of why they reach conclusions about guilt that differ from judges' conclusions, been limited to the assumptions of the judiciary. A ground-breaking study into hung juries[3] by researchers from the National Center for State Courts (NCSC) in 2000–2001 provides a rich source of data from which we attempt to develop a more complete understanding of acquittals in the modern context. Using data information provided by judges and juries for more than three hundred criminal trials conducted in 1999–2000 in four jurisdictions—the Bronx, Maricopa and Los Angeles Counties, as well as the District of Columbia—we seek to understand the meaning of acquittals. While we did not collect this data, we recognized its potential to answer long-neglected questions about the meaning of acquittals and the role of juries in the process of arriving at acquittals in the modern context. We are greatly indebted to the work of the NCSC researchers for developing a rich source of data that allowed us to undertake the research for this book.

Acknowledgments

This book would not have been possible without the support of our colleagues and friends. Many people—more than we can name—contributed to the ideas presented in this book. Colleagues at the School of Criminology and Criminal Justice, School of Law, and Institute on Race and Justice supported our work on this project and encouraged our continued scholarship on issues of justice. We are grateful to the members of the Northeastern University School of Criminology and Criminal Justice writing seminar for their thoughtful feedback on early versions of chapters. Particularly, we thank Nicole Rafter, who leads the workshop. From the initial book proposal to the development of substantive chapters, she provided invaluable guidance on strategies for framing an empirically rich book, as well as read our work as we went along. We are both greatly indebted to Jack McDevitt for his insight into the serious problems of justice that we sought to address through our research and writing. He helped foster this interdisciplinary partnership and continually supported our collaborative law and social science approach. Thank you to the graduate and undergraduate research assistants at the Institute on Race and Justice who helped us find newspaper articles, dug through archival records, and assisted with the formatting of numerous data tables. In addition, at the very real risk of underinclusion, we would like to thank Stan Fisher, Jim McCloskey, Michael Meltsner, Jonathan Oberman, Michael Radelet, and Steve Subrin for their feedback and intellectual contributions to our thinking about the issues addressed in this book.

We are extremely grateful to Paula Hannaford-Agor, Valarie Hans, Nicole Mott, Thomas Munsterman, and the research team at the Center for State Courts, who originally collected much of the data that we use in this book to examine questions about jury decision making and acquittals. While their data was originally collected for a different purpose—to provide an empirical picture of hung juries—we found it to be well suited to addressing other types of questions about jury decision making, particularly in illuminating the circumstances in criminal cases where judges and juries disagreed about the correct legal outcome. We recognize the immense effort that it took to collect the original data from court records and detailed surveys of judges, attorneys, and jury members participating in criminal trials. By facilitating public access to their data through the Inter-University Consortium for Political and Social Research, the National Center for State Court research team has facilitated new avenues for research beyond the original designs of their project. Our research would not have been possible without access to such a rich and unique source of data about judge and jury perceptions of the facts presented in criminal trials.

We extend a heartfelt thanks to the editorial staff at New York University Press. In particular, we would like to thank our editor, Ilene Kalish, and her assistant, Aiden Amos, for their continued support and encouragement of this project. They provided helpful feedback and suggestions throughout all stages of this project. Additionally, we are grateful to the reviewers, whose thoughtful suggestions and comments greatly improved the book.

Finally, we would like to thank our respective spouses, Fran and Shea, without whose continued support and encouragement this project would remain only a disconnected set of ideas and ambitions. Thank you for allowing us the many late nights and weekend hours we spent conducting analysis and writing. Your willingness to provide both a sounding board for new ideas and the patience to allow us space to think and write made this book possible.

1

Introduction

Invisible Innocence

> A woman who was acquitted of beating her husband to death
> with a baseball bat cannot be declared innocent because
> enough evidence pointed to her guilt, the California Supreme
> Court ruled unanimously Thursday.[1]

This headline is not an oxymoron. Jeanie Louise Adair, tried for the murder of her husband in 1999, was found "not guilty" by the jury. She then went to court to do what California law permitted: secure a formal judicial determination that she was factually innocent of the crime. The California Supreme Court refused her request because the prosecution had presented enough evidence that it would have been permissible for the jury to return a guilty verdict. Because a different jury, looking at the identical evidence, may have come to a different conclusion, she can never be declared innocent. Her status —found not guilty but not declared innocent—confronts virtually every person a jury acquits of criminal charges. Precisely because there is a gap between a verdict of not guilty and an affirmative determination that the defendant is innocent, those who administer the criminal justice system can, and typically do, treat acquittals as counterfactual. In essence, "they are all guilty" whether the state succeeded in proving it or not. As Edwin Meese, United States attorney general under President Ronald Reagan, once explained, "But the thing is, you don't have many suspects who are innocent of a crime. That's contradictory. If a person is innocent of crime, then he is not a suspect."[2]

At first blush, the data regarding case outcomes seem to support this view both when Meese spoke and today. Only one out of every one hundred individuals formally charged with a crime will be found not guilty following a trial.[3] And a not guilty verdict does not necessarily signal actual innocence. One can be acquitted for reasons unrelated to actual innocence (e.g., because the state's evidence is shaky or a jury's sentiment overwhelms its commitment to accuracy or the defendant is an accomplished liar), so even the one in one hundred who is acquitted is not necessarily innocent of the crime charged. Indeed, many observers suggest that it is more likely that an acquitted person is *guilty* than that she is innocent.[4]

Judges in criminal cases tell jurors that they must presume that the accused are not guilty of the crimes charged. They also tell jurors that prosecutors are obliged to introduce evidence to persuade them beyond any reasonable doubt that the defendants are guilty. If the state succeeds in doing so, then juries must convict. If the state fails to eliminate reasonable doubt about guilt, juries must acquit. A not guilty verdict says something definitive about the evidence that the state introduced: it was insufficient to eliminate all reasonable doubt about guilt from the minds of the jurors. But acquittals do not answer, nor even address, the question of whether defendants are *factually innocent.* All we know is that the juries were not persuaded that the defendants committed the crimes charged.

Designed to ensure that the innocent are protected to the greatest extent humanly possible, this arrangement results in what has been aptly termed *adjudicatory asymmetry,* the belief that guilt is based on a factual conclusion concerning the defendant's behavior whereas an acquittal reflects only an absence of proof.[5] We know (or believe we know) that the convicted are guilty of the crime because the evidence has eliminated every reasonable doubt. We do not know that the acquitted are innocent; the not guilty verdict may be a product of the government's very high burden of proof in a criminal case or the jury's failure to follow instructions or the failure of a key witness to testify as expected or a jury's dislike of the law involved or a distrust of the state's witnesses. Any of these reasons may result in reasonable doubt about guilt, and that doubt exonerates.

Because it is not an affirmative declaration of innocence, an acquittal does not preclude the state or others from showing that the defendant committed the crime in question when the test is whether the defendant's guilt is more probable than not. For example, in one of the most famous criminal prosecutions of the last quarter-century, the jury in the criminal case acquitting O. J. Simpson of murder did not preclude a different jury finding that it was more probable than not that he did commit the murder in the civil suit when the victim's families sought money damages.[6] Nor does the acquittal necessarily preclude a judge from giving Simpson a longer sentence than would otherwise be appropriate if he is convicted of a different crime.[7] Finally, should Simpson ever be charged with even more crimes, the state may be able to introduce evidence of the murders of Nicole Simpson and Ronald Goldman to demonstrate a pattern of criminal behavior. In his case, at least, prosecutors, courts, and most of the rest of us do not believe that his acquittal meant he was innocent.

Acquittals are essentially invisible. We know very little about why juries or judges conclude that defendants are not guilty. Because the vast majority of research concerning those accused of crime is based upon sentencing or prison data, we also know very little about those who are found not guilty; the acquitted have no race, gender, or social class. In practice, most prosecutors, defense counsel, and judges encounter the acquitted very infrequently. If we combine criminal cases resolved through guilty pleas and dismissals (the overwhelming majority) with the relatively few cases resolved by verdicts after trial, we find that an acquittal occurs approximately once in every one hundred cases.[8] Given these statistics, it is perhaps not surprising that, with a notable exception, acquittals have remained unexamined by social scientists, legal scholars, and policymakers. Rather, they are treated as random events "signifying nothing" about the actual guilt or innocence of those prosecuted for crime.

Our collective indifference to acquittals reverberates beyond the injustice of ignoring, in a subsequent civil suit or criminal prosecution, the possibility that a jury acquittal signals innocence. If we do not know *why* the jury acquits, we can ignore the possibility that innocents are charged and prosecuted fully. An acquittal can be (and typically is) treated as a *failure* by the police, the prosecutor, the jury, or any combination of those entities to do their respective jobs appropriately rather than as the successful exoneration of the innocent. We can ignore claims that plea bargaining may force the innocent falsely to admit guilt simply to avoid the draconian penalty attached to the conviction of certain crimes. If we ignore acquittals—if we accept that "defendants are acquitted for many reasons, the least likely being innocence"[9]—we reduce criminal justice outcomes to extremely accurate, if sometimes harsh, convictions and very inaccurate, if sometimes emotionally understandable, acquittals. To paraphrase, convictions are from Mars, acquittals from Venus.

What We Think We Know about Acquittals

What we think we know about acquittals comes essentially from three sources: (1) a study of nearly four thousand mid-twentieth century criminal jury trials by University of Chicago law professors Harry Kalven and Han Zeisel,[10] considered the seminal study of judge-jury decision making, and a handful of studies conducted to attempt to replicate its conclusions; (2) depictions of acquittals in popular culture; and (3) anecdotes. The picture is incomplete. Anecdotes and media presentations focus upon the counterintuitive: "guilty man acquitted" and "innocent man convicted" stories are more interesting than trials in which juries arrive at correct verdicts. They tell us little about the frequency or nature of trials in which the jury produced accurate results. Although Kalven and Zeisel provided an in-depth analysis of the *trial judge's* explanation for the reasons why the jury acquitted when the judge would have convicted, they were not able to provide any direct information about what the people who decided the case, the jurors themselves, thought or believed. In this book, we have been able to extend our understanding of acquittals through utilizing new data gathered from jurors, judges, prosecutors, and defense counsel in four jurisdictions: the Bronx, the District of Columbia, Los Angeles, and Maricopa County, Arizona. Although these data were originally collected and analyzed by the National Center for State Courts (NCSC) in 2002 to study hung juries,[11] they are a unique source of information to help us develop a more complete understanding of acquittals in the modern context.

The American Jury, published in 1966, contained an analysis of the results of a survey conducted in the mid-1950s. Kalven and Zeisel asked hundreds of judges to assess jury verdicts in terms of how the judges would have decided the cases. They found that judges agreed with the jury verdicts in 78 percent of all cases; when they disagreed, juries were far more likely to acquit when the judges would have convicted (19 percent of all cases) than they were to convict when the judges would have acquitted (3 percent of all cases). Judges and juries agreed that acquittals were appropriate in only 14 percent of all cases. Sir William Blackstone insisted, "The law holds, that it is better that ten guilty escape, than that one innocent suffer";[12] and Kalven and Zeisel's data suggested that something like this was occurring.

Kalven and Zeisel were not content simply to report that juries were more acquittal prone than judges. They sought to explain *why* juries were more lenient than judges in nearly one out of five cases. Noting that a significant majority of all cases in which the juries were more lenient than the judges involved issues of both fact and values, the authors suggested that because of the existence of "evidentiary difficulty," the juries were "liberated" to consider nonevidentiary factors—"sentiments," in their lexicon—in resolving the questions of fact. More simply put, close cases "liberated" the juries to consider values; and this consideration frequently resulted in juries acquitting when the judges would have convicted.[13] As they eloquently put it, the jury "yields to sentiment in the apparent process of resolving doubts as to evidence. The jury, therefore, is able to conduct its revolt from the law within the etiquette of resolving issues of fact."[14] Apparently, judges were immune from the influence of sentiment.

Kalven and Zeisel's liberation hypothesis has largely guided our understanding and interpretation of jury decision making and has arguably shaped the direction and scope of social science research on juries since its publication.[15] Their work, and its impact on our understanding of acquittals, is the focus of the next chapter.

The representation of trials and their outcomes in popular culture resonates with Kalven and Zeisel's finding that juries embrace senti-ment when jurors acquit those whom judges would have convicted. Courtroom scenes and trials are so common in movies, television, and literature that a majority of our experience with criminal adju-dication and our expectations of it come from things we see or read as opposed to our direct experiences.[16] Although the representation of trials and their outcomes in the American media is not static, little attention has been paid to the experiences of defendants who are ac-quitted of crimes.[17] Unlike real life, where the facts are contested, in fictional accounts, the viewer or reader is generally let in on the truth through flashbacks to the events in question. Heroic lawyer characters, either defense lawyers fighting tirelessly for their (possibly) wrongfully accused clients or prosecutors upholding the values and wisdom of the state, then represent the truth that as audience members we al-ready understand.[18] Rarely do fictional judges or juries return verdicts that contradict this truth, comforting the public that through the ag-gressive presentation of the defense and prosecution cases, the legal process arrives at the morally, if not always legally, correct result.

Anecdotes from those who practice criminal law also tend to con-firm the view that to be charged is to be factually guilty. Advocates for a zealous defense seem to delight in the irrelevance of a defendant's potential or actual innocence to their work. As noted criminal defense attorney Alan Dershowitz asserted,

> The Perry Mason image of the criminal lawyer saving his innocent client by uncovering the real culprit is television fiction; it rarely hap-pens in real life. Almost all criminal defendants—including most of my clients—are factually guilty of the crimes they have been charged with. The criminal lawyer's job, for the most part, is to represent the guilty, and—if possible—to get them off.[19]

Defense lawyer Martin Erdmann famously opined in an article in *Life* magazine extolling his virtues, "I have nothing to do with justice. Jus-tice is not part of the equation."[20] Not surprisingly, prosecutors tend to agree that defense victories are counterfactual. When a jury acquit-ted the actor Robert Blake of murder in 2005, the district attorney for

Los Angeles County informed the press that the jury was "incredibly stupid."[21]

Anecdotes suggest that actual trials are lessons in civics, and acquittals are the price society pays for taking so seriously the obligation that the government has to be able to demonstrate guilt convincingly in open court. No criminal case in the past quarter-century has captured the public attention as much as the O. J. Simpson murder trial, a case in which the verdict is almost universally perceived as historically inaccurate. As one commentator characterized it, criminal adjudication is an administrative process, with trials operating as the occasional adjudicatory hearing designed to assure that the government is administering fairly.[22]

How Often Acquittals Occur

Statistics of criminal case dispositions in the largest urban counties in the United States (see table 1.1) indicate that 68 percent of the individuals charged with felony offenses were actually convicted of crimes (either felonies or misdemeanors). Of those who were convicted, the overwhelming majority (approximately 97 percent) pled guilty. Dismissals accounted for another 23 percent of the cases, acquittals but 1 percent. The remaining approximately 8 percent of cases were either disposed through alternatives to traditional criminal punishment or resolved in the following year.[23] This pattern has been very consistent over time. In the last sixteen years that adjudication data have been reported by the U.S. Bureau of Justice Statistics, acquittals have consistently accounted for only 1 percent of all case outcomes.[24]

According to the Bureau of Justice Statistics data, only 3 percent of all criminal cases were actually resolved through trials in which judges or juries rendered verdicts of guilt or innocence.[25] Of the small proportion of cases that did go to trial, approximately one-third resulted in acquittals. Thus, although acquittals represented only a tiny fraction of criminal dispositions, they represented a much larger proportion of those rare cases that did go to trial.

TABLE 1.1

Adjudication Outcomes for Felony Defendants in Large Urban Counties (2004)

Most serious arrest charge	No. of defendants	% convicted	Convicted of felonies			Convicted of misdemeanors			Not convicted		
			Total	% plea	% trial	Total	% plea	% trial	% dismissed	% acquitted	% other outcome*
All offenses	51,256	68	59	57	2	9	9	—**	23	1	9
Violent offenses	11,091	61	52	49	3	9	9	—	34	1	5
Property offenses	15,934	72	62	60	2	10	9	—	20	—	8
Drug offenses	19,022	67	60	58	1	8	8	—	19	—	14
Public-order offenses	5,209	72	61	59	2	11	10	—	23	1	6
Weapons	1,587	71	61	59	2	9	8	1	27	1	2
Driving-related	1,642	81	73	70	3	8	8	—	12	1	7

Source: Tracy Kyckelhahn and Thomas Cohen, "Felony Defendants in Large Urban Counties, 2004." Statistical Tables, Table 19, "Adjudication Outcome for Felony Defendants, by Most Serious Arrest Charge, 2004," Bureau of Justice Statistics, Washington, DC.

Note: Eleven percent of all cases were still pending adjudication at the end of the one-year study period and are excluded from the data in this table. Data on adjudication outcomes were available for 99 percent of those cases that had been adjudicated during the study period. Detail may not add to total because of rounding.

* Includes diversion and deferred adjudication. Murder defendants were followed for an additional year.

** Denotes less than .05 percent.

When Acquittals Are Legally Appropriate

As a technical matter, an acquittal reflects the fact finder's judgment that the state has failed to offer evidence sufficient to establish the defendant's guilt beyond a reasonable doubt. This leaves open the possibility that the state was correct that the defendant committed the crime but simply failed to persuade twelve laypersons or a judge that this was the case. Double jeopardy precludes the state from appealing acquittals, so there are no appellate court rulings clarifying when an acquittal is appropriate and when it is not. When the jury or judge returns a not guilty verdict, *legal* inquiry ceases. Those acquittals that do result in further popular or scholarly inquiry (e.g., O. J. Simpson) support the view that acquittals tell us little other than that juries are capable of behaving irrationally.

Actual innocence is difficult to verify. Courts virtually never address or rule upon the question of whether defendants are truly innocent. In a jury trial, the judge's role is to determine whether there is sufficient evidence to permit the jury to return a verdict of guilty. If there is no jury, then the judge must determine whether she is persuaded of the defendant's guilt beyond a reasonable doubt. Neither situation requires the judge to determine whether the defendant is actually innocent of the crime charged.[26] Once either the judge or the jury decides that the state's case for guilt is unpersuasive, their work is done; their verdicts of not guilty leave open the question of whether they believe that the defendants are actually innocent. It is a question that they are neither asked nor expected to answer. Thus, although any serious evaluation of the quality of criminal justice rendered requires an inquiry into whether the innocent are prosecuted and acquitted, an explicit answer cannot be found in the results of the adjudicatory process itself. Because a claim of actual innocence requires a judgment that goes beyond that which official governmental bodies make, such claims are readily and frequently disputed.[27]

A focus upon acquittals requires a rethinking of the definition of innocence commonly employed by scholars examining the problem of wrongful convictions. Taking a Caesar's wife approach to the definition of innocence, these investigators have adopted a conservative "wrong man" definition of factual innocence.[28] If the defendant was involved in the behavior described as criminal, the case was excluded from consideration even if that individual was innocent of any crime. This significantly underinclusive approach makes sense when the goal is to establish that mistaken convictions occur. It complements our most powerful tool for establishing wrongful convictions, DNA evidence establishing that the biological evidence is not from the prisoner.[29]

If we examine appropriate acquittals (rather than wrongful convictions), the acquitted *should include all people who did not commit the crimes charged even if their manifest behavior might have aroused legitimate suspicion.* Some, perhaps most, of the acquitted are people who have nothing to do with the crime; whether acting in good or bad faith, the state's witnesses incorrectly identify them as the criminals. Some of the acquitted may have engaged in behaviors that the state seeks to characterize as criminal but are innocent because they lack the required mental state or their conduct is legally justified. Examining the extent to which the innocent are acquitted requires a definition of historical accuracy that reflects the substantive law.

The criminal law defines serious felonies in terms of both state of mind and act, and it acknowledges that even when defendants do the acts with the prohibited state of mind, they may nonetheless be justified or excused. The forgetful man who places a necktie in his bag and leaves the store without remembering that he has done so is not guilty of larceny. Larceny requires a *purpose* to deprive another of his property permanently. By definition, the forgetful person in this example does not have such a purpose. The jury that acquits this person has rendered a historically accurate verdict. A woman who shoots and kills her abusive husband insists that she acted only because she was convinced that he was about to kill her. If she actually and reasonably thought she was about to die and she reasonably believed that she could save herself only by using deadly force, she has committed no crime. A jury that acquits her has absolved an innocent person. To suggest that these are acquittals of people who are not really innocent ignores the fundamental structure of our criminal law. Acquittals are historically accurate whenever juries correctly determine that either the defendants did not engage in the prohibited conduct or, if they did so engage, either they lacked the state of mind required to make the conduct criminal or their actions were the products of appropriate beliefs that justify their actions.[30]

This adjudicatory asymmetry that guilt rests upon a factual conclusion concerning the defendant's behavior whereas an acquittal reflects only an absence of proof complicates any effort to understand the fate of those who are actually innocent. The first consequence of this asymmetry—ignorance—we have already noted. We know far more about why the innocent are occasionally *convicted* than we do about those instances in which they are appropriately acquitted. Recent advances in forensic science such as DNA evidence collection has focused increased attention on the problem of mistaken convictions. According to the Innocence Project, as of this writing, there have been 235 post-DNA exonerations in the United States since the early 1990s.[31] Exonerations are newsworthy and frequently result from formal legal inquiries. "Man bites dog" is a more interesting story than "dog bites man."

We also hear (if not necessarily learn) a great deal about the opposite problem, the guilty person who is erroneously acquitted. One "knows" immediately when the guilty have been acquitted because the prosecutors or police can point to evidence in their possession—confessions, criminal records, statements by codefendants—that, had they been permitted to present it to the jury, would have demonstrated guilt. Or, through interviewing jurors, one can learn of their mistakes in attempting to apply the law. Also, the official language of the law, appellate decisions, repeatedly provides examples of the guilty going free. According to the United States Supreme Court, to ensure adherence to the mandates of the Fourth (search and seizure), Fifth (right to remain silent and to call witnesses), and Sixth (right to counsel) Amendments to the United States Constitution, evidence seized in violation of these constitutional provisions typically cannot be considered by judges or juries in determining the defendants' guilt. This doctrine, the exclusionary rule, has generated (and continues to generate) considerable distress. For example, in *Brewer v. Williams*,[32] involving the abduction and murder of a ten-year-old girl who had simply left her parents for a moment to go to the washroom, the majority found the defendant's confession inadmissible in evidence because he had been questioned without his lawyer being present. Chief Justice Burger dissented in no uncertain terms: "The result in this case ought to be intolerable in any society that purports to call itself an organized society."[33]

When the innocent are *acquitted*, however, the matter ends there. Prosecutors can blame acquittals upon the denseness of the juries, the chicanery of defense counsel, or questionable rulings by the trial judges. The police can point to the relative ineptitude of the prosecutors. The judges can identify the juries' credulity. Whatever the explanation and by whomever offered, typically the matter ends there. Appellate courts have no power to reverse the judgment.

Second, the asymmetry between the official determination of guilt and no determination of actual innocence feeds the belief that those charged with crimes are guilty. Despite maxims to the contrary, the presumption of guilt, not the presumption of innocence, permeates the criminal adjudicatory system. There are no formal events or pronouncements to contradict this view. All results, including acquittals and dismissals, can be rationalized on the grounds that guilty defendants "beat" the charge rather than that innocent persons were vindicated. Moreover, in contrast to the absence of any procedure to determine whether acquitted persons are innocent, we do have formal processes for determining that people juries have acquitted are really guilty after all. As noted, although the O. J. Simpson civil suit is the most obvious public manifestation of this phenomenon, it is found in criminal cases as well. For example, if the defendant is prosecuted for a crime (e.g., an armed robbery at knife point on July 1) and the state wishes to prove a pattern of criminal behavior, the prosecutor can introduce evidence of a similar crime (an armed robbery using a screwdriver on February 1) even though the defendant has been *tried and acquitted* of that supposedly similar crime. This practice does not offend due process, the Supreme Court has held, because the earlier acquittal did not mean that the defendant was innocent but only that the state had failed to prove guilt beyond a reasonable doubt.[34] Thus, the "acquitted but guilty" can be made to suffer for their crimes. That judges routinely and appropriately make findings of fact that acquitted defendants are in fact guilty but never make findings of fact that acquitted persons are innocent confirms the view that it is only the guilty who are charged and, necessarily, only the guilty who are convicted.

Herbert Packer suggested that there were two competing ideologies of criminal justice administration: the crime control model and the due process model.[35] These reflect the tension between the need for a criminal process that deals efficiently with a large mass of cases and concern for the privacy of individuals and for limiting state power. Former attorney general Edwin Meese's assertion, noted at the outset of this chapter, that "if a person is innocent of crime, then he is not a suspect,"[36] reflects the core assumption of the crime control model: it is the executive (e.g., police and prosecutors), as opposed to the judiciary, who makes the significant decisions about guilt.[37] From this premise, which its proponents assert as an empirical matter, follows the presumption of guilt. This, in turn, justifies an essentially administrative approach to the guilt-determination process. The result is a core belief shared by virtually all personnel who work within the criminal justice system that defendants formally accused of crimes are guilty.[38]

The pervasive problem of crime fuels the belief that we do not prosecute the innocent. Because resources to combat crime effectively are scarce, triage is essential. Personnel and funds must be allocated where they will be most productive. Police, prosecutors, judges, and correctional officials make rational decisions about how to proceed in light of the enormity of the problem and the lack of adequate resources.[39] Police officers are not going to waste time arresting and presenting to the prosecutor suspects who have not engaged in serious wrongdoing. The overwhelming numbers of arrests they do make are of people caught in the act or known to the victims or witnesses at the scene.[40] If, however, the police err, the prosecutors are not likely to squander resources proceeding against suspects they believe did not commit crimes or, more commonly, against whom only weak cases exist. Indeed, there are informal sanctions (e.g., pretrial detention and the denial of bail despite inadequate evidence) that can be and are imposed in such cases.[41] Defense counsel aids in this process by ensuring that those who are genuinely innocent come to the attention of prosecutors and are extruded from the system. Certainly, by the time of trial, it is the guilty alone who stand before the judges or juries.[42]

Those who stand trial are protected by numerous adjudicatory devices designed to help ensure that any innocent person who stands trial will be acquitted. The acquittals and dismissals that occur reflect an overly compassionate criminal justice system in which the guilty are released to guarantee that no innocent person is ever convicted.[43] The guilty are acquitted along with the innocent both because no adjudicatory system, however constituted, can achieve perfect accuracy and because we embrace values other than achieving the highest possible level of factual accuracy. These values are found in three clusters. The first cluster, which commands the greatest attention from courts and commentators, includes our regard for individual privacy, mistrust of the state, desire to control police-citizen interactions, and preference for broad discretion not to prosecute. The second cluster of values, exemplified by concepts such as the presumption of innocence and the demand that guilt be established beyond a reasonable doubt, reflects a preference that errors made be ones that result in false negatives (acquitting the guilty) rather than false positives (convicting the innocent). Commitment to the adversary system represents the third cluster of values. This includes the preference for a system of justice in which advocates can free guilty persons by outperforming adversaries in front of passive fact finders rather than a system in which the decision makers (state employees) control the gathering, presentation, and analysis of evidence.

The belief that the vast majority of the acquitted really are guilty rests on the assumption that neither the police nor the prosecutors will pursue criminal charges against innocent people. This belief solves a problem that may otherwise exist: how to justify the vast disparity in resources available to the state compared to those available to the criminally accused. As judge and legal scholar Richard Posner put it,

> I can confirm from my own experience as a judge that indigent defendants are generally rather poorly represented. But if we are to be

hardheaded we must recognize that this may not be entirely a bad thing. The lawyers who represent indigent criminal defendants seem to be good enough to reduce the probability of convicting an innocent person to a very low level. If they were much better, either many guilty people would be acquitted or society would have to devote much greater resources to the prosecution of criminal cases. A bare-bones system for the defense of indigent criminal defendants may be optimal.[44]

Defense counsel commonly do not challenge the dominant assumption that the acquitted, like the convicted, are guilty. Anecdotal evidence suggests that defense counsel generally presume that defendants are guilty.[45] Even if the reality is not as extreme as one may conclude from data showing that acquittals represent less than 1 percent of all adjudicatory outcomes, there is no reason to doubt the observation that criminal defense lawyers who restrict their practices only to the innocent will have little to do. In addition to being rare in the population of those who plead or go to trial, the presence of actual innocents in any attorney's practice will be obscured by the insistence of many of the guilty that they are in fact innocent. Defense lawyers need to begin with the premise that what really matters is what the prosecution can prove, not what the defendants insist happened.[46] Ethical rules push in this direction: defense lawyers who encourage their clients to acknowledge guilt in private conversations are defense lawyers who have placed themselves and their clients in an awkward situation if the clients insist upon testifying. Does she place her duty to the client ahead of her duty as an officer of the court and permit the defendant to testify even if she believes that the testimony will be false? To solve this problem, many defense counsel embraced "don't ask, don't tell" long before it emerged as a policy of the military.

Ideology matters as well. At a minimum, defense counsel view their role as forcing the government to secure convictions in an open and lawful manner. Securing acquittals for the guilty serves the important end of forcing the government to follow its own rules even in its treatment of the most despised members of the community. While essential, securing acquittals of the innocent does not necessarily send a more powerful message about the government's commitment to following its own rules than the acquittal of guilty persons against whom the government simply failed to amass persuasive evidence.

Defense counsel likely subscribe to the dominant assumption that the majority of clients they defend are actually guilty because any other view may render their work emotionally and practically unsupportable. Consider this description by a defense lawyer of the effect of a belief in innocence upon the behavior of a defender:

> Given the defense lawyer's typical relationship to truth, there is a stunning change in perspective when a lawyer represents someone who is innocent. Suddenly, there is nothing more important than the truth, nothing more sacrosanct. Now, the lawyer who is ordinarily indifferent to the truth is outraged that the system is indifferent to it. Sometimes the defense lawyer representing a client he or she believes to be innocent is downright desperate. Gone is the cocky irreverence that characterizes many defenders. Gone is the nonchalance. Defenders who seek to vindicate a factually innocent person wear their hearts on their sleeves: "Please, please, please," they beg, "my client is really innocent." They are willing to lay themselves bare before the most recalcitrant prosecutor. They are willing to be thought of as naïve.[47]

The typical outcome of a criminal case is a conviction based upon the defendant's entry of a guilty plea. Few want to do work that regularly results in injustice to their clients. Those whose work it is to negotiate plea agreements for their clients need to believe that what they are doing serves their clients well rather than poorly. Because all agree that the vast majority of all those clients are in fact guilty, defense counsel may be unlikely to perceive, much less believe, that there is a risk that their advice to their client to accept a plea bargain may result in the conviction of the innocent.

Believing that those charged are guilty also eases the conscience of those who administer criminal justice in our society. No one wants to participate in a practice that they believe routinely imprisons the innocent or compels the innocent to plead guilty to crimes they have not committed in order to avoid very severe sentences. A prosecutor securing an indictment will not know typically whether the case will be one of the 97 percent that do not go to trial (ending in a guilty plea, dismissal, or deferral) or one of the 3 percent that go to trial.[48] Trials are unpredictable; but to the extent that prosecutors have initial questions about whether defendants will be convicted, they take comfort from the knowledge that acquittals are extremely rare outcomes.

Yet the typical justifications for treating acquittals as historically erroneous are hardly persuasive. The screening process for accepting a case for prosecution is concerned with the existence of a prima facie case, not the validity of a defense. Police and prosecutors are arguably no more adept at determining whether witnesses are telling the truth than twelve jurors devoted to answering that question.[49] The small percentage of defendants who resist plea bargains and insist on trial may all be counting on deficiencies in the prosecutions' cases rather than their own innocence, but there is no a priori reason to believe this is true. Even though some defendants undoubtedly do engage in witness intimidation, there is neither data nor reason to assume that even a substantial fraction of those who go to trial do so.[50] Those who chose trial do so in the face of sentencing regimes that explicitly authorize judges to increase a convicted defendant's sentence precisely because he insisted upon going to trial and authorize an ever greater increase if the defendant also testified, albeit unpersuasively, in his own behalf.[51]

For the few cases that do go to trial, judges and juries do not necessarily arrive at similar judgments about guilt. Kalven and Zeisel found that judges and juries agreed that the defendants should be acquitted in fourteen out of one hundred cases but *disagreed* about the appropriateness of acquittals in twenty-two out of one hundred cases. Thus, of the 36 percent of cases in which either the judges or juries or both thought acquittals were appropriate, judges and juries *agreed* that the defendant should be acquitted less than 40 percent of the time.

Things have not improved in the past fifty years. In a study of nearly four hundred felony jury trials conducted by the NCSC,[52] which we will discuss at length in succeeding chapters, juries returned acquittals in 27 percent of the cases whereas judges indicated that they would have acquitted, had these been bench trials, in 19 percent of those cases. The impression of a reasonably high level of agreement between judge and jury about innocence dissipates when we examine the degree of actual overlap between judge and jury assessments. Judges were prepared to acquit in 7 percent of the cases even though the jury had found the defendant guilty, and juries acquitted in 16 percent of the cases even though the judge would have convicted those defendants. Overall, the judges and juries agreed that acquittal was the appropriate disposition in only 11 percent of the case while disagreeing about innocence in twice as many cases (23 per cent).

Out of one hundred jury trials, then, judges and juries agreed to acquit in eleven, and agreed to convict in about sixty-six. They disagreed about acquittal in 23 percent of cases. Thus, contemporary judges and juries agree on the appropriateness of acquittals in only one-third (11 percent) of all the total cases (34 percent) in which either the judge or the jury is prepared to find the defendant not guilty. Given evidence of disagreement between judges and juries about when it is appropriate to acquit a defendant, it may be more comforting to believe that all defendants are guilty and that acquittals are mere artifacts of the burden of proof. Otherwise, we might have to confront seriously the question of whether the difference is attributable to the willingness of judges to convict the innocent or to the willingness of jurors to acquit the guilty.

So what is to be said about the 1 percent of defendants who are actually acquitted? If pretrial screening really eliminates every innocent person, then the tiny acquittal rate represents a spectacularly low error rate for a process as fraught with uncertainty as the determination of contested historical fact whether by plea or after trial. However, notice that pretrial screening would have to achieve an even more astounding error rate, a false positive error rate of zero, if among the millions who go to judgment, there are no innocents. No criminal justice system can possibly operate with such tiny error rates, and no serious commentator suggests that ours does.[53] Given the inevitability that some innocents will not be dismissed through pretrial screening, to what extent do the *acquitted* overlap with the *innocent*? In the remainder of this book, we explore that question.

We have investigated the meaning of acquittals primarily through a detailed analysis of data from nearly four hundred criminal trials originally collected by the NCSC.[54] These data, obtained from the lawyers who presented the evidence, the jurors who decided the cases, and the judges who presided over the trials, offer more detailed and nuanced information about acquittals than has been available to those who previously investigated acquittals. We describe these data and our approach in detail in chapter 3 and use the data to examine particular patterns of acquittals in chapters 4 through 6. In the next chapter, we explore what we know about the presence and fate of the innocent through previous investigations of pretrial dismissals and trial outcomes, including, most prominently, Kalven and Zeisel's monumental work, *The American Jury*.

2

Judge and Jury Decisions to Acquit
What We Know from Social Science Research

In October 1955, the Subcommittee on Internal Security of the Senate Judiciary Committee took a break from its normal business of searching for subversives to conduct a hearing into recordings of jury deliberations allegedly conducted by researchers at the University of Chicago. While conceding that it was an unusual topic for the subcommittee to investigate, James O. Eastland of Mississippi, chairman, explained that the hearing was justified because "anything which undermines or threatens the integrity of the jury system necessarily affects the internal security of the United States."[1] The recordings in question, which apparently had the potential to threaten internal security, were undertaken by a research team from the University of Chicago Jury Project as part of a $1.4 million ($11.8 million in 2011 dollars) empirical investigation of the American jury. Researchers had secretly tape-recorded five civil jury trial deliberations in the hopes of verifying survey responses from jurors about how they made decisions with the actual recorded processes of the deliberations. Committee members took the research team to task for violating the sanctity of the jury room and the trust of the American people. Members of the subcommittee and the U.S. attorney general publicly censured the Chicago Jury Project and its principal researchers for the tape-recording incidents. As Kalven and Zeisel, coauthors of the major publication from the project, *The American Jury,* noted when the book appeared in

1966, "One of the distinctions of the jury study is that it is a research project that has a Purple Heart."[2]

Unlike many congressional hearings, this one bore fruit. Following the hearing, Congress and thirty state legislatures banned the recording of jury deliberations. The recordings taken for the Chicago Jury Project were never published or analyzed, nor was there an analysis of the questionnaires directed to the juries. Perhaps because of this experience, Kalven and Zeisel's seminal study of the jury was based virtually entirely upon the thousands of questionnaires filled out by judges. *The American Jury* did not include any information from the perspective of jurors about how the juries made decisions or whether or not the jurors agreed with the judges' assessments of the evidence and outcomes. For all of its elegance of expression, analytic power, eminence, and influence, *The American Jury* analyzes only judges' speculations about why juries decide as they do. The liberation hypothesis, perhaps its major finding, rests upon judges' views of the reasons why juries disagree with the way the judges would have resolved the case. The disapproval of the recording of jury deliberations manifested in the Subcommittee on Internal Security hearings and in the state laws banning such a practice has for decades hampered social scientists' efforts to explore how juries make decisions in actual trials. As a result, the judicial lens through which case outcomes were evaluated in *The American Jury* has continued to influence our understanding of how juries arrive at acquittals and to shape the direction of social science research into jury decisions.

The Chicago Jury Project

The Chicago Jury Project was born out of a desire to understand how juries arrive at verdicts. Noting that throughout the first half of the twentieth century, the American jury system had been under attack, scholars at the University of Chicago hoped to establish "that the jury is an efficient model of deciding cases, despite the clogging of the dockets, that it can be strengthened and preserved, and that the doubts that have arisen about the jury system in various parts of this country and in the world, as for example in England, where the jury system has been much limited, are not well established."[3]

Supporters of the American jury system advanced four main arguments: (1) jury trials are essential to help protect against the actuality of corruption and prejudice by judges and the public's perception of the same,[4] (2) juries keep the administration of the law in accordance with the wishes of the community,[5] (3) juries are superior fact finders to judges,[6] and (4) the public has more trust and confidence in the legitimacy of the law when citizens actively participate as members of juries.[7] Opponents of the American jury system offered two main arguments: (1) jury trials are inefficient, unnecessarily slowing the processing of cases and ultimately delaying justice[8] and (2) jurors are inferior fact finders to judges because they do not understand the law, are unaware of previous court decisions, and generally are unable to follow judges' instructions.[9]

The investigators sought to provide hard data about how juries actually operate. Our understanding of juries up until the 1950s was mainly deductive, based on logical assumptions and anecdotal experiences rather than inductive examination. The researchers wanted to subject some of the assumptions about the operation and effectiveness of juries to empirical testing. They were particularly interested in knowing "to what extent they [juries] understand the instructions of the judges, to what extent they are able to handle difficult problems of evidence, to what extent it might be possible to speed up the jury system, so as to avoid the clogging of the courts in the urban centers and at the same time to preserve the jury system."[10] Because it was impossible to observe the decision-making processes of real juries directly, the research team utilized a number of different methodologies to understand the jury process indirectly. Four of the primary methods used in the Chicago Jury Project are described in some detail to provide an overview of the research strategy.[11]

The first part of the project involved the collection and analysis of information about a sample of real criminal and civil cases. Researchers reached out to federal and state trial judges, asking them to participate in the project. Over 550 judges agreed. Throughout the course of the study, judges provided information about 3,576 criminal cases over which they had presided.[12] Judges received questionnaires to fill out about each of their cases. They were asked to fill out the first part of each questionnaire to provide background information about the case, including the presentation of evidence and testimony, their instructions to the jury, and the main issues before the jury prior to the jury rendering its verdict. Judges were asked to indicate how they would have decided the cases and the punishments they would have imposed had they tried the cases without juries. Once the jury returned its verdicts, the judge was asked to complete information concerning the final verdict of the jury and the punishments imposed. The judges were also asked to indicate whether or not they agreed with the decisions of the juries and to explain the reasons why the jury verdicts might have been different from the judges' decisions had they decided the cases.[13] The data were intended to inform our understanding of "the frequency and nature of judge-jury differences."[14] Data from the judge questionnaires provided the primary source for Kalven and Zeisel's analysis in *The American Jury.*

The second method was to conduct interviews with the general public and a subgroup of recent jurors in a medium-sized midwestern city about their attitudes toward the courts and the jury process generally. In 1955, 102 people from the general population of Peoria, Illinois, were randomly selected for interviews. An additional 225 interviews were conducted with individuals in Peoria who had served on juries in twenty trials (thirteen civil and seven criminal cases between 1953 and 1954).[15] The interviews were intended to gather information about the public's attitude toward and experience with the courts. The research team wanted to determine whether individuals who had recently served on juries had more positive attitudes toward the courts and the legal process than the general public. The interviews were also used to assess whether people who had other personal interactions with the courts, such as being witnesses or parties in legal cases, changed their attitudes toward courts and the law. A number of scholarly publications examining the perceptions of jurors about their experiences resulted from these interviews.[16] The third part of the study involved field work with jurors who served on real cases. Brief interviews were conducted with approximately fifteen hundred jurors who served on 213 criminal juries in Chicago and Brooklyn. With the permission of the courts, jurors were interviewed immediately after their service to find out how the first ballot votes of the juries compared to their final verdicts. Additionally, the interviewers asked jurors questions about their "willingness to convict on circumstantial evidence and approve a death penalty,"[17] about their experiences serving on the juries, and about their willingness to serve on future juries. Intensive studies of approximately eighteen cases were also conducted by field observers who watched entire trials and then interviewed judges, attorneys, and jurors following the trials.

The final method involved experimental research with mock juries aimed at understanding the processes through which jurors deliberate and arrive at verdicts. Because researchers could not observe actual jury deliberations, they depended upon jury simulations. Led by social psychologist Fred Strodtbeck, researchers selected individuals to observe fictitious trials. Those individuals were then divided into small groups, similar to actual juries, to deliberate on the outcomes of the cases. The simulated deliberations were observed by researchers, and mock jurors were interviewed during the research process. A number of scholarly articles detailing the deliberative process resulted from the Chicago Jury Project mock jury experiments.[18]

In the original study design for the Chicago Jury Project, researchers did not anticipate observing or recording the deliberations of actual jurors. The team accepted that their understanding of jury decision making would be limited to indirect measures. However, an opportunity to observe actual jury deliberations presented itself in November 1953 when Paul Kitch, an attorney in Kansas and a University of Chicago alumnus, approached federal judges in Wichita, Kansas, about the possibility of recording jury deliberations in the federal court. Kitch had heard about the Chicago Jury Project through professional circles and expressed concern that the researchers would not be able to draw reliable conclusions about the decision making of juries without actually observing the deliberation process first-hand. Kitch wrote to Judge Delmas Hill, the chief of the Federal District Court in Wichita, Kansas, proposing a series of rules to guide the tape-recording of jury deliberations for the purposes of research and asking for the court's permission for such recordings. Judge Hill agreed to allow the recordings in his court and eventually the chief judge of the U.S. Appeals Court for the Tenth Circuit also agreed to the secret tape-recording.[19]

The research team seized upon the opportunity to tape-record jury deliberations because it provided a chance to test whether their assumptions about jury decision making and the deliberative process derived from the mock juror experiments, surveys, and post-trial questioning of jurors actually occurred in real-life deliberations. With such recordings, researchers would also be able to "learn whether post-trial interviews with jurors permit reconstruction of the events of the jury room."[20] Through listening to real jury deliberations, researchers potentially would be able to improve the design of research questions and experimental methodologies and to extend the team's understanding of the deliberative process. The decision to tape-record jury deliberations and the reaction to it markedly changed the direction and scope of the Chicago Jury Project.

Following the agreement by the federal district court in Wichita to allow the tape-recording, the research team installed concealed microphones in the jury room and a recording machine in the coat closet of the chief judge's private office. During 1954, five jury deliberations (all civil) were tape-recorded with the permission of the presiding judge and the attorneys in each case.[21] In each case, the jurors were unaware that the deliberations were being tape-recorded and had not consented to anyone listening in on their deliberations. Only two members of the Chicago Jury Project research team had access to listen to the recordings during deliberations to ensure the machinery was working properly. No personnel of the court were present during the tape-recording of the sessions. In accord with the agreement with the court, after the juries deliberated and verdicts were reached, the tape-recordings from all five cases were shipped to the University of Chicago. Nothing was done with the tape-recordings until the court notified the research team that each case had reached final disposition. At that point, the tape-recordings were to be transcribed and any identifying information, such as names or locations, was to be redacted from the transcripts.

Despite the efforts of the research team to maintain secrecy, information about the tape-recording experiment circulated in the legal community. In the year following the tape-recording, Judge Hill asked to play one of the recordings at a conference of judges held in Colorado to help demonstrate a particular problem with the way jury members interpret instructions from judges.[22] Some participants at the judges' conference raised concern about the fact that juries had been secretly tape-recorded. Within a few months of the judges' conference, on October 7, 1955, the *Washington Post* ran an editorial condemning the secret tape-recording of jury deliberations as undermining the jury process and depriving litigants of their rights to fair trials. The attorney general of the United States publicly censured the secret tape-recording and the U.S. Senate Subcommittee to Investigate the Administration of the Internal Security Act and Other Internal Security Laws, Committee on the Judiciary, held a special hearing on October 12, 1955. Members of the Chicago Jury Project testified before the subcommittee about the secret tape-recording of jury deliberations in Wichita, Kansas, and the justification for the jury project more broadly. Following the hearing, Congress enacted a statute prohibiting the secret tape-recording of juries, even for the purposes of research; and legislators in over thirty states enacted laws similarly prohibiting the tape-recording of jury deliberations.[23]

The public censure and fallout from the secret tape-recording project changed the nature and focus of the Chicago Jury Project. The most notable publications from the project were primarily based on the opinions and perceptions of judges about jury decision making. The voice of jury members themselves, so central to the research design of the Chicago Jury Project, was largely abandoned in an effort to distance the research and the research team members from the jury tape-recording scandal.

Although the research team collected extensive information about jury decision making through interviews with members of the public and former jurors in Peoria, Illinois, conducted interviews with jurors who served in criminal cases in Chicago and Brooklyn, and experimented with mock juries, the results of these investigations have arguably been less influential to our understanding of juries than the survey data from judges reported in *The American Jury*. From this work, we know what the *judges thought* the juries had done, not what the jurors themselves indicated they had done. *The American Jury*, which has been influential in subsequent efforts to understand criminal juries, reflects the judges' views of the reasons juries may agree or disagree with the way the judges would have decided the cases.

Understanding Judge-Jury Disagreements: Findings from The American Jury

Using the data from the judges' questionnaires in 3,576 criminal trials, Kalven and Zeisel sought to discover how often judges disagreed with the verdicts that juries rendered and how judges explained those disagreements. The agreement between judges and juries was remarkably high. In 78 percent of the cases, the judges and the juries would have reached the same verdicts. Kalven and Zeisel reported that when judges and juries disagreed, juries were far more likely to be lenient than judges. Kalven and Zeisel identified three types of disagreements between judges and juries: (1) disagreement as to whether defendants were guilty of *any* of the crimes for which they were on trial (66 percent of all disagreements), (2) disagreements as to whether defendants were guilty of *some* of the crimes with which they were charged (17 percent of all disagreements), and (c) disagreements in which the juries were hung on one or more of the charges against the defendants (17 percent of all disagreements). Each type of disagreement was in the same direction: juries were far more likely to be more lenient than judges than the other way around. Thus, in 88 percent of the disagreements about overall guilt or innocence, the juries were more lenient than the judges; in 85 percent of the disagreements as to guilt of some of the charges, the juries were more lenient than the judges; and in 79 percent of the disagreements arising from hung juries, the juries were more lenient than the judges.[24]

Relying solely upon the judges' written accounts of the reasons juries arrived at verdicts with which they disagreed, Kalven and Zeisel identified five different explanations. They cited sentiments about the law, sentiments about the defendant, evidence factors, facts only the judge knew, and disparity of counsel. Weighting these factors, Kalven and Zeisel concluded that differing evaluations of the evidence accounted for 54 percent of all disagreements, sentiments about the law and the defendant for another 40 percent, and facts that only the judge knew and disparity of counsel the remaining 6 percent.[25] Dividing these explanations into facts and values[26] (a term they used interchangeably with "sentiment"), they showed that 42 percent of the normal disagreement cases (those in which the juries were more lenient than the judges) involved disagreements about both facts and values.[27] From these findings, they posited the liberation hypothesis that a combination of facts and values explained a significant number of judge-jury disagreements. They explained that when the case was close on the evidence,[28] the jury was liberated from the dictates of the law and could, and did, give expression to sentiment[29] in arriving at its verdict. As they stated, "The sentiment gives direction to the resolution of the evidentiary doubt: the evidence makes it possible for the jury to respond to sentiment *by liberating* it from the discipline of the evidence."[30]

Kalven and Zeisel never stated explicitly that when judges and juries disagree about guilt, the judges are factually correct and the juries are in error. Rather, they employed metaphors to suggest this is the case. Thus, the judges' views of the cases were the "baseline representing the law,"[31] while the close cases in which the juries came to different conclusions constituted a "war with the law," albeit a "modest and subtle one."[32] They asserted that "most but not all of the time" when juries *agreed* with judges, the juries were "not importing values of [their] own" into their decisions about guilt or innocence.[33]

The situation changed dramatically when juries and judges *disagreed* about guilt. In those situations, "two-thirds of the disagreements with judges are marked by some jury response to values."[34] Kalven and Zeisel continued, "The upshot is that when the jury reaches a different decision from the judge on the same evidence, it does so not because it is a sloppy or inaccurate finder of facts, but because it gives expression to values which fall outside the official rules."[35] Thus, they concluded that "the jury's sense of justice leads it to policies that differ from official legal policies."[36] This conclusion reflected the popularly understood genius of the jury system that tempered the rigors of the law with the common sense of the community.

The Legacy of The American Jury *and Our Modern Understanding of Judge-Jury Disagreements*

Kalven and Zeisel's research was conducted at the dawn of the civil rights movement, before police forces, judges, and juries began to reflect more accurately the race and gender of the general population. It was conducted before DNA analysis revealed the vulnerability of previously uncontestable convictions in serious cases. Their data also predated the constitutional revolution in the way our society investigates crime and adjudicates guilt.

The demographics of defendants in felony courts have changed substantially since the time of Kalven and Zeisel's study as well. In the cases Kalven and Zeisel examined, representing courts in forty-seven of the forty-eight states (Hawaii and Alaska had not yet been admitted to the union) and the District of Columbia, 73 percent of all defendants were White and the remaining 27 percent were Black.[37] Today, White felony defendants make up only 29 percent of defendants in the seventy-five largest counties in United States, 42 percent are Black, 28 percent are Hispanic, and 2 percent are "Other Race."[38] The percentage of defendants who are female has more than doubled, increasing from 7 percent in the 1950s to 18 percent in 2002; and twice as many defendants are under the age of twenty today than in the 1950s.[39] These changes have the potential to produce a markedly different set of trial outcomes than those reported by Kalven and Zeisel in the 1960s. The Supreme Court cases dealing with the constitutional requirements for the conduct of trials, including those relating to the racial composition of the jury, rest in part on such an assumption.[40]

The American Jury and the Courts

Two years after the publication of *The American Jury*, the Supreme Court of the United States, in the case of *Duncan v. Louisiana*,[41] confronted the question of whether the Constitution required states to afford criminal defendants the right to jury trials in serious cases. The Court noted that the constitutional right to a jury trial in a serious criminal case reflected

> a profound judgment about the way in which law should be enforced and justice administered. A right to jury trial is granted to criminal defendants in order to prevent oppression by the Government. . . . If the defendant preferred the common-sense judgment of a jury to the more tutored but perhaps less sympathetic reaction of the single judge, he was to have it.[42]

The Court found support for its view in Kalven and Zeisel's *American Jury*. Responding to the objection that "juries are incapable of adequately understanding evidence or determining issues of fact, and that they are unpredictable, quixotic, and little better than a roll of dice,"[43] the Court referenced Kalven and Zeisel:

> Yet, the most recent and exhaustive study of the jury in criminal cases concluded that juries do understand the evidence and come to sound conclusions in most of the cases presented to them and that when juries differ with the result at which the judge would have arrived, it is usually because they are serving some of the very purposes for which they were created and for which they are now employed.[44]

These sentiments have been reaffirmed in recent Supreme Court cases limiting judicial power to enhance sentences under state and federal guideline systems.[45]

Twenty years after its original publication, *The American Jury* was invoked by both sides in the debate over racial disparities in death sentences. In *McCleskey v. Kemp*,[46] the majority rejected the argument that racial disparities rendered Georgia's capital punishment scheme unconstitutional, noting that "it is the jury's function to make the difficult and uniquely human judgments that defy codification and that 'build discretion, equity, and flexibility into a legal system.'"[47] The dissent responded with its own reference to Kalven and Zeisel's work:

> The considerable racial disparity in sentencing rates among these cases is consistent with the "liberation hypothesis" of H. Kalven and H. Zeisel in their landmark work, *The American Jury* (1966). . . . Thus, it is those cases in which sentencing evidence seems to dictate neither life imprisonment nor the death penalty that impermissible factors such as race play the most prominent role.[48]

When the Supreme Court determined that the Constitution prohibited the death penalty for crimes committed by juveniles, Justice Scalia, in dissent, invoked *The American Jury* to argue that the majority's "startling conclusion undermines the very foundations of our capital sentencing system, which entrusts juries with 'mak[ing] the difficult and uniquely human judgments that defy codification and that "buil[d] discretion, equity, and flexibility into a legal system."'"[49]

Duncan, McCleskey, and *Roper* are three of the twenty-five different Supreme Court decisions (as well as more than 150 decisions of other courts) in which *The American Jury* has been cited as support for propositions concerning the behavior of juries.[50] No other work of social science relating to jury behavior has been as widely or as approvingly referenced by courts. These citations are a tribute to the eminence of the authors, the breadth and sweep of their empirical and analytic work, and the mostly reassuring message about juries they presented.

Empirical Studies of Judge-Jury Agreement in the United States

Since Kalven and Zeisel posited the liberation hypothesis in 1966, researchers investigating the factors that inform judge and jury verdicts have relied upon analysis of small samples of cases, experimental designs, or interviews with decision makers. These various methodologies have strengths and limitations. Judge-jury verdict comparisons of actual criminal trials necessarily involve judges rendering hypothetical judgments while juries render real ones. It is possible that judges may be less punctilious in evaluating the evidence when it is not their responsibility to decide the case. The opinions they indicate they would render may be influenced by what the juries have already done.[51] However, reasoning from other empirical approaches presents even greater challenges. If the studies are archival, judges and juries are by definition not deciding the same cases.[52] Simulations and mock jury experiments also pose challenges because, no matter how realistic the presentations, the participants are aware that their decisions have no genuine consequences.[53]

Many of the studies that compare judge and jury decision making involve civil rather than criminal cases.[54] Although these studies are informative, they do not necessarily represent the experience of judges and juries in the criminal justice system. The burden of proof in a civil case is "more probable than not"; in the civil setting, justice is achieved when the parties are afforded a fair process for making their cases before disinterested adjudicators. Criminal justice seeks a higher end: that the state convicts and punishes only those who actually committed the crime. The law in many civil cases invites decision makers to consult values in determining whether or not defendants *behaved* appropriately (e.g., Were the defendants' behaviors "unreasonable"? Were the products "unreasonably dangerous"?). In the few serious criminal cases in which juries are asked to consider reasonableness, they are typically asked in terms of the reasonableness of the defendants' *beliefs* about the conduct or intentions of other persons (Did the victims consent? Were the victims threatening?). The very studies that show that juries are more lenient than judges in criminal cases also indicate that there is no particular direction to leniency in civil cases: when they disagree, judges are as likely to be more lenient than juries as the other way around.[55] Although it may be reassuring in civil cases that judges and juries agree most of the time and that their level of agreement equals that of scientists engaging in peer reviews or physicians diagnosing physical illnesses,[56] it is less than reassuring that judges and juries disagree in approximately one-quarter of all criminal trials as to whether the defendants committed the crimes.[57]

Until recently, attempts to replicate Kalven and Zeisel's findings in criminal trial decisions have been quite limited. In 1986, researchers who tested Kalven and Zeisel's theory directly in a small number of cases reported that liberation occurred in those cases that were close on the evidence. To examine the effect of legally irrelevant factors on juror votes in fourteen sexual assault cases involving evidence characterized as "weak" and twenty-four such cases involving evidence characterized as "strong," juror sentiment was measured through (1) assessment of the defendants' attractiveness, (2) any references to the defendants being employed or unemployed, (3) any negative comments about the victims' moral character, and (4) juror perceptions of the victims' responsibility for the assaults.[58] Hard evidence was classified as eyewitness testimony, physical evidence, recovered weapons, and physical injuries to the victim. Reskin and Visher concluded that the effect of extralegal factors was confined to weak cases in which evidence about the defendants' guilt or innocence was more equivocal. Their finding that extralegal variables have the greatest role in cases in which the legal evidence is equivocal was consistent with the tenor of Kalven and Zeisel's finding.

In another analysis of the juror interviews from the same group of sexual assault trials, Visher[59] suggested that juror decisions are dominated by evidentiary as opposed to victim or defendant characteristics and that juror attitudes have little explanatory power with respect to case outcomes. She concluded that relevant evidence variables[60] alone accounted for 34 percent of the variance in case outcomes. Adding victim and defendant characteristics variables into these models increased the explained variance by only 8 percent, and adding juror characteristics and attitudes increased the explained variance only an additional 2 percent.[61]

Based on recent reanalysis of the data originally collected by Kalven and Zeisel using more sophisticated multivariate regression analysis techniques, researchers have called into question a central premise of Kalven and Zeisel's hypothesis, the notion that evidentiary strength and juror sentiment are independent phenomena.[62] Researchers found a strong relationship between defendants' lack of criminal records and the perceptions of judges that jurors were sympathetic to the defendants. They further found that judges' perceptions that jurors were sympathetic to defendants diminished after controlling for the severity of the cases and criminal records. These findings suggest that the liberation hypothesis may not actually work as Kalven and Zeisel posited. Instead, the presence or absence of particular evidentiary factors may actually result in juror sympathy for the defendant. If so, this requires a methodology that controls for these factors independently.

Because jurors are more likely than judges to have demographic characteristics that may result in identification with (and leniency toward) defendants, extralegal factors such as defendant or juror race may be expected to affect jury decisions.[63] Numerous studies have suggested a relationship between juror characteristics and jury leniency toward same-race defendants,[64] but this relationship appears strongest when the evidence supporting guilt is mixed or weak.[65] Other jury research, however, has suggested a more complex relationship among juror race, interpretation of evidence, and liberation,[66] with researchers sometimes finding no measurable relationship between defendant and juror race and case outcomes.[67]

Those applying the liberation hypothesis to other criminal justice decisions, particularly sentencing decisions, have achieved mixed results.[68] Consideration of extralegal factors appears to be constrained when judges sentence offenders convicted of more serious crimes such as murder, rape, and robbery; but these same judges appear liberated to consider extralegal factors such as race in sentencing decisions in less serious cases.[69] There is only mixed support for the liberation hypothesis in the disposition of murder cases at various stages of the criminal justice process. Although victim characteristics affect the processing of murder cases, the effects are not clearly limited to a particular level of case severity.[70]

The liberation hypothesis has also been utilized by scholars examining the effect of defendant and victim race on jury decision making.

Principles from the liberation hypothesis have been used to conclude that the race of defendants and victims has significant effects only under conditions of less-than-clear defendant culpability and ambiguous evidence.[71] In an important study cited in *McCleskey v. Kemp*, Baldus, Woodworth, and Pulaski[72] found the race of the victim predictive of capital sentences only in those cases in which the legal evidence was neither particularly strong nor particularly weak.

Robbenolt, in reviewing the research comparing judge and jury decision making, noted, "Compared to the extensive study of the decision making of jurors and juries, there has been relatively little examination of trial judges' decision making, and even fewer studies have directly compared the decision making of judge and jury."[73] There are many reasons why one may anticipate that juries will decide cases differently than judges. Juries are "one-shot" versus repeat players.[74] They decide collectively rather than individually, they are not legally trained, and they are more likely to be ethnically diverse than the judiciary. Being novices and being under the direction of judges, they may also respond in their verdicts to both verbal and nonverbal cues provided by judges.[75] Yet Robbenolt observed,

> The most notable conclusion to be drawn from this emerging literature is that the decision making of judges and jurors are [sic] strikingly similar. While there is evidence of some differences, there is a high degree of agreement between groups, they appear to decide real cases quite similarly, and they show a great deal of similarity in responding to simulated cases designed to examine a variety of legal decision making processes.[76]

When juries do disagree with judges, the research has shown consistently that juries exhibit greater leniency toward the defendants.

In a survey of judges conducted by Alschuler and Rodriquez at the University of Chicago,[77] one-third of the 142 judges who responded had observed juries acquit individuals whose guilt the judge believed to have been convincingly demonstrated during the previous year.[78] This represented thirteen percent of all the acquittals observed by the responding judges (87 of the 659 full acquittals observed by surveyed judges).[79] Assuming that the judges' opinions were valid,[80] the other 572 (87 percent of all acquittals) *were* responsive to the evidence. Assuming that the judges correctly identified cases in which patently guilty defendants were freed by juries (commonly known as jury nullification), the remaining acquittals (572 defendants, or 25 percent of all cases observed by the judges) were by the same measure appropriate.

In a four-jurisdiction study by the NCSC designed in part to replicate Kalven and Zeisel's original findings, researchers confirmed that, holding the strength of the case constant, juries were more likely to acquit than judges.[81] This was true whether one employed the judge's or the jury's assessment of the strength of the evidence, confirming Kalven and Zeisel's best-known observation: judges appear to have a lower conviction threshold than juries. However, questions concerning the reasons for this pattern remained unanswered. Are jurors prone to acquittal in the sense that they are either moved by sentiment or are unduly credulous while the judge responds objectively to fact? Or are judges prone to conviction in the sense that they cannot accurately identify the innocent in any but the most obvious case?[82] We discuss the NCSC data and its promise for answering these questions in more detail at the end of this chapter.

Empirical Studies of Judge-Jury Agreement in the United Kingdom: The Search for Wayward Verdicts

Scholars outside the United States have arrived at strikingly similar conclusions about judge and jury disagreement as those found for the American jury. Responding to a report by the Association of Chiefs of Police in the United Kingdom expressing concern that nearly four out of ten persons tried in higher courts were acquitted, Sarah McCabe and Robert Purves examined the results of 475 defendants brought to trial between 1968 and 1970. Of these, 112 changed their pleas to guilty, 58 received direct acquittals from the trial judges, and juries acquitted 115 and convicted 151.[83] The investigators determined that there were five categories of acquittals: policy prosecution, failure of witnesses, defendant's explanation, wayward verdict, and other. Thirteen percent of the acquittals were treated as wayward whereas 87 percent were, in the view of the investigators, understandable given the nature of the prosecution and the evidence adduced. Overall, 9 percent of all jury verdicts (both convictions and acquittals) were viewed as wayward acquittals.[84] This statistic was remarkably consistent with the findings of Kalven and Zeisel, who reported that 7 percent of all jury acquittals were "meritless."[85]

John Baldwin and Michael McConville[86] conducted an investigation of jury verdicts in Birmingham and London during the latter part of the 1970s. Their conclusions challenged those of McCabe and Purves in terms of the reasonableness of acquittals. Exploring the views of the judges, the defense solicitors, the prosecution solicitors, and the police involved in the cases, they found that at least one of these groups had serious doubts about whether the acquittals were justified in two out of three acquittals and that at least three of the four groups had those views in one out of four acquittals.[87] Indeed, they found that even the defense solicitors had serious doubts in 10 percent of the acquittals.[88] Baldwin and McConville focused upon acquittals about which both the judges and one of the other survey respondents had serious misgivings. They characterized some 36 percent of all acquittals in Birmingham as questionable acquittals.[89]

Despite the differences in times and legal systems, there is remarkable consistency between the findings of McCabe and Purves (5.6 percent of trials result in perverse acquittals), Kalven and Zeisel (7 percent of trials result in meritless acquittals), and Alshuler and Rodriguez, whose survey in 1997–1998 found that judges believed that there had been jury nullification (the acquittal of the obviously guilty) in 4 percent of criminal trials.[90] Baldwin and McConville reported a higher rate of questionable acquittals (11 percent of all trials),[91] although they eschewed characterizations such as "perverse" or any other term suggesting that a verdict was outside the acceptable range of what a jury ought to do. Put the other way around, across studies researchers found that, in the view of expert observers, acquittals were legally appropriate in between 20 percent and 38 percent of the trials studied.

In the American studies (Kalven and Zeisel, Alschuler and Rodriguez, and NCSC, described above), researchers placed the figure at around 25 percent.

These studies do not, indeed cannot, show us how many of the acquitted were actually innocent. Nor do they show that the acquitted were actually guilty of the crimes charged. What the studies do show is that, their broad discretion to both dismiss charges and strike plea bargains notwithstanding, prosecutors win only about seven out of ten trials and that in the vast majority of the losses, the judges see the outcomes as understandable based on the evidence presented. Even if we assume that judges are invariably correct in their assessments of lawless acquittals, these account for only a small fraction of all acquittals and reveal nothing to us about acquittals viewed as lawful.[92]

In the following chapters, we reexamine the question of the relationship between jury verdicts and potential innocence through an analysis of data collected by the NCSC in concert with numerous other existing studies. As described briefly above, researchers from the NCSC collected data on judge and jury decision making in 401 non-capital felony jury cases originating in four courts in the United States (Central Criminal Division of the Los Angeles County Superior Court, California; the Maricopa County Superior Court, Arizona; the Bronx County Supreme Court, New York; and the Superior Court of the District of Columbia) between 2000 and 2001.[93] This data, while originally intended to help researchers understand hung juries, expanded significantly on the kinds of information collected and analyzed for *The American Jury* and provides an opportunity to learn more about how juries arrive at acquittals. In addition to gathering data directly from the jurors who decided the cases and the lawyers who presented them (as opposed to judges only), the NCSC study researchers also secured information about the backgrounds of the jurors and lawyers, including race, gender, and prior experience with and assessment of the criminal justice system. This information was not collected in the survey instruments employed by Kalven and Zeisel, which were drafted and distributed in the 1950s (although they did seek information about the race and gender of the defendants and victims with those instruments). In their brief discussion in *The American Jury* of the effect of defendant and victim race, Kalven and Zeisel expressed skepticism that their data indicated a distinctive response by juries to race.[94] The NCSC data permits a considerably more fine-tuned assessment of the potential roles of race and gender in the resolution of criminal cases.

The NCSC data also included information secured from surveys of 3,497 individual jurors serving on the studied cases about the factors that informed their decisions, particularly their assessments of credibility and their sentiments about the law and the defendants.[95] Jurors were asked questions about their perception of the complexity and strength of the case, skill of attorneys, and evidence presented in court. Jurors also responded to questions about the deliberation process and their reaction to the final verdict. Additionally, NCSC researchers collected information from the case record concerning charges, demographic information about defendants and victims, the jury selection process, and evidence presented at trial. This information, coupled with the survey data, provided the basis for determining whether Kalven and Zeisel's explanation for judge-jury disagreement found support among today's jurors. More significantly, with the NCSC data, researchers could examine the factors that lead to judges and juries agreeing about guilt and innocence as well as those that generate disagreement. This unique source of data cannot tell us whether judge or jury decisions are factually correct, but they can be the basis for determining whether the factors associated with these outcomes are logically related to decisions about guilt or innocence.

3

Screening for Innocence

Erdmann walks to the far end of the cell and Santiago meets him at the bars. Erdmann puts his toe on a cross strip between the bars and balances Santiago's folder and papers on his knee. He takes out a Lucky Strike, lights it, and inhales. Santiago watches, and then a sudden rush of words starts violently from his mouth. Erdmann silences him. "First let me find out what I have to know," he says calmly, "and then you can talk as much as you want." Santiago is standing next to a chest-high, steel-plate partition. On the other side of it, a toilet flushes. A few steps away, Rodriguez is talking through the bars to his lawyer, "If you didn't do anything wrong," Erdmann says to Santiago, "then there's no point even discussing this. You'll go to trial."

Santiago nods desperately, "I ain't done nothing! I was asleep! I *never* been in trouble before." This is the first time since his initial interview seven months ago that he has had a chance to tell his story to a lawyer, and he is frantic to get it all out. Erdmann cannot stop the torrent, and now he does not try. "I never been arrested," Santiago shouts, "never been to jail, never been in *no* trouble, no trouble, *nothing*. We just asleep in the apartment and the police break in and grab us out of bed and take us, we ain't done nothing. I *never* been in trouble, I never saw this man before, and he says we did it. I don't even know what we did, and I been here 10 months, I don't see no lawyer or nothing, I ain't had a shower in two months, we locked up 24 hours a day. I got no shave, no hot food, I ain't *never* been like this before, I can't stand it. I'm going to kill myself, I got to get out, I ain't—"

Now Erdmann interrupts, icily calm, speaking very slowly, foot on the cross strip, drawing on his cigarette. "Well, it's very simple. Either you're guilty or you're not. If you're guilty of anything you can take the plea and they'll give you a year, and under the circumstances that's a very good plea and you ought to take it. If you're *not* guilty, you have to go to trial."

"I'm not guilty." He says it fast, nodding, sure of that.

"Then you should go to trial. But the jury is going to hear that the cop followed you into the building, the super sent him to apartment #3-A, he arrested you there, and the man identified you in the hospital. If they find you guilty, you might get 15 years." Santiago is unimpressed with all of that.

"I'm innocent. I didn't do nothing. But I got to get out of here. I got to—"

"Well, if you *did* do anything and you are a little guilty, they'll give you time served and you'll walk."

"That's more like it. Today? I walk today?"

"If you are guilty of something and you take the plea."

"I'll take the plea. But I didn't do nothing."

"Then you'll have to stay in and go to trial."

"When will that be?"

"In a couple of months. May be longer." Santiago has a grip on the bars.

"You mean if I'm guilty I get out today?"

"Yes." Someone is urinating on the other side of the partition.

"But if I'm innocent, I got to stay in?"

"That's right." The toilet flushes. It's too much for Santiago. He lets go of the bars, takes a step back, shakes his head, turns around and comes quickly back to the bars.

"But, *man*—"[1]

We have no way of knowing the guilt or innocence of Santiago, Martin Erdmann's client. What we do know is that if Santiago wished to achieve freedom now and worry about the consequences of a conviction later, pleading guilty made sense. The prosecutor assigned to Santiago's case and the judge who accepted the plea could (and would) believe that their work had led to the conviction and sentencing of a guilty individual. We know Erdmann's view: his work had "nothing to do with justice."

Assuming that Santiago was innocent (we have no way of knowing), why was pleading guilty to a crime he did not commit his shortest and safest route to freedom?

The Screening of the Innocent

In the United States, we currently employ a two-tier approach to the problem of sorting the innocent from the guilty following arrest. The first tier is the screening by prosecutors that supposedly eliminates the overwhelming majority of the innocent from those against whom judgments are sought. The second is the formal system of adjudication and review through which participants seek to ensure that the innocents who have survived the screenings by the prosecutors are rescued from the injustice of false convictions.

The initial screening significantly determines the kinds of errors committed in the adjudicatory phase. If all innocents are effectively screened out before charges are brought, all adjudicatory errors should be false negatives: only the guilty will be acquitted.[2] There should be no false positives (convictions of the innocent) because there should be no innocent people among those who go to trial or plead. However, the less effectively the initial screening eliminates those who are innocent prior to adjudication, the greater the likelihood that adjudicatory errors will involve both convictions of the innocent and acquittals of the guilty.

Our only formal method of determining whether or not cases are pursued through judgment against the guilty and not the innocent is to examine the results of the adjudicatory process: the number of people found guilty and the number of people found not guilty. That the overwhelming majority of all defendants who receive judgments are found guilty (roughly 97 percent)[3] seems to be confirmation that the screening process is working very well.

Data on Screening

The processing of criminal cases from arrest through the initiation of formal charges to disposition results in a substantial winnowing of defendants at each stage. Police arrest only a fraction of those who commit crimes. Prosecutors charge only a fraction of those arrested;[4] and in some jurisdictions, more than half of those charged have their cases dismissed prior to final disposition. Whether those who are left to face serious prosecution are overwhelmingly guilty, as this dismissal rate appears to suggest, depends upon the reasons cases are dismissed.

The Bureau of Justice Statistics reports data on case processing and adjudication in the largest urban counties in the United States. For every one hundred felony defendants arraigned in the state courts, sixty-nine were prosecuted, twenty-three were dismissed for a variety of reasons, and eight underwent pretrial diversion or similar programs. Of those prosecuted, sixty-eight were convicted—sixty-five through a guilty plea, three following trial. Only one out of the one hundred was acquitted following trial.[5] This pattern is a persistent one. Approximately two-thirds of defendants are convicted and one-third are disposed of through dismissal, diversion, or acquittal, although acquittals make up only 1 percent of all case outcomes.[6] Ten years earlier, the statistics were nearly identical: approximately 28 percent of all those charged with felonies or misdemeanors were not convicted, and only 1.5 percent secured an acquittal.[7]

When one considers individual jurisdictions, however, there appears to be variation in the distribution of those formally charged whose cases are ultimately adjudicated. Seventeen jurisdictions participating in a study conducted by the NCSC Network reported dismissal rates in felony cases ranging from 2 percent in Ventura County, California, to 26 percent in Washington, DC.[8] The explanation offered for the difference was that the prosecutors in Ventura County did a much more rigorous job of screening before charging than did the prosecutors in Washington, DC. A detailed study of a jurisdiction embracing a "rigorous charging, no plea bargaining policy" revealed a dismissal rate of 13 percent.[9]

The Bureau of Justice Statistics

In 1992, the U.S. Bureau of Justice Statistics released a study in which the reasons why cases are dismissed following the filing of original charges were categorized into "diversion," "other prosecution," "evidence," "witness," "due process," "interest of justice," "covered by another case," and "other."[10] The three categories that seem to have the most to do with concern for innocence ("interest of justice," "evidence," and "witness") accounted for between 20 percent (in St. Louis, Missouri) and 51 percent (in Denver, Colorado) of all postcharge dismissals.[11] The average dismissal rate for potentially innocence-related reasons for the nine jurisdictions studied was 36 percent, with Los Angeles, New York City (Manhattan), Portland, Oregon, and Denver, Colorado, all reporting more than 40 percent dismissals related to innocence.

The 1992 BJS figures confirm that most dismissals appear unrelated to concerns about establishing the guilt of the defendants. Among those dismissals that were potentially innocence related, the categories were too broad to reveal the precise evidentiary deficiencies that resulted in dismissal. In most jurisdictions, the cases dismissed for reasons of evidence outnumbered the cases in which dismissal was attributed to witness;[12] and each of these categories outnumbered the dismissals attributed to interests of justice.[13] If we assume that the categories of "evidence" and "witness" referenced deficiencies in the prosecution's case, dismissals due to weaknesses in prima facie cases were more common than dismissals attributed to the strength of the defendants' cases. There is no surprise here: only very confident defense counsel lay their entire case before prosecutor in efforts to end the case with pretrial dismissals.

If we assume a dismissal rate of approximately 25 percent of all cases in which felony charges are filed and further assume that 36 percent of these dismissals are for innocence-related reasons (whether weaknesses of the prosecutors' cases or strengths of the defendants'), then it is arguable (but hardly provable) that 9 percent of all formal criminal charges are dismissed because of concerns that the defendants are innocent. Even if the figure is much lower than this (and it may well be), the likelihood is that far more of the innocent are freed by prosecutors before trial than by juries or judges following trial.

The Zeisel Study

The results from the 1992 BJS study[14] assign a less expansive role of evidentiary concerns than Hans Zeisel found in his analysis of New York court data. Sampling approximately nineteen hundred felony arrests made in New York City in 1971, Zeisel tracked information about each case from arrest to disposition.[15] He collected biographical information on each defendant and then selected 369 cases for more intensive study. From this subsample of cases, he interviewed the main criminal justice actors (judges, prosecutors, defense counsel, and, where possible, the defendants) to provide insight into how the cases were processed.

Zeisel's court respondents (mainly judges, prosecutors, and defense counsel) explained dismissals primarily in evidentiary terms, sometimes adding nonevidentiary considerations to the mix.[16] The most frequent explanation for dismissals was the failure of complaining witnesses to testify. In more than half of the cases, the witnesses did not come forward because of prior relationships between the defendants and the victims, because the defendants also accused the complainants of criminal behavior, because restitution was made, or because of some other connection between the victims and defendants. One need not endorse the appropriateness of the reasons[17] to note that dismissals such as these have little to do with a passion to protect the innocent.

About one-half of the dismissals reported by Zeisel involved specific evidentiary deficiencies consistent with innocence (as opposed to the simple failure of complainants to pursue the charges).[18] As noted previously, in the 1992 BJS study,[19] the figure of evidentiary concerns related to innocence was a third lower, 36 percent. Given the vast differences in the data and categories employed, it may be impossible to reconcile the Boland et al. (1992) and Zeisel (1982) results.[20] Even assuming that the more fine-grained Zeisel study is the more authoritative one, those data show that about one-half of the dismissals are for evidentiary reasons consistent with innocence and one-half are attributable to other causes. Whichever figure is accepted, some of the pretrial screenings resulting in dismissals represent winnowing those who may have been charged with crimes they did not commit.

Zeisel noted that the dismissal rate in New York City was quite comparable to the rates of robbery suspects not prosecuted to trial in Germany and Austria.[21] He suggested,

> The loss between arrest and [proof beyond a reasonable doubt] appears to be the unavoidable result of the judicial safeguards built into all Western law enforcement systems, requiring probable cause for arrest and proof beyond a reasonable doubt for conviction. Like the steam engine in the course of transforming heat into motion, civilized law enforcement must allow a large part of its energy to go to waste.[22]

The image is arresting but a bit misleading. Freeing the innocent is not "blowing off steam"; it is a central goal of criminal justice administration.

Prosecutors' Effectiveness in Screening for Innocence

In typical criminal cases, prosecutors make ex parte determinations that defendants should be charged. Prosecutors rely upon the information presented to them by the police in determining whether the evidence that the police have gathered is sufficient to persuade juries of the defendants' guilt. Typically, prosecutors decide to file charges without speaking with either the defendant or anyone speaking on the defendant's behalf. Once the charges are filed, prosecutors rarely re-examine the fundamental question of guilt or innocence.[23]

Following the filing of formal charges (whether by grand jury or by information), prosecutors may be in contact with defense counsel in connection with pretrial motions or for the purpose of talking about pleas. Prosecutors interact with the police concerning the cases with respect to upcoming court dates, and prosecutors are probably first to talk extensively to the actual witnesses as trial dates approach. At these points, prosecutors may learn that key witnesses will not come forward, that the forensic evidence is much weaker than originally thought, or that the witnesses will not say what the prosecutors had originally understood they were going to say. This information may result in dismissals of the charges on the grounds that the state will not be able to persuade juries of guilt and the defendants cannot be induced to plead. In all likelihood, this is how most erroneously charged defendants secure relief. Prosecutors typically have a harder time establishing false propositions than true ones. However, unless defense counsel call defendants' claims of innocence to prosecutors' attention, prosecutors will likely think about the dismissals in terms of whether they can prove guilt, not in terms of whether defendants actually committed the crimes.

What happens if prosecutors do revisit the question of guilt and innocence prior to trial? This depends upon the bases for the defendants' claims of innocence. One expects pretrial screening to be most effective in those cases in which the defendant claims that the police have arrested and charged the wrong person. Claims of mistaken identity are amenable to verification and resolution through investigation. In theory, innocent defendants through their lawyers will inform prosecutors that they are innocent and point prosecutors to individuals who can confirm that the defendants were elsewhere when the crimes were committed. The police discounted the claims (assuming the defendants made them when arrested) when they presented the defendants to the prosecutors to be charged. Prosecutors concurred (assuming the police informed them of defendants' claims) when they authorized the filing of charges. If defense counsel can make persuasive cases that these decisions were erroneous and persuade the prosecutors that more investigation is needed, the prosecutors may deploy investigative resources to resolve the questions.

The same cannot necessarily be said for claims of innocence founded upon a lack of intent or claims that the defendant's conduct was justified. With respect to claims of self-defense, lack of purpose, and the like, both police and prosecutors may decide that defendants should, quite literally, "tell it to the judge." The more that guilt or innocence turns upon moral evaluations of the defendant's conduct, the more likely that neither the police nor the prosecutors will take responsibility for making the determinations.

There are at least three reasons for this. First, unlike cases in which there are credible claims that defendants are the wrong persons, in cases involving claims of innocence related to mens rea[24] and defenses, there is no question of the ability of the prosecution to make a prima facie case of guilt. The defendant cannot effectively raise the claim that he lacked mens rea nor present an affirmative defense without conceding that he is the person who committed the act that the prosecutor insists constitutes the crime.

Second, police and prosecutors may well think that it is not their role to evaluate the strength of defenses or the claim that the defendant lacked the forbidden state of mind. The police will consider that they have completed their job when they apprehend the persons who committed the acts that appear to be crimes. Prosecutors have a broader role, but their ability to resolve the bona fides of claims of lack of mens rea and their interest in doing so may be quite limited in ordinary cases. This is a very difficult thing to measure, and the tools available (e.g., a lie detector test) are of quite limited utility. Indeed, it is not clear that there is anything inappropriate about the police and prosecutors leaving these questions to judges and juries.

Third, prosecutors do not learn about claims of innocence unless defense counsel opt to put them forward prior to trial. Typically, there are no formal procedures for arguing innocence to prosecutors prior to the filing of charges or trial. This does not mean that such arguments are not made and taken seriously, at least in the rare cases when defendants have resources and are well represented.[25] Nonetheless, typical criminal defendants have neither resources nor effective representation prior to indictment; nor do typical criminal cases begin with investigations of which defendants are aware.

The overwhelming majority (over 95 percent) of cases that are not dismissed result in guilty pleas.[26] The existence of plea bargaining, coupled with the recognition that it is appropriate for innocents to plead guilty when they believe that they will be mistakenly convicted, calls into question the accuracy of some of those pleas.[27] As Erdmann explained to Santiago, a defendant may find an inaccurate admission of guilt to be very much in his interest.[28] Those in jail while awaiting trial may be tempted to plead to "time served" if this will result in their immediate release.

The *Federal Sentencing Guidelines* make explicit what has long been implicit in plea bargaining: criminal defendants can be punished through increased incarceration for insisting upon trial and for testifying in a manner the judge believes to be false. On the other hand, if defendants choose to plead guilty, they can be rewarded with reductions in their sentences.[29] Rational defendants may choose the certainty of reduced sentences over the uncertainty of sentences following trials, particularly when the differences between the sentences are stark. In *North Carolina v. Alford*,[30] the choice confronting the defendant was between the certainty of a long prison term if he pled guilty and the possibility of a death sentence if he went to trial and was convicted by a jury. The Supreme Court saw no constitutional infirmity in the state accepting a guilty plea to the lesser offense under these circumstances, even through Alford insisted he was innocent.

The innocent can and do make such choices. John Dixon of New Jersey pled guilty to sexual assault and received a forty-five year sentence in return in 1991. He explained his plea on the grounds that he feared an even longer sentence if he went to trial and was convicted. Ten years later, he was exonerated through DNA testing.[31] William Kelley of Pennsylvania pled guilty to third degree murder only to be released two years later when DNA established that another had committed the crime. A psychiatrist testified that Kelly had been trying to please his interrogators when he confessed to the crime.[32]

We do not suggest that a high percentage of those who plead guilty are actually innocent of the crimes to which they plead. We do suggest that some of those who plead guilty make a rational decision that their freedom will be enhanced rather than diminished by acknowledging guilt of crimes they did not commit. However, given the vast number of defendants who plead guilty to resolve serious criminal charges each year, the absolute number of innocents who plead guilty may well be in the thousands. The presence of innocents among those against whom charges are dismissed suggests what logic dictates: winnowing by the police does not result in elimination of the innocents from the pool of those against whom the state proceeds. The presence of innocents among those who plead guilty also suggests that prosecutors are not omniscient; many innocents are forced to judgment. Many plead guilty in return for reduced sentences; some insist upon trials and are acquitted.

Curiously, recent data indicate that federal judges acquit a higher percentage of defendants than do juries. The Department of Justice, Bureau of Justice Statistics, reported that for fiscal year 2009, 35 percent of the defendants who were tried by federal judges sitting without juries were acquitted as opposed to 12 percent of those whose cases were decided by juries.[33] Seven times as many defendants were convicted by federal juries as by federal judges.[34] In the federal system, at least, those with the most information (the judges) are the most likely to acquit.[35]

Judicial beneficence has been explained on the grounds of selection effects. Those who are innocent desire the most accurate fact finding and believe that they can find this from judges more readily than from juries. On the basis of this view, defendants with weak cases are the ones who seek jury trials; so it is not surprising that juries return guilty verdicts at a higher rate than judges.[36] This may explain the different acquittal rates between judges and juries in those systems in which the choice between jury or judge trial is the defendant's alone. It does not explain the results in federal courts where, under the Federal Rules of Criminal Procedure, the prosecution must agree before juries can be waived.[37]

Screening Failures: What We Know about Acquittals

We began this chapter with a journalist's description of a lawyer, Martin Erdmann, advising his client that pleading guilty would result in immediate freedom while insisting upon innocence would prolong incarceration. Consider another individual, charged with a crime he insisted that he did not commit, who refuses a plea offer. The following excerpt is from Bernard Malamud's fictionalized retelling of the ritual murder trial of Menahim Beilis in czarist Russia.

An old pink-faced man came into the cell dressed in winter clothes. He wore a black cape and black gaiters and grasped a gnarled cane. Berezhinsky followed him in, carrying a slender chair with a delicate back, and the old man sat in it erectly, several feet from the fixer, holding the cane in gray-mittened hands. His watery eyes wandered. He told Yakov he was a former jurist of high repute, and that he came with good news. An excitement so thick that it felt like sickness surged through the fixer. The former jurist said this was the year of the three-hundredth anniversary of the Rule of the House of Romanov and that the Tsar, in celebration, would issue a ukase amnestying certain classes of criminals. Yakov's name would be listed among them. He was to be pardoned, and permitted to return to his village. The old man's face flushed with pleasure. The prisoner clung to the wall, too burdened to speak. Then he asked, Pardoned as a criminal or pardoned as an innocent? The former jurist testily said what difference did it make so long as he was let out of prison. It was impossible to erase the sins of the past, but it was not impossible for a humane ruler, a Christian gentleman, to forgive an evil act. The old man sneezed without snuff and peered at his silver watch. Yakov said he wanted a fair trial, not a pardon. If they ordered him to leave the prison without a trial they would have to shoot him first. Don't be foolish, said the former jurist, how can you go on suffering like this, caked in filth? The fixer moved his chains restlessly. I have no choice, he said. I have just offered you one. That's not a choice, said Yakov. The former jurist tried to convince the prisoner, then gave up

in irritation. It's easier to reason with a peasant. He rose and shook his
cane at the fixer. How can we help you, he shouted, if you are so pig-
headed. Berezhinsky, who had been listening at the spy hole, opened
the door and the old man left the cell. The guard came in for the chair
but before taking it, he let Yakov urinate in the can, then dumped the
contents on his head. The fixer was left in the chains that night. He
thought that whenever he had been through the worst, there was always worse.[38]

In reality, Menahim Beilis refused to acknowledge guilt for a crime he
never committed and went to trial. He was acquitted. It is to that topic
—the relationship between those who refuse to plead and the outcome
of their trials—that we now turn.

Approximately one-third of all cases that go to trial result in an acquittal.[39] According to the traditional view of plea bargaining, these
are the close cases in which defendants are willing to turn down plea
bargains.[40] But what makes a case "close"? Because plea offers are
theoretically adjusted to reflect the likelihood of acquittal, acquitted
defendants' decisions to refuse the bargains may reflect their beliefs
that juries will not convict them, possibly because they did not commit the crimes.

Recent data are consistent with the view that many trials occur
because defendants claim innocence. In the NCSC data described
earlier, the defense counsel identified claims of innocence as the reason why there were no pleas in nearly half of the jury trials.[41] As illustrated in table 3.1, prosecutors in the NCSC study data identified
defendants' claims of innocence as the reason why there were no pleas
in only 25 percent of the cases, suggesting either that defense counsel
did not identify the claims as those of innocence in plea negotiations
or the prosecutors did not hear them that way. Indeed, prosecutors
and defense counsel *agreed* that claims of innocence were the reason
why plea bargaining failed in only 25 out of 173 (14 percent) of the
cases examined.[42]

As we described in the previous chapter, studies of acquittals, both
in the United States and in the United Kingdom, conducted over the

TABLE 3.1
Prosecution and Defense Explanations of Failure of Plea Bargaining (NCSC Data)

Prosecution explanation	Defense explanation				
	Defendant claimed innocence	Defendant refused to plea	No plea offered	No plea agreement reached	Total
Defendant claimed innocence	14.5% (25)	3.5% (6)	1.1% (2)	5.8% (10)	24.9% (43)
Defendant refused to plea	17.3% (30)	5.2% (9)	1.1% (2)	9.8% (17)	33.5% (58)
No plea offered	11.0% (19)	0.% (0)	5.8% (10)	7.5% (13)	24.3% (42)
No plea agreement reached	5.8% (10)	1.7% (3)	0.% (0)	9.8% (17)	17.3% (30)
Total	48.6% (84)	10.4% (18)	8.0% (14)	32.9% (57)	100.% (173)

Source: Analysis of 2002 data from Hannaford-Agor et al., *Are Hung Juries a Problem?*
Note: Number of cases is given in parentheses.

past fifty years have been surprisingly uniform in their findings. The vast majority of acquittals are viewed by judges as either factually accurate or factually inaccurate but legally sound. A small minority of acquittals are viewed as lawless.[43]

Despite the differences in times and legal systems, the consistency of the findings is remarkable. These studies indicated that prosecutors win only about seven out of ten trials; that judges believed most of their losses were understandable based on the evidence presented; and that acquittals that in the judges' opinions were lawless accounted for only a small fraction of all acquittals. However, the studies provided little information about the characteristics of lawful acquittals.[44]

Explaining Lawful Acquittals

What accounts for lawful acquittals? Some acquittals are undoubtedly attributable to evidentiary failures. Witnesses disappear or claim not to remember the incidents in question or become confused on cross-examination. Judges may rule that relevant and persuasive evidence is inadmissible.[45] Some acquittals are attributable to the burden of proof. The state introduces all the available evidence as persuasively as it can, but the jury or judge retains a reasonable doubt as to guilt. This can occur even if the evidence is sufficient to persuade everybody that the defendant is *probably* guilty. Many acquittals probably result from the interplay between evidentiary shortcomings and the burden of proof. Finally, some acquittals may result from the defendants' ability to present their versions of events to decision makers who are not necessarily committed to the idea that the defendants are guilty. Defendants' cases may consist of either presenting affirmative evidence of their innocence, pointing out shortcomings in the prosecutions' evidence, or some combination of the two.

Both innocent and guilty defendants can be lawfully acquitted for any of these reasons. Knowing *why* juries acted does not answer definitively the question of whether their judgments were factually accurate. However, knowing the reasons for the acquittals may help answer the question that every acquittal raises: Why wasn't the evidence that persuaded the police and prosecutor of the defendant's guilt sufficient to persuade the judge or jury? The official story reflects the premise of the liberation hypothesis: juries are swayed by irrelevancies such as the personal characteristics of the people who testify or argue before them, or juries make legal mistakes in deciding in terms of unattainable standards of proof. When cases are close on the evidence—as all observers agree is true of most acquittals—juries are free to decide cases according to their values instead of pursuant to the evidence.[46] The message is consistent: the acquitted are not actually innocent but are instead beneficiaries of a generous legal system or decision makers who permit their values to determine the outcomes.[47] The traditional answer to the question of how many of the acquitted are innocent is that there are a few of them,[48] although we really do not know.

This view rests on a series of assumptions. First, prosecutors proceed only against the guilty. Second, their judgments that defendants are guilty are superior to those of juries because prosecutors, like judges, have more information about the defendants and the crimes (particularly whether the defendants have committed crimes in the past) than do the juries. Third, prosecutors and judges are more skilled than laypeople at evaluating evidence (particularly credibility); their evaluations of conflicting stories are the correct ones. Fourth, the prosecutors' heavy burden of proof and the vagaries of litigation inevitably result in some acquittals that are legally appropriate but factually in-accurate. Each of these points is contestable, which suggests that the claim of universal guilt among those who go to trial is overstated.

Yet, a fifth point speaks most tellingly against the view of prosecu-torial omniscience. Frequently, jurors have more relevant information upon which to base judgments about guilt than prosecutors possess when they decide to file charges. Juries are typically the first remotely neutral decision makers to hear the defendants' stories from the de-fendants or, more important, other witnesses. The simplest explana-tion for acquittals may be that it is only at trial that defendants can actually tell their stories.

The Belief That Prosecutors Only Proceed against the Guilty

The American Bar Association canons suggest that prosecutors should not proceed in cases unless they believe that the defendants are guilty.[49] However, this can be a very awkward requirement. Take, for example, the following scenario. There is a shooting in a bar. The witnesses present a very confusing picture of what happened. The de-fendant insists that he acted in self-defense after the victim said, "I'll kill you," and reached inside his pocket. No weapon is found on or near the victim. The victim has a reputation in the community as a violent person.

What does it mean, in this situation, that the prosecutor must be-lieve the defendant is guilty before pressing charges? Prosecutors who genuinely believe they know the truth in cases of this nature have ac-cess to insights denied the rest of humanity. On the other hand, the facts are more than sufficient to justify a belief that the defendant killed unlawfully. What prosecutors probably believe is that there is sufficient evidence here that the community, through the institution of the jury, should make the judgment as to guilt or innocence.

These kinds of ethical problems disappear if prosecutors become convinced of the defendants' guilt, something quite likely to occur given the ease with which advocates can come to believe in the jus-tice of their causes. Prosecutors will proceed appropriately regardless of whether they have any actual basis for being convinced beyond any doubt that the defendants did the crimes. Jury verdicts reflecting that doubt are hardly challenges to the integrity of such prosecutorial decisions.

In the situation just described, the jury has the same information as the prosecutor but comes to a different conclusion. There are also cases in which the disagreement between the jury or judge and the prosecutor may reflect the different information available to them. Despite the traditional assumption that prosecutors know more than the juries, as noted, this need not be the case. Frequently, prosecutors will have less information when they decide to charge defendants with crimes than do the juries that decide guilt or innocence.

The rules purporting to limit the evidentiary use of prior criminal records frequently mean that in this area at least juries have less information about the accused than do the prosecutors. These very differences in information may be part of what results in juries acquitting when prosecutors believe in guilt. This does not mean that the prosecutors are correct and the juries wrong. Rather, although the prosecutors may have information about the accused beyond that which is presented to the juries, the additional information about prior criminal records may not prove what the prosecutors may believe it does, that the defendants' past bad deeds are evidence of guilt in the present cases.

The evidentiary rules limiting the use of prior criminal records speak to the universal perception that the existence of prior criminal records may prove too much. In evidentiary terms, the prejudice may outweigh the probative value of the prior convictions. However, the rules are also irrational. They prohibit the most persuasive evidence, prior criminal behavior that is similar to the behavior charged in the current case, while embracing the questionable proposition that prior convictions of just about any crime are some evidence that the defendants are lying in the current cases. In terms of the relationship between prior records and actual innocence, we should remember that the vast majority of the DNA exonerations involve individuals with prior records.

The problem is not that criminal records may not represent some evidence that the defendants may have committed the crimes, but rather that the significance of the prior criminal records turns heavily upon how the state came to identify the accused as the perpetrators. In cases that rest heavily on eyewitness testimony (e.g., sexual assault committed by a stranger), the existence of prior criminal records adds very little (perhaps nothing) to the prosecutions' cases if the witnesses identified the accused from pictures in police files of those with records for the same kind of crimes. Had the eyewitnesses picked other faces out of the photographs shown them from the sex crime files, the cases against those persons would be just as strong as the cases against the actual defendants. There is nothing particularly distinctive about rape suspects with prior records for sexual assault when they are identified from an array of people with histories of criminal sexual assault. Prior criminal records would be more persuasive evidence of guilt if the defendants were identified independently of those records (e.g., by the victims seeing them on the street rather than by identifying them from police files).

A dominant rationalization for indifference to the possibility of adjudicatory errors has always been that "even if he didn't do this crime, he did another for which he has not been held responsible." This rationale is particularly problematic when the charges against the accused derive significantly from their records of prior criminal activity. The problem is worse than simply ignoring the fundamental strictures of due process and justifying punishment based on crimes that have not been established with appropriate proof in open court. To the extent that the very fact of the prosecution depends upon the defendants' presence in police files, the rationalization may be more readily characterized as "even if he didn't do this crime, he did another crime in the past, and it is okay to punish him a second time for that crime."

The point should not be overstated. A police record is some evidence of a disposition (willingness) to commit crimes, and starting an otherwise unformed investigation by focusing on those who have committed this kind of crime in the past is a rational and appropriate approach. Indeed, ignoring that information would be professional incompetence. Most crimes are committed by recidivists. However, the prosecutions' awareness and the juries' ignorance of the extent of defendants' criminal records does not mean that the prosecutors are correct and the juries are in error whenever the juries acquit. Nor does it mean that the defendants are actually guilty even if the juries' acquittals are legally appropriate. The probative value of prior records is dependent in significant part upon the role that those records play in focusing the state's attention on the defendants and upon the extent to which there is persuasive evidence unrelated to the prior records that establishes guilt.

The NCSC data described earlier[50] reveal doubt about whether the juries' ignorance of defendants' criminal records explains why juries acquit when more informed decision makers (the judges) would convict. As illustrated in table 3.2, the NCSC data suggest that it is whether or not the defendants have criminal records, not whether the juries learn about them, that has the greatest influence on acquittal or conviction decisions. Although juries acquitted nearly twice as often when defendants had no prior records than when they had such records (45 percent vs. 23 percent), there was very little difference between the acquittal rate when defendants had records of which juries were unaware and the acquittal rate when defendants had records of which juries were aware (23.8 percent vs. 21.1 percent).

Judges' assessments of guilt or innocence followed the same pattern. Judges were nearly twice as likely to indicate that they would have found the defendant not guilty in cases in which defendants had no

TABLE 3.2
Verdicts in Cases according to Defendants' Criminal Records and
Juries' Awareness of Criminal Records (NCSC Data)

Defendants' criminal records/jury awareness	Hung jury or conviction	Acquittal	Total
Unknown	62.5% (10)	37.5% (6)	100% (16)
No known arrests or convictions	55.0% (33)	45.0% (27)	100% (60)
Jury does not learn of defendant's criminal record	76.2% (138)	23.8% (40)	100% (168)
Jury does learn of defendant's criminal record	78.8% (52)	21.2% (14)	100% (66)
Total	71.9% (223)	27.1% (87%)	100% (310)

Source: Analysis of 2002 data from Hannaford-Agor et al., *Are Hung Juries a Problem?*
Note: Number of cases is given in parentheses.

records compared with those cases in which defendants had records of which judges were aware but juries were not.[51] Although judges may have information about defendants' criminal histories that is denied to the juries, that information does not appear significant in the judges' assessments of whether defendants ought to be acquitted.

On occasion, prosecutors will have information other than the defendants' prior criminal records that may render their judgments about the defendants' guilt more reliable than the juries'. The operation of the exclusionary rules or information from undisclosed informants may result in prosecutors making more reliable decisions about guilt than juries. To the extent that the excluded evidence is highly probative of guilt (e.g., the proceeds of crime or contraband that it is illegal to possess), the prosecutors' judgments about the defendants' guilt are likely to be correct. However, these situations are extremely rare. The exclusionary rule affects the decision to prosecute in a small number of cases but rarely has a role in cases in which prosecutors have decided to go forward. Prosecutors screen out between 0.2 and 0.8 percent of all adult felony cases because of illegal searches.[52] No comparable data exist with respect to the number of cases in which prosecutors have reliable information from informants that points to the defendants' guilt but do not call the informants as witnesses at trial. There surely are such cases, but the likelihood is that informants are not used either because they do not offer admissible evidence or because their testimony is not likely to be credited by juries at trial.

Beyond the situations in which prosecutors are denied the ability to introduce probative evidence or decide not to do so to serve broader law enforcement interests, prosecutors may also have superior information that juries do not consider for other reasons. Witnesses may fail to appear in a timely fashion or may testify unconvincingly. Witnesses may also be precluded from telling their stories because of aberrant judicial rulings.

The cases in which prosecutors actually possess probative evidence of guilt that they cannot share with juries probably represent a very small percentage of acquittals. Kalven and Zeisel found that information that the judges alone knew accounted for only a tiny percentage

(2 percent) of the disagreements concerning guilt between judges and juries.[53] If one looks exclusively at the cases in which juries acquit when judges would have convicted (as opposed to cases in which the disagreements are about the charges, the juries hang, or the juries convict when the judges would have acquitted), judges mentioned that they had information not available to juries in 7 percent of cases.[54] Virtually all the facts that Kalven and Zeisel's respondents identified would also have been known to the prosecutors: about the only information available to the prosecutors that the judges would not know would have been the information coming from informants the prosecutors decided to protect.

Kalven and Zeisel's data relating to information known only to the judge focused on a subset of acquittals, the ones in which judges and juries disagreed. Judges agreed with the jury's verdict of acquittal in 14 percent of the cases. One cannot know what secret information the prosecutors might have possessed in those cases, but there is no reason to believe that the percentage was any higher than that possessed by the judges in the disagreement cases. Nor is it likely that the ratio has shifted dramatically since Kalven and Zeisel did their study.[55] Jury conviction rates appear to have remained stable.[56] There does not appear to have been a significant decrease in the ability of prosecutors to present incriminating information to juries.

The Belief That Prosecutors Evaluate the Evidence Differently

Prosecutors may be correct and juries in error if prosecutors have superior abilities to evaluate the evidence. Evaluation typically means determining which witnesses to believe. There may also be cases that are sufficiently complicated (e.g., securities fraud) that, due to the limitations of the adversary system (and, possibly, the adversaries), juries simply do not understand what the evidence means. These cases are relatively rare.[57] Most criminal prosecutions are not nuanced affairs calling for subtle understanding of complex information. If we are to credit the prosecution rather than the juries because the prosecutors have superior understanding (as opposed to superior information),

this understanding will typically be related to knowing which witnesses to believe and which to discount.

There is no empirical support for the view that a single professional
is better at determining credibility than a group of amateurs sharing
information. The studies can and do show that professionals arrive at
similar judgments about who is telling the truth, but they do not show
that these judgments are more accurate than those arrived at by non-
professionals. If anything, the judgments are likely to be less accurate
because they are made according to shared professional norms, at least
some of which are without sound empirical bases.

We also have no reason to believe that, among professionals, prosecutors are better than judges in determining questions of credibility. After all, judges sitting by themselves acquit on occasion.[58] When
they do so, they are necessarily disbelieving evidence that prosecutors
found persuasive. Even if one ignores the lack of any data suggesting
that professionals are better at discerning truth telling than amateurs,
when professionals do disagree (as they do when judges enter acquittals in bench trials), nothing suggests that the prosecutors are correct
and the judges in error.[59]

The Prosecutors' Burden of Proof and Vagaries of Litigation

The prosecutors' burden to persuade juries beyond a reasonable
doubt appears to mean that many who are guilty will be acquitted. The
question of innocence does not arise. The trial is focused on whether
the state's evidence of guilt is thoroughly persuasive. If it is not, juries
should find defendants not guilty even if the juries are persuaded that
the defendants probably committed the crimes. Because it is lawful to
acquit the guilty, it seems logical that that is what happens. The acquitted are guilty people against whom prosecutors were unable to mount
persuasive cases.

The scant data that we have do not provide support for this view.
We know that judges believe that juries ignore their obligations to convict when the evidence leaves no reasonable doubt in around 15 percent of all acquittals.[60] This means that the vast majority of acquittals

are legally appropriate in the sense that judges can understand how juries may find the state's cases unconvincing beyond a reasonable doubt. Kalven and Zeisel[61] concluded that, in those cases in which judges would have convicted but juries acquitted (about 17 percent of the entire sample of cases),[62] the major source of the disagreement between the judges and the juries was their differing evaluations of the evidence (as opposed to differences in what the authors characterized as values or a combination of evidence and values).[63] They also noted that the cases in which judges treated the jury verdict as being without merit were much more likely to involve disagreements concerning values than disagreements about the evidence.[64]

There is nothing surprising in these data: it makes sense that judges are most disapproving of decisions that appear to rest on extralegal factors rather than on evaluations of the evidence. It is the other side of the coin that deserves attention: that most disagreements between judges and juries concerning guilt involve differing interpretations of the evidence.[65] This too is logical. If it is then a matter of interpretation, it becomes important to know who is better at interpreting the evidence. No data suggest that judges are invariably or even predominantly more correct in evaluating the evidence than juries. Most verdicts of acquittal probably represent accurate responses to the evidence presented.

That acquittals are responsive to the evidence does not mean that the acquitted are innocent. At the same time, acquittals that are responsive to the state's evidence surely do not mean that the defendants are guilty. Some (probably most) of the failure to persuade may be attributable to the state's failure to provide very convincing evidence, but this raises the question of why the evidence is unconvincing. On rare occasions, this occurs because the courts forbid the state from introducing probative evidence, prosecutors choose to withhold such evidence, or juries do not understand the evidence. Sometimes it occurs because of the skill of the opposing lawyers or the ineptitude of the prosecutors. On other occasions, it results from the inability of truthful and perceptive witnesses to communicate effectively with juries. Some cases are simply not free from doubt, and the doubt goes to the defendants. Finally, sometimes the state fails in its proof because the defendants are innocent and the state is trying to establish propositions that are not true.

The Belief That Some Information Is Not Available to Prosecutors

Innocent defendants typically have far more information about their behavior in relation to the crimes than do the prosecutors. In these instances, the information available to the juries from both the prosecution and the defense is more complete than the information available to the prosecutors who made the decisions to proceed to trial. Here, at a minimum, there are no a priori reasons to conclude that prosecutors' conclusions that defendants are guilty are more accurate than judges' or juries' conclusions that defendants are not guilty.

Juries tend to hear a coherent recounting of the defendants' stories to a far greater extent than do police and prosecutors. Kalven and Zeisel found that most (82 percent) of defendants in criminal trials testified in their own defense;[66] but in the NCSC data, this occurred in only one-half the cases.[67] Our criminal process encourages innocent defendants to withhold their stories until trial.[68] If police investigations were concerned solely with establishing what happened as opposed to establishing cases against the leading suspects, innocent defendants may be well advised to speak with the police and tell them what they wish to know. A disinterested, open-minded search for the truth, however, does not necessarily characterize police investigation of crime. Studies of police investigations indicate that the police tend to arrive at judgments about who committed crimes relatively quickly and the remainder of the investigation is focused upon building the cases against those persons.[69] Most questioning of prospective defendants is undertaken with this goal in mind.[70] Once the police have made an arrest, defendants are affirmatively advised of their rights to remain silent; and defendants are, indeed, well advised to do so.

The decision whether to charge someone with a crime is made by the prosecutor. The only judicial question is whether there is probable cause to detain the prisoner, and the test for probable cause is quite minimal. Moreover, judges make these decisions ex parte. Those arrested have no realistic opportunity to present their stories until after they are formally charged with crimes. In typical jurisdictions, this occurs when the accused are assigned lawyers or given opportunities to secure the services of lawyers. At this point, they can tell their stories to these individuals, who are on their side and are obliged to keep the stories confidential.

The NCSC data revealed that what defendants tell their lawyers about their innocence is related to the ultimate outcomes of the cases. The NCSC survey instrument included questions of both prosecutors and defense counsel to indicate why there had been no pleas in the cases in question. The juries acquitted in almost one-half (46 percent) of the cases when the defense counsel indicated that there were no pleas because the defendants insisted that they were innocent. In contrast, there were acquittals in only 18 percent of the cases in which the pleas were not entered for some other reason (see table 3.3).

We have noted that juries may receive more information than the police or the prosecutors. The more information juries receive from the defendants, the more likely juries are to acquit the defendants. Using the data from the NCSC study, for example, consider the stepwise progression in acquittals as we move from cases in which there is no defense evidence to those in which the defendant alone testifies to those in which at least one witness testifies but not the defendant and, finally, to those in which both the defendant and at least one other witness testifies (see table 3.4). When juries were confronted with what was likely to be the same evidentiary picture as the prosecutors (e.g., the evidence of guilt was either uncontested or contested by

TABLE 3.3
Acquittal Rates by Defense Counsel Reasons for No Pleas (NCSC Data)

Explanation	Hung or conviction	Acquittal	Total
Defendant claimed innocence	54.3% (57)	45.7% (48)	100% (105)
Bargaining failed for other reasons	81.8% (81)	18.2% (18)	100% (99)
Total	67.6% (138)	32.4% (66)	100% (204)

Source: Analysis of 2002 data from Hannaford-Agor et al., *Are Hung Juries a Problem?*
Note: Number of cases is given in parentheses.

TABLE 3.4
Comparative Progression of Information Supplied to Juries

	Hung or conviction	Acquittal	Total
No defense witnesses testify	83.3% (65)	16.7% (13)	100% (78)
Defendant alone testifies	78.4% (47)	21.6% (13)	100% (60)
At least one defense witness testifies without defendant	65.1% (54)	34.9% (29)	100% (83)
Defendant and at least one defense witness testify	58.6% (51)	41.4% (36)	100% (87)
Total	70.4% (217)	29.6% (91)	100% (308)

Source: Analysis of 2002 data from Hannaford-Agor et al., *Are Hung Juries a Problem?*
Note: Number of cases given in parentheses.

the defendants alone), they convicted in more than 80 percent of the cases. When juries confronted evidence that the prosecutors or police were unlikely to have considered (e.g., evidence provided by witnesses other than the defendant), the acquittal rate literally doubled, increasing from 16.7 percent to 34.9 percent.[71] Perhaps the state's one-sided view of the evidence results in more accurate judgments about innocence than juries' views of both sides of the stories, but why this should always be so is a mystery.

Reginald Heber Smith and Herbert Ehrmann cautioned in their 1922 study of courts in Cleveland, Ohio, that "the service performed by juries does not lend itself to appraisal by the statistical method. Without knowing the facts in each case, one is not able to conclude whether or not an acquittal, disagreement, conviction, or verdict was or was not justified."[72] Acquittals are *legally* accurate whenever juries conclude appropriately that the state has failed to present evidence to persuade them of the defendants' guilt beyond a reasonable doubt. However, even when the juries' not guilty verdicts are appropriate, we still do not know whether they are *factually* accurate. Acquittals are factually accurate when juries determine correctly that defendants either did not engage in the prohibited conduct or, if they did so engage, that they either lacked the state of mind required to make the conduct criminal or that their actions were products of appropriate beliefs that justify them.[73]

The criminal law requires proof beyond a reasonable doubt, and it is possible that it is the state's failures to amass and present evidence persuasively rather than defendants' actual innocence that result in acquittals. The state's key witnesses may leave town without informing prosecutors, and yet judges insist that the trials go forward. Juries may find eyewitnesses to be unconvincing even though everything they say is entirely correct. In some cases, even if all available prosecution witnesses testify accurately, there are some questions that the witnesses cannot answer definitively. For example, did the defendant really believe that the laptop he took from the library was the one he had left there the night before? If the answer is yes, he is not guilty of larceny. But we have no way to know definitively what was actually in his mind on that occasion. Similarly, defendants' claims of self-defense are dependent upon whether they were actually in fear for their lives or limbs; but juries have only the defendants' trial testimonies and the observations of those present from which to form judgments.

We cannot know definitively the extent to which juries' verdicts of not guilty result in freeing factually innocent defendants. What we can do is explore the extent to which jury verdicts respond to factors consistent with factual innocence. In the next chapters, we have taken advantage of a unique opportunity to use the NCSC database to explore the factors distinguishing the cases in which juries acquitted from those in which they convicted. The database also provides information about judges' and lawyers' views of those same factors in the same cases. As shall be seen, contemporary juries, like those in Kalven and Zeisel's day, are more likely to acquit than judges. But, contrary to Kalven and Zeisel, jurors disagree with judges because they assess the evidence differently, not because they yearn to liberate the guilty. In the end, the question of who is correct, the judges or the juries, depends upon who assesses the evidence correctly, not who is most moved by sentiment.

4

Understanding Why Judges and Juries Disagree about Criminal Case Outcomes
Are Jury Verdicts an Expression of Sentiment?

The pizza man was charged with hiring assassins to kill a Genovese crime family associate. The evidence was robust. The baker was charged with helping him. The evidence was less robust. But the pizza man was working at a restaurant on Friday when the baker was convicted of murder. "The irony, the irony, the irony!" cried the victim's sister, Assunta Rozza, throwing her arms in the air. Mafia historians may long debate the split verdict, but one distinction was clear: The pizza man entrusted his fate to a jury, the baker to a judge.[1]

A Brooklyn baker convicted of cooking up a hit on a Genovese loan shark got the minimum on Monday after a judge took the unusual step of criticizing the jury that cleared his co-defendant. Mario Fortunato, 60, was convicted in a bench trial of planning and helping to execute the November 30, 1994, shooting at a Williamsburg social club. He was sentenced to 15 years to life. Co-defendant Carmine Polito had his fate weighed by a jury, not the judge, and got off. "Although I'm not supposed to criticize a jury verdict, I had to disagree with it," said Brooklyn Supreme Court Justice Joel Goldberg, who found

Fortunato guilty after the jury cleared Polito. "The evidence against Mr. Polito is overwhelming . . . the evidence was not that strong against Mr. Fortunato," Goldberg said. "It reached a result that doesn't speak justice at all for anyone." Fortunato and Polito were charged with planning and helping to whack Sabato (Tino) Lombardi. The shooting also severely wounded his cousin, Michael (Cookie) D'Urso. Polito chose a jury trial and Fortunato, to separate himself from the seeming mountain of evidence against Polito, chose a bench trial. The hit man and D'Urso—a mob informant who brought down dozens of Genovese mobsters in unrelated cases—testified against both men. "What has happened is unbelievable," Fortunato said in a statement read by his lawyer on Monday. "Carmine Polito is home. I am in jail. This is not justice."[2]

A Brooklyn baker convicted of a mob hit walked out of prison a free man Friday after an appellate court overturned his 2008 conviction.[3]

The case of the baker and the pizza man reflects a phenomenon that concerns observers of our criminal justice system—how can a judge and a jury look at the same evidence and arrive at radically different conclusions as to what it shows? If they do arrive at different conclusions, which one is correct? The judge who was certain that Fortunato and Polito both participated in the murder or the jury that acquitted Polito? And if the judge was correct, why did the appellate court overturn his verdict?

In the United States, we have resolved this conundrum by insisting that the jury serves values that transcend accurate fact finding. At the height of the due process revolution, the Supreme Court confronted the question of whether the United States Constitution required states to afford criminal defendants the right to a jury trial in a serious case. In concluding that the Constitution did impose this requirement, the Court did not base its ruling on the view that juries were more accurate fact finders than judges. Rather, it noted that the constitutional right to a jury trial in a serious criminal case reflected "a profound judgment" that a criminal defendant had a right to a jury in order to prevent "oppression by the government."[4]

The Court in *Duncan v. Louisiana* found support for the view that juries provide a distinctive and valuable voice on the question of guilt or innocence affirmed in Kalven and Zeisel's *American Jury*. *Duncan* is just one of the twenty-fix different Supreme Court decisions (as well as more than 150 decisions of other courts)[5] that cites *The American Jury* for support of a proposition concerning the behavior of juries. It is a fair statement that no other work of social science relating to jury behavior has been as widely or as approvingly referenced by courts. These citations are a tribute to the eminence of the authors, the breadth and sweep of their empirical and analytic work, and the mostly reassuring message about juries that the work conveys. On occasion, both the majority and the dissent in the same opinion draw sustenance from Kalven and Zeisel's work. In *McCleskey v. Kemp* (1987) the majority of the United States Supreme Court rejected the argument that racial disparities rendered Georgia's capital punishment scheme unconstitutional, quoting Kalven and Zeisel when they noted that juries need to make "difficult and uniquely human judgments."[6]

Despite the prominence and influence of Kalven and Zeisel's research, it provides little guidance on how we should assess those cases where juries disagree with judges on guilt. If juries do rely on personal or community sentiments about the law or the defendant to arrive at an acquittal in opposition to a judge's opinion that the defendant is guilty, as Kalven and Zeisel's liberation hypothesis predicts, does this mean the jury's verdict in the decision is incorrect and the judge is correct? The appellate court in the Brooklyn baker mob case illustrated at the beginning of this chapter certainly did not think so, overturning the conviction of the judge when a jury found the defendant's codefendant not guilty. Judge and jury disagreements continue to raise questions about whether jury decisions made in opposition to the view of the judge are more or less accurate or just than a decision about which the judge and jury agree.

Kalven and Zeisel[7] drew their conclusions about why juries disagreed with judges entirely from survey responses by judges about their perceptions as to why juries arrived at a different conclusion than they would have in various cases. No attempt was made to verify that the conclusions of judges about why the jury disagreed with him were in fact correct. Research for *The American Jury*[8] was conducted over fifty years ago at the dawn of the civil rights movement, before the composition of police forces, judges, and juries began to reflect more accurately the race and gender of the general population. The research was conducted before DNA analysis exposed the vulnerability of previously uncontestable convictions in serious cases. The data also predated the constitutional revolution in the way courts conduct criminal adjudication.[9] The demographics of defendants in felony courts have changed substantially since the time of Kalven and Zeisel's study as well.[10] These changes have the potential to produce both a markedly different set of trial outcomes and a different level of judge-jury agreement than those reported by Kalven and Zeisel in 1966.

This chapter examines the liberation hypothesis through analysis of data from an empirical study of criminal court case outcomes conducted by the National Center for State Courts (NCSC) a half-century after Kalven and Zeisel. Before turning to an exploration of the behavior of contemporary juries, we first examine the findings of Kalven and Zeisel in more detail and then describe how the hypothesis has fared when tested by subsequent investigators in a variety of contexts. Having set the stage, we then turn to the main business of this chapter, which is an analysis of whether the data from the NCSC study provides support for Kalven and Zesiel's explanation of why juries and judges disagree about guilt. As we shall see, judges and juries continue to disagree in a significant number of cases, and *judges* continue to believe that values or sentiment explain the jury's decision to acquit someone whom the judge thought guilty. Jurors provide a very different explanation for their decisions—they acquit when they find the state's evidence unpersuasive or the defendant's evidence persuasive or both. To a large extent, they follow instructions and acquit when they were told to acquit—because the evidence presented to them did not establish that the defendant committed the crime.

The Liberation Hypothesis

Based on their analysis of survey responses from over five hundred judges presiding over three thousand criminal trials, Kalven and Zeisel[11] found that 94 percent of judge-jury disagreements could be explained through a combination of differing views of the evidence and sentiment. They concluded that the combination of evidence and sentiment, especially in cases close on the evidence, freed jurors to consider extralegal values in determining their verdicts rather than being guided by the strict dictates of this law: the liberation hypothesis. This conclusion was also in keeping with the common understanding of the jury system as the mechanism for tempering the rigors of the law with the common sense of the community.

Researchers have conducted several studies since the publication of *The American Jury* that provide moderate support for Kalven and Zeisel's findings. In 1986, Reskin and Visher observed trials and conducted post-trial interviews with jurors in thirty-eight sexual assault trials. They found that while legal and evidentiary factors were primary motivators for a juror's decisions, jurors indicated that they relied on extralegal factors in those cases that they believed were weak in that the evidence about the defendants' guilt tended to be equivocal. However, additional research the following year using the same data by Visher[12] suggested that jurors based their decisions more on the evidence presented at trial than on the characteristics of either victims or defendants and that juror attitudes had little explanatory power with respect to case outcomes. More recent research has found that extra-evidentiary influences that are specifically related to the case, such as charge severity, pretrial publicity, and trial complexity, affect jury verdicts, but only when the evidence presented by the prosecution is ambiguous or weak, providing moderate support for the liberation hypothesis.[13]

The liberation hypothesis has also been employed by researchers investigating capital punishment to conclude that the race of defendants and victims significantly affects decisions as to punishment in those cases in which the culpability of the defendants is less than clear and the evidence is ambiguous.[14] Seminal research conducted in the 1990s by David Baldus and colleagues on racial disparity and the application of the death penalty found that the race of the defendant and the race of the victim were most important in determining whether or not a defendant was sentenced to death in cases that were close on the evidence.

Extralegal factors such as defendant and victim race may be expected to affect jury decision making more than judge decision making because jurors are more likely to have demographic characteristics similar to those of the defendants, resulting in jurors identifying with the defendants and thus being more lenient toward them.[15] Numerous studies suggest a relationship between the racial composition of the jury and jury leniency toward same-race defendants.[16] This effect seems strongest when the evidence supporting guilt is mixed or weak,[17] thus supporting the liberation hypothesis. Other research, however, indicates that the relationship among juror race, interpretation of evidence, and liberation is more complex. Pennington and Hastie suggest that jurors employ a complex cognitive process, commonly referred to as the story model of juror decision making, by which they evaluate the degree to which evidence presented at trial comports with their own life experiences. For some jurors, particular facts that are introduced at trial are more salient than others because they match preexisting cognitive schemas that jurors hold.[18]

Some scholars have attempted to apply the principles of the liberation hypothesis to other criminal justice decision makers. Keil and Vito[19] suggested that considerations of defendant and victim race were not confined to legally ambiguous cases, and Baumer, Messner, and Felson[20] concluded that the effects of victim characteristics were not limited to cases of a particular level of severity. In examining sentencing, they found that judges were constrained in their consideration of extralegal factors when sentencing defendants convicted of more serious crimes (rape, murder, robbery) but were less so when sentencing defendants convicted of less serious crimes.[21]

More recently, Gastwirth and Sinclair's[22] reanalysis of the original Kalven and Zeisel data using more sophisticated multivariate regression techniques called into question many of the findings from *The American Jury*. Specifically, they found a strong relationship between a defendant's lack of a criminal record and the perception of judges that jurors were sympathetic to the defendant. In fact, they argue that in Kalven and Zeisel's original data, judges' perceptions that jurors were sympathetic to defendants (apparently because of the defendant's lack of criminal record) diminished after controlling for the severity of the cases.[23] These more recent findings suggest that the liberation hypothesis may not provide as persuasive an explanation for judge-jury disagreement as Kalven and Zeisel posited.

The techniques used by researchers to investigate the factors involved in judge and jury verdict decision making have generally been limited to analysis of small samples of cases, experimental designs, or interviews with the decision makers. When researchers attempted to compare verdicts of judges and juries in actual criminal trials, of necessity, the judges were asked to render hypothetical verdicts while the juries rendered actual verdicts. The judges' lack of actual responsibility for deciding the case might have resulted in them not being as conscientious as jurors in evaluating the evidence. Also, the judges' decisions could have been affected by what the juries had already done. In studies based on archival evidence, respondents were quite possibly deciding different cases. In research based on simulations and mock jury experiments, no matter how realistic, participants knew that their decisions had no genuine consequences.[24]

Studies of comparisons of judge and jury decision making involving civil rather than criminal cases are informative but do not necessarily reflect the experience of judges and juries in the criminal justice system. The burden of proof in civil cases and criminal cases is different. Justice in civil cases may be achieved by ensuring that all parties are afforded a fair process for making their cases before disinterested adjudicators. In criminal cases, justice is predicated on ensuring that only those who actually commit crimes are convicted. In many civil cases, jurors are expected to consult values in determining the appropriateness or reasonableness of the defendants' behavior. In criminal cases when juries are asked to consider reasonableness, it is typically in connection with the reasonableness of the defendants' beliefs about the conduct or intentions of other persons.

Although juries are more lenient than judges in criminal cases, investigations of civil cases have revealed no particular direction to leniency: judges are just as likely as juries to favor plaintiffs over defendants as the other way around.[25] Robbenolt found that the few studies that investigate how trial judges make decisions reveal that judges and jurors are very similar in their decision making.[26] However, when the two groups disagree, juries are usually more lenient toward the defendants than are judges.

In the NCSC study designed to replicate Kalven and Zeisel's study,[27] which we examine in detail in this book, researchers expanded the kinds of information collected and analyzed, producing a considerably more fine-tuned assessment of the potential role of race and gender in the resolution of criminal cases (a detailed description of the NCSC methodology can be found at the end of chapter 2). The researchers confirmed that juries were more likely to acquit than judges when the strength of the cases was held constant.[28] Thus, as Kalven and Zeisel had suggested decades earlier,[29] judges have a lower conviction threshold than juries. In this chapter we examine why this is so.

The Liberation Hypothesis as Explanation for Judge-Jury Disagreement Today

We begin our inquiry by exploring the question of whether the constitutional revolution in criminal procedure and the demographic changes in both courts and communities noted previously have affected the *distribution* of agreement versus disagreement cases reported by Kalven and Zeisel. If contemporary judges, like their counterparts in the 1950s, require less evidence to convict than do jurors (and are therefore more likely to convict than jurors), evidence that fails to meet the judges' lower standard of proof should certainly fail the juries' higher evidentiary expectations.

Analyzing data collected in the 1950s, Kalven and Zeisel found

TABLE 4.1
Judge-Jury Outcomes: The National Center for State Courts (NCSC) Survey and Kalven and Zeisel Study Data (Excluding Hung Juries)

		Juries' verdicts		
Data source	Judges' verdicts	Acquitted % (N)	Convicted % (N)	Total % (N)
NCSC	Acquitted	12.5% (35)	6.0% (17)	23.1% (65)
		67.3%	*32.7%*	*100%*
	Convicted	17.1% (48)	64.4% (181)	76.9% (216)
		21.0%	*79.0%*	*100%*
	Total	29.5% (83)	70.5% (198)	100% (281)
Kalven and Zeisel	Acquitted	14.2% (479)	2.3% (79)	16.5% (558)
		85.8%	*14.2%*	*100%*
	Convicted	17.9% (602)	65.6% (2217)	83.5% (282)
		21.4%	*78.6%*	*100%*
	Total	32.0% (1081)	68.0% (2296)	100%(3379)

Sources: National Center for State Courts, *Caseload Highlights*; Kalven and Zeisel, *The American Jury*.
Note: Italicized percentages indicate the proportion of judge verdicts that are in agreement with jury verdicts for each data source. For example, in 67.3% of the cases where the judges would have acquitted in the NCSC data, the jury also acquitted, and in 32.7% of the cases where the judge would have acquitted, the jury convicted.

that juries were more likely to come to the same conclusion as judges when the judges would have acquitted than when the judges would have convicted. Today, juries are more likely to agree with judges' decisions to convict than they are with judges' decisions to acquit. Table 4.1 shows the findings from Kalven and Zeisel, recalculated to exclude hung juries, and the comparable data from the NCSC survey.[30] The italicized percentages show the degree to which the juries agree with the judges' assessments of guilt or innocence.

Kalven and Zeisel presented their fundamental findings concerning judge-jury agreement in two important tables, tables 11 and 12, which differed only in terms of their treatment of hung juries. Kalven and Zeisel's table 11 showed the extent of judge-jury agreement in cases in which juries convicted, acquitted, or hung. In their table 12, they collapsed the jury verdict categories from three to two by treating cases in which the juries hung as though half of them ended in convictions and half of them ended in acquittals. Although a table showing judge-jury agreement with respect only to convictions and acquittals may be easier to follow than a table that includes hung juries, Kalven and Zeisel never presented a serious rationale for dividing the hung juries between guilty verdicts and acquittals rather than simply omitting them. We were unable to find any data from the NCSC sites concerning what happened to those defendants whose trials ended in hung juries. Kalven and Zeisel relied on the advice of an experienced prosecutor who estimated that, in the end, about half of those whose trials ended in hung juries were acquitted. A study in nine counties suggested that of the small number of hung cases that were retried (approximately 3 percent) nearly 70 percent resulted in convictions.[31] Given this uncertainty, we have chosen to omit hung juries in the presentation of our findings because our focus is upon cases in which judges and juries disagree about guilt and innocence. Also, we could see no reason to assume that half of the trials that end in hung juries are actually acquittals. As it turns out, our finding that the direction of judge-jury agreement has changed holds true regardless of whether one excludes hung juries entirely (as we have done here), keeps hung juries in the calculation, or divides hung juries between convictions and acquittals as Kalven and Zeisel did.

Table 4.1 reveals, as Eisenberg et al.[32] reported, that the direction of judge-jury disagreement (i.e., juries acquit when judges would convict more often than they convict when judges would acquit) has remained unchanged since Kalven and Zeisel. If we look at judge-jury agreement, however, the situation has changed. Table 4.1 also shows that in more than forty years there has been practically no difference between the rate of judge-jury agreement as to who is guilty (79 percent from the NCSC data and 79 percent from Kalven and Zeisel) but that there is a more substantial difference in the rate of agreement about acquittals (67 percent from the NCSC data and 86 percent from Kalven and Zeisel). Unlike juries studied in the 1950s, contemporary jurors are more likely to agree with judges' decisions to convict than they are to agree with judges' decisions to acquit.[33]

The shift in the pattern of agreement may reflect the shift in the judges' views of the closeness of the cases.[34] Judges in Kalven and Zeisel's study were more likely to consider cases clear for conviction

(52 percent) than close (43 percent) or clear for acquittal (5 percent).[35] Contemporary judges view criminal cases differently; only 38 percent of the NCSC judges considered a case clear for conviction while more than half felt the case was close (53 percent) and nearly one-tenth thought the case was clear for acquittal (9 percent).[36] Disagreements between judges and juries as to when acquittals are appropriate seem to be a logical outgrowth of the increasing number of cases at the margin combined with the different views of judges and juries concerning when doubt is reasonable.

Consistent with Kalven and Zeisel's findings that liberation occurs most frequently in cases that are close on the evidence, the NCSC data confirms that judges are least likely to consider cases close (46 percent) when the judges agree with the juries that the defendants are guilty. They are next most likely to view cases as close (62 percent) when the judges agree with the juries' decisions to acquit. Finally, they are most likely to view cases as close (66 percent combined) when either the juries or the judges acquit while the other convicts. The 23 percent gap between cases in which judges and juries agree about conviction and cases in which juries are more lenient suggests, consistent with Kalven and Zeisel, that cases that judges view as close on the evidence are likely to produce disagreement either in the direction of liberation or in the direction of reverse liberation, which refers to judge and jury disagreements in which the jury would convict where the judge would acquit. Indeed, approximately two-thirds (65 percent) of the cases in which either judges, juries, or both thought the defendants should be acquitted were viewed by the judges as close on the evidence as opposed to 45 percent of the cases in which judges and juries agreed about guilt.

The ratio of liberation to reverse liberation decisions has narrowed considerably since Kalven and Zeisel's study (from 8 to 1 in the 1950s to 2 to 1 today), and the number of cases that appear to be close seems to have increased. As noted, while juries remain more lenient than judges, contemporary judges and juries have reversed the pattern of fifty years ago and are now more likely to agree about who is guilty than about who is not guilty. The relatively clear vision of guilt and innocence reported by the Kalven and Zeisel respondents appears to have clouded over the years.

In addition to the NCSC data providing a modern perspective on judge-jury agreement, it also permits us to compare the judges' *predictions* of the juries' verdicts with the verdicts actually rendered. Although the results are less than definitive on the point, comparing judges' predictions of juries' verdicts with the results reached by the juries provides some indication of how well judges understand jury behavior. If judges can successfully predict before the fact whether juries will disagree with them, the judges' after-the-fact explanations of *why* the juries disagreed may well justify Kalven and Zeisel's treatment of judicial insight into jury behavior. If judges prove not to be adroit at predicting how juries will decide cases, relying upon judges' explanations for jury deviations from "accurate" (the judges') fact finding requires firmer support than Kalven and Zeisel's assertion that judges, through long exposure, understand jury behavior.[37] In their original study, Kalven and Zeisel did not ask judges to predict juries' decisions, so there is no way to compare the NCSC judges with those responding in the 1950s.

The NCSC data indicates that judges predict juries will agree with their decisions 84 percent of the time regardless of the nature of the decisions.[38] Table 4.2 indicates that judges appear to know whereof they speak when they predict juries will convict. The picture changes when one turns to acquittals. Judges are not as proficient at predicting

TABLE 4.2
Jury Outcomes and Judges' Predictions

| | Jury outcomes | | |
Judges' predictions	Acquitted	Convicted on at least one count	Total
Acquittal	65.1% (56)	14.1% (29)	29.1% (85)
	65.9%	*34.1%*	*100%*
Conviction on at least one count	34.8% (30)	85.9% (177)	70.9% (207)
	14.5%	*85.5%*	*100%*
Total	100% (86)	100% (206)	100% (292)

Note: Number of cases is given in parentheses. Italicized percentages indicate the proportion of judges' perceptions that are in agreement with jury outcomes.

acquittals, nor is the agreement between judges and juries as high with respect to acquittals. Indeed, rather than the judges predicting outcomes correctly 85 percent of the time, as is true when judges predict juries will convict, their predictions that juries will return not guilty verdicts are accurate only 65 percent of the time. As noted earlier, juries return defense verdicts in only 67 percent of the cases in which judges indicate they would have found for the defense.

Understanding Why Judges and Juries Disagree Today

Focusing now on the cases in which judges and juries disagree, we have explored the effects of a range of factors, including jury sentiment, that result in either judges or juries concluding that defendants are not guilty. Here we have examined the liberation hypothesis that in close cases, juries but not judges are moved through sentiment to find defendants not guilty. In the present analysis, we have overcome many of the limitations of efforts to replicate the liberation hypothesis through expanding the analysis to a full range of felonies prosecuted in urban courts in four different jurisdictions.[39]

We have not directly tested what Kalven and Zeisel actually found: *that judges explain jury disagreements in part by suggesting that juries are moved by values rather than fact.* The data does not permit such an inquiry (judges were not asked to explain why juries disagreed with them in the NCSC data).The liberation hypothesis, however, stands for a proposition grander than judges' explanations of disagreements. According to the hypothesis, *when juries in close cases are more lenient than judges, this occurs in part because jurors (as opposed to judges) are actually moved by sentiment.* Because the NCSC data permits us to compare the role of sentiment in cases of agreement as well as disagreement and because we can consider the views of the jurors as well as the judges, we can examine whether juror sentiment plays a distinctive role when juries are more lenient than judges in close cases.

The claim that juries are moved by sentiment to acquit those whom judges view as guilty fuels the perception that not guilty verdicts indicate little about the actual innocence of defendants. It contributes to the view that "they are all guilty of something" even if the state cannot prove it in court. In this analysis, we actually test whether jury sentiment distinguishes cases in which judges and juries disagree on the outcomes and whether sentiment has the strongest effect on judge-jury disagreement in cases that are close on the evidence.

The data used to answer these questions was originally collected and analyzed by the NCSC as part of a study on hung juries.[40] The NCSC collected information from trial courts in the Central Criminal Division of the Los Angeles County Superior Court, California; the Maricopa County Superior Court (Phoenix), Arizona; the Bronx County Supreme Court, New York; and the Superior Court of the District of Columbia, between 2000 and 2001. Data were collected on noncapital felony trials in each jurisdiction. The data from this study included case information about the nature of the charges, demographic information on the offenders and victims, voir dire, trial evidence and procedures, and jury deliberations for 401 separate criminal cases, though complete information was available for only 334 cases.[41] In addition to case information, questionnaires designed to elicit information about their perception of the case proceedings and outcomes were submitted to the judges who presided over the cases, the prosecution and defense attorneys, and individual jurors. These additional sources of data provide a unique opportunity to examine the sources of judge-jury disagreement, and, possibly, to find some indication of whether judges or juries provide the more reliable judgments as to the guilt of the accused.

To test the effect of juror sentiment in those cases in which judges and juries disagreed on the outcomes of the cases, we compared the effects of legal and extralegal variables on judge-jury agreement and disagreement. Agreement and disagreement were measured as (1) agreement on guilt, (2) agreement on acquittal, (3) disagreement on acquittal in which judges would convict but juries acquit, and (4) disagreement on guilt in which judges would acquit but juries convict.[42] Through this analysis, we sought to understand broadly whether differences between judge and jury outcomes were explained through the notion that judges were guided by facts and juries by sentiments or values or whether judges and juries responded to evidence in distinctive ways.[43] To evaluate whether juror sentiment had a distinctive role when juries were more lenient than judges in cases that were close on the evidence, we calculated a series of interaction terms to examine the effect of jury sentiment in those cases that juries indicated were close on the evidence compared with those cases that juries did not think were close. We separately modeled interaction terms to measure the effect of jury sentiment in cases that judges indicated were close on the evidence because judges and juries might disagree about the degree to which particular cases were close.

Outcome Measures

We measured the effect of jury sentiment on four possible case outcomes: (1) judge and jury agreed on conviction; (2) judge would convict, but jury acquitted; (3) judge and jury agreed on acquittal; and (4) judge would acquit, but jury convicted. The outcome variable was created by combining information on the actual verdicts rendered by the juries in each of the cases analyzed here with information provided by the judges about the verdicts they would render if the cases had been decided in bench trials. We then recoded case outcomes into categories for each specified judge-jury agreement outcome.[44]

Independent Measures

Kalven and Zeisel[45] attributed nearly 60 percent of the disagreements in which juries were more lenient than judges to evidentiary factors and 40 percent to jury sentiment about the law and the defendants. We created a series of variables to measure aspects of both of these important and distinct phenomena.[46]

Evidentiary factors. Strength-of-the-evidence variables reflected the evidence admitted at trial and its presentation by either the prosecution or defense. The original NCSC data included separate measures of the total number of witnesses and number of exhibits presented by the prosecution and defense. To measure the magnitude of the evidence presented by either the prosecution or defense, we combined measures of witnesses and exhibits to create additive measures of the total number of prosecution exhibits and witnesses and the total number of defense exhibits and witnesses. We also included subjective measures of the judges' perceptions of the importance of real or demonstrative evidence (treated as a factor combining the judge's evaluations of the importance of real evidence, expert testimony, and exhibits for each case).

We included additional indicators of factors that resulted in improving the defendants' cases. The quality of the defense case may be more important than the quantity of the prosecutions' witnesses or real evidence. When the defense puts forward no witnesses, the defendant testifies alone, or a defense witness testifies alone, the jury is much more likely to convict than when a defense witness or witnesses testifies in combination with the defendant.[47] To account for the quality of the defense cases, we included a variable to measure weak defense cases (defined as no witnesses presented by the defense or only the defendant or a witness testifying alone) or strong defense cases (defined as a witness for the defense and the defendant testifying together).

In addition to traditional measures of evidentiary strength, the defendant's criminal history matters. Defendants with criminal records are more likely to be convicted than those without such a record, even when juries do not learn of the criminal histories.[48] Information on the defendants' criminal histories was captured in the original NCSC data in a variable indicating whether juries learned about defendants' criminal histories (measured as yes, no, or no criminal history). We recoded this variable into a variable to measure whether defendants had criminal histories.

Analysis of the NCSC data reveals that a defendant's claim of innocence predicts disagreement between the judge and jury as well.[49] The defendant's insistence upon innocence as a reason for not accepting a plea has no direct analogue in the Kalven and Zeisel typology but was included in the present analysis with the other evidentiary variables indicative of the defense case.[50] In the NCSC survey, lawyers were asked to explain the reasons the cases had resulted in a trial rather than a plea. This open-ended question was coded into common response categories: (1) because the defendant claimed he was innocent, (2) because the defendant refused to plead, (3) because no offer was made, and (4) because the parties could not agree on an appropriate plea. The reason why the defendant did not plead may come to the attention of the judge but is not admissible in evidence for consideration by the jury as showing whether or not the defendant committed the crime. The reason plea bargaining failed was recoded in the present analysis as a variable measuring whether or not the failure of the plea was due to a defendant claiming innocence or was due to any other reason.

Jury sentiment. Kalven and Zeisel explained 40 percent of the disagreement when juries were more lenient than judges in terms of the juries' beliefs about the defendants and about the law.[51] In the NCSC study, researchers attempted to explore this issue by asking individual jurors the following questions designed to tap into their sentiments:

1. Did they believe the law was fair in this case?
2. Was the legally correct outcome fair?
3. Would a conviction be too harsh?
4. How much sympathy did they have for the defendant?

These questions were all measured on 7-point scales, where 1 represented the lowest assessment (*least unfair, least sympathetic*) and 7 represented the highest assessment (*most unfair, most sympathetic*).[52] To assess the effect of individual juror sentiment on case outcomes, we aggregated the data from individual jurors for each case to represent an average jury response for each case. A score measuring sentiment toward the law was created by taking the mean of the available score for fairness of the law and fairness of the legal outcome ($\alpha = .75$). A separate score measuring sentiment toward the defendant was created by taking the mean of scores for sympathy toward the defendant and consequences of conviction ($\alpha = .72$).

Closeness of case. Kalven and Zeisel's liberation hypothesis asserts that jurors feel most likely to consider sentiment in those cases that are close on the facts.[53] The NCSC questionnaire asked both judges and juries, "All things considered, how close was the case?" Respondents were provided a 7-point scale ranging from 1 (*evidence strongly favors prosecution*) to 7 (*evidence strongly favors defense*). Responses in the middle of the 7-point range (3–5) indicated the cases were close; the evidence seemed to favor neither the prosecution nor the defense. To measure closeness of the case, we created a variable where responses 1–2 and 6–7 indicate that evidence in the case favored either the prosecution or the defense and responses 3–5 indicate the case was close. Although measures of strength of a case and judge or jury perceptions of case closeness might appear to be measures of the same phenomenon, the correlation between the objective measures of strength of the evidence (number of witnesses and number of exhibits presented) and judge or jury perceptions of closeness of the case was weak and not significant. As a result, separate measures were calculated for judge and jury perceptions of case closeness.

Severity of charge. The NCSC data included detailed information on the type of offense charged for each count in each case. Sixteen different offense types were included in these data. To control for the effect of different types of charges, we created an 8-point classification scale corresponding with the severity of the offense.[54] In cases involving multiple counts, we coded the most serious charge.

Location. The community in which a case is heard may be a critical factor in determining the degree of judge-jury agreement on case outcomes. Overall, cases in the NCSC data were fairly evenly distributed across the four courts; however, as reported originally by Eisenberg et al.,[55] there were striking differences in the outcomes of cases by site. To account for this variation, we created variables to measure whether the same kind of trial was heard in each of the four courts.

Race of the defendant. Defendants in the NCSC data were classified as White non-Hispanic (10 percent), White Hispanic (25 percent), Black non-Hispanic (55 percent), Black Hispanic (3 percent), Asian (1 percent), or another race (5 percent). We created variables to measure the race of the defendants.[56] Information was collected on defendant gender, but only 8 percent of all defendants were female. As a result, given the relatively small number of cases that included female offenders (27 out of 334), there was too little variation in defendant gender to include it in subsequent analyses.

Findings

Table 4.3 provides information about the distribution of evidentiary factors and sentiment by each of the four different case outcomes. The type of defense presented distinguishes significantly between judge-jury agreement and disagreement cases. When the defense presented either no witness or only the defendant as a witness, judge-jury agreement about guilt was quite robust (76 percent and 69 percent, respectively). When the defendant and a witness both testified, however, agreement about conviction decreased to 49 percent. Not surprisingly, judges and juries were most likely to agree about acquittal in those cases in which defendants and supporting witnesses testified together.

Judges and juries were significantly more likely to agree about case outcomes in those cases in which the defendants had criminal histories, agreeing to convict 71 percent of the time. The relatively small fraction of defendants (19 percent) without criminal records were acquitted in nearly half (48 percent) of the cases. Judges believed that defendants without criminal records should be acquitted at the considerably lower rate of just over one in four cases (28 percent). The lack of a criminal history may have moved juries toward acquittal in many cases in which judges believed defendants were guilty.

Although juries may not know the reasons defendants refuse to plead, defendants' claims of innocence to their attorneys had strong, positive effects on jury acquittal. Juries acquitted in 44 percent of all cases in which this was the reason the defendants did not plead; judges agreed with the juries that the defendants were not guilty in half of these cases. Perhaps defendants insist that they are innocent to encourage their lawyers to behave vigorously on their behalf. Perhaps they insist on their innocence although they know themselves to be

TABLE 4.3
Descriptive Information and Variance: All Variables by Case Outcome

Descriptors	Judge and jury convicted	Judge would convict; jury acquitted	Judge and jury acquitted	Judge would acquit; jury convicted
Site**				
Los Angeles	78.5% (51)	9.2% (6)	10.8% (7)	1.5% (1)
Maricopa	70.5% (55)	3.8% (3)	17.9% (14)	7.7% (6)
Bronx	50.8% (31)	24.6% (15)	13.1% (8)	11.5% (7)
Washington, DC	56.0% (42)	32.0% (24)	8% (6)	4.0% (3)
Crime category				
Violent	69.1% (94)	14% (19)	11% (15)	5.9% (8)
Nonviolent	61.5% (91)	19.6% (29)	13.5% (20)	5.4% (8)
Victims				
0 victim	59.6% (68)	22.8% (26)	12.3% (14)	5.3% (6)
1+ victims	67.1% (110)	13.4% (22)	12.8% (21)	6.7% (11)
Race**				
White	73.3% (22)	3.3% (1)	16.7% (5)	6.7% (2)
Black	67.1% (102)	20.4% (31)	8.6% (13)	3.9% (6)
Hispanic	57.3% (43)	14.7% (11)	21.3% (16)	6.7% (5)
Other	50.0% (9)	22.2% (4)	5.6% (1)	22.2% (4)
Defendant claims of innocence**				
No	78.4% (69)	9.1% (8)	8% (7)	4.5% (4)
Yes	50.9% (56)	21.8% (24)	21.8% (24)	5.5% (6)
Criminal history**				
No prior	43.1% (25)	29.3% (17)	19% (11)	8.6% (5)
Prior criminal history	70.5% (146)	14% (29)	10.6% (22)	4.8% (10)
Testimony type*				
No witness	76.1% (51)	13.4% (9)	4.5% (3)	6.0% (4)
Only defendant	69.2% (36)	11.5% (6)	13.5% (7)	5.8% (3)
Defendant and other witness together	49.4% (40)	21.% (17)	21% (17)	8.6% (7)
Public defender				
No	61.7% (79)	21.9% (28)	11.7% (15)	4.7% (6)
Yes	65.9% (91)	11.6% (16)	14.5% (20)	8% (11)
Means (no. of cases)				
Number of witnesses	7.99 (157)	7.75 (48)	6.94 (35)	6.47 (15)
Number of exhibits	21.14 (155)	15.69 (42)	12.94 (32)	15.57 (14)
Judge				
Prosecutor skillful*	5.02 (187)	5.08 (49)	4.25 (36)	4.53 (17)
Importance of evidence factor*	.15 (186)	.14 (49)	−.63 (36)	−.32 (17)
Close case (judge)**	2.65 (186)	3.21 (48)	5.00 (36)	4.65 (17)
Jury				
Prosecutor skillful*	5.14 (177)	4.53 (46)	4.02 (35)	4.50 (16)
Sympathy for defendant*	3.09 (177)	2.76 (46)	2.69 (35)	2.87 (16)
Fairness of the law**	5.94 (176)	5.31 (46)	5.39 (35)	5.37 (16)
Just consequences to defendant**	3.58 (175)	3.14 (46)	3.03 (35)	4.16 (16)
Fairness of legally correct outcome **	5.61 (176)	5.05 (46)	5.36 (35)	5.14 (16)
Trust police**	5.27 (176)	4.77 (46)	5.17 (35)	4.94 (16)
% jurors female	55.75 (175)	61.85 (45)	63.45 (35)	56.84 (16)
% jurors black**	23.96 (176)	38.52 (46)	21.38 (35)	21.92 (16)
Close case (jury)**	2.71 (177)	4.86 (46)	5.00 (36)	3.69 (16)

* p < .05; ** p < .01

guilty because they believe that the states' cases are weak. However, defendants sophisticated enough to claim innocence to manipulate their lawyers may well be sophisticated enough to believe their defense counsel when counsel inform them that judges may increase their sentences if they are convicted after trial and may increase them even more if the defendants take the stand and insist unsuccessfully upon their innocence. Defendants may also decline plea bargains on the grounds of innocence because they are, in fact, innocent. At a minimum, juries (who are ignorant of plea offers and their refusal) respond more positively to defendants who refuse to plead on the ground of innocence than to those who refuse to plead on other grounds.

Although judge and jury outcomes did not vary significantly with respect to objective measures of evidence presented in the cases (measured as the total number of exhibits or witnesses presented for both sides), the judges' perceptions of the importance of real or demonstrative evidence (measured as a factor combining the judge's evaluation of the importance of real evidence, expert testimony, and exhibits for each case) was a significant predictor of judge-jury disagreement. The skillfulness of the prosecuting attorney had an interesting effect on case outcomes. Judges and juries each ranked the skill of prosecuting attorneys on a scale of 1 to 7 (1 = *least skillful*, 7 = *most skillful*). In those cases in which judges would have convicted but the juries acquitted, judges were significantly more likely to think prosecutors were skillful than in cases in which juries convicted even though the judges would have acquitted (*mean* = 5.08 and 4.53, respectively).[57] Jurors were less moved by skillful prosecutors. There was virtually no difference in jury perceptions of prosecutor skill in those cases in which they acquitted when the judges would have convicted (4.53) and those cases in which they convicted when the judges would have acquitted (4.50). Earlier findings suggested that juries are more interested in the defense case than are the judges; apparently, judges are more affected by the skill of the prosecutor than are juries.

Kalven and Zeisel explained 40 percent of the disagreement when juries were more lenient than judges in terms of the juries' sentiments about the defendants and about the law. According to the NCSC data, juries felt the law and legally correct outcomes were most fair in those cases in which they agreed with the judges that the defendants were guilty (mean = 5.94 and 5.61, respectively). They felt that both the law and the legally correct outcome were least fair when they acquitted and the judges would have convicted (5.31 and 5.05, respectively). Juries had the least amount of sympathy for defendants or concern about the consequences of convictions in those cases in which they acquitted (either with or without judges' agreement). Trust in the police also distinguished agreement from disagreement cases. The juries that acquitted in disagreement with judges exhibited lower levels of trust in the police (4.77 on a 7-point scale) than those that agreed with judges on conviction or acquittal (5.27 and 5.17, respectively).

Turning to measures of case closeness, we found that judges and juries convicted in the cases in which they perceived the evidence was heavily in favor of the prosecution (average rating of 2.65 and 2.71, respectively). They acquitted in cases in which the evidence was heavily in favor of the accused (average rating of 5.0 each). With respect to the views of the judges and the jurors in the cases in which they disagreed, the discrepancy seemed to flow from the evaluation of the evidence: when juries acquitted although the judge would have convicted, juries tended to characterize the evidence as strong for the defense (4.86 on a 7-point scale). The judges evaluated the same cases as moderately strong for the prosecution (3.21 on a 7-point scale). When the situation was reversed, judges viewed the evidence as favoring the defendants (4.65); and juries were very much in the middle (3.69). These results are consistent with a view of adjudication as a rational, evidence-weighing, and evidence-evaluating process. Alternatively, the disagreements may be explained as products of the decisions to convict or acquit rather than as logical steps in arriving at those decisions (e.g., "Since I voted to acquit the defendant, I must have believed that his case was strong or the state's case was weak or both."). However, the data does not appear to support the claim that juries acquit when *juries* find the evidence close.

In terms of other factors that may predict case outcomes, we found that as reported originally by Eisenberg et al.,[58] there were striking differences between the jurisdictions studied and case outcomes. There was an almost 20 percent difference between agreement on outcomes of cases heard in the Bronx and Washington, DC, on the one hand, and Maricopa and Los Angeles, on the other. Jurors and judges agreed (combined agreement on convictions and agreement on acquittal) in almost nine out of ten cases in the western communities and in two out of three cases in the East. The disagreements typically occurred in cases in which the juries acquitted although the judges would have convicted. This was not true in Maricopa, where juries were more likely to convict when judges would acquit than the other way around. Bronx and Washington, DC, juries were almost three times as likely to find defendants not guilty whom the judges would have convicted than were juries in Los Angeles and six times as likely as those in Maricopa.

The race of juries had a strong effect on judge-jury agreement. A significantly higher proportion of jurors were Black in those cases in which judges would have convicted but the juries acquitted (39 percent Black) as opposed to cases in which the judge and jury agreed or the judge would have acquitted and the jury convicted (22 percent Black). The role of race of the defendant was intriguing. Juries and judges were in virtual lockstep when the defendants were White (combined agreement on conviction or acquittal of 90 percent) but reached consensus approximately 75 percent of the time when the defendants were either Black or Hispanic. Whites were most likely to be convicted by juries, Blacks were next most likely (71 percent), and Hispanics were least likely (64 percent). The figures would have been quite different had the judges' views of guilt prevailed: judges would have found 87 percent of Blacks guilty, 77 percent of Whites guilty, and 72 percent of Hispanics guilty. As these figures suggest, judges and juries disagreed most sharply about the guilt of African Americans, with the judges being harsher in 20 percent of the cases and the juries harsher in only 4 percent. This was in stark contrast to their respective views of White defendants (although the numbers were extremely small—judges would have acquitted two White defendants whom the jury convicted while convicting one whom the jury acquitted). Juries liberated Hispanics in 15 percent of the cases and engaged in reverse liberation in 7 percent.

We now turn to the heart of our inquiry, examining whether and how evidentiary and nonevidentiary factors explain disagreements between judges and juries. Do jury sentiment and the liberation hypothesis based upon it provide an explanation for judge-jury disagreement in the modern data? To accomplish this task, we measured jury sentiment in the NCSC data using five separate indicators of jury beliefs: (1) fairness of the law, (2) fairness of the legally correct outcome, (3) harshness of a conviction, (4) sympathy for the defendant, and (5) trust in the police. To arrive at some understanding of the role of sentiment, we examined a range of other possible contributors to disagreement. Because case outcome is a multicategory variable representing judge-jury agreement about conviction or acquittal and judge-jury disagreement about conviction or acquittal, multinomial regression analysis was used to help isolate the degree to which variables illustrative of jury sentiment affected outcomes in those cases in which judges and juries disagreed on the verdicts. For a full discussion of the multinomial regression modeling, see appendix A.

The analyses presented in appendix A confirm that judge and jury outcomes did differ in cases that were close compared to cases that were clear on the evidence, but these analyses did not actually confirm Kalven and Zeisel's thesis that juries' sentiments about the law and about defendants is what explains judge and jury disagreements. It appears that some sentiments have a role consistent with Kalven and Zeisel's theory (e.g., the relationship among outcomes, trust in the police, and fear of harsh consequences) but the effect is inconsistent in others (e.g., belief in the fairness of the law, sympathy for the defendant).

Jury assessments of the closeness of the evidence strongly predict judge-jury disagreements. (See Table A.1 for multinomial regression result.) Juries were most likely to acquit and judges to convict in those cases *juries* viewed as being close on the evidence. Judges' opinions about the closeness of the evidence, however, were not predictive of judge-jury disagreements on the case outcomes. This finding stands in opposition to Kalven and Zeisel's original claim that when judges thought that cases were close on the evidence, jury sentiment led to jury disagreement with the judges' verdict. Kalven and Zeisel did not have the benefit of knowing objectively how juries felt about the closeness of the case or their actual sentiments and instead relied on judges' perceptions of these factors.

The degree to which jury sentiment actually explained disagreement in close cases cannot be addressed through multinominal regression modeling. To explore this question, we partitioned cases in the NCSC data by both judges' perceptions of closeness (close or clear) and jury perceptions of closeness (close or clear). Tables 4.4 and 4.5 present the results that we discuss in more detail below.[59]

Table 4.4 follows Kalven and Zeisel in that the *judge's* view of case closeness was used to identify the cases in which to look for evidence of the liberation hypothesis. However, unlike Kalven and Zeisel's analysis, it includes the mean scores of *jury* reports of the five measures of sentiment across judge and jury outcomes. The liberation hypothesis identified juror sentiments as a major cause of pro-defendant, inaccurate fact-finding. Although hardly infallible, the jurors' descriptions of why they believed they acted should provide a more reliable indication of what actually moved jurors toward a particular decision than the reports of judges with no personal knowledge of jury sentiments beyond the fact that juries disagreed with their decisions.[60]

Table 4.5 departs from Kalven and Zeisel's methodology and examines the role of jury sentiments in the cases that *juries* identified as close on the evidence. If the liberation hypothesis accurately describes what happens to juries in cases that are close on the evidence, one should expect the effect of sentiments to be particularly prominent when juries believe the cases to be close. This should be particularly true because liberation (jury acquits when the judge would convict) was present in more than 30 percent of the cases that juries deemed to be close on the evidence, in contrast to only 23 percent of the cases that judges deemed to be close.

The Judge's Evaluation of Whether the Case Is Close

According to table 4.4, as suggested by the liberation hypothesis, when judges considered the cases to be close on the evidence, certain jury sentiments (i.e., the fairness of the law, the fairness of the legally

TABLE 4.4

Means of Jury Sentiment by Outcome: Judges' View of Closeness of Case

Descriptor	Both convicted	Judge convicted; jury acquitted	Both acquitted	Judge acquitted; jury convicted	Overall
Closeness**					
Judge thinks case close	54.1% (79)	23.3% (34)	15.1% (22)	7.5% (11)	100% (146)
Jury sentiment					
Judge thinks case close					
Fairness of the law	5.82	5.19	5.49	5.42	5.59
Fairness of legally correct outcome**	5.50	4.99	5.36	5.16	5.34
Consequences of conviction harsh	4.23	4.34	4.17	4.43	4.26
Sympathy for the defendant	3.08	2.73	2.78	2.96	2.95
Trust in police*	5.17	4.78	5.31	4.60	5.06

Descriptor	Both convicted	Judge convicted; jury acquitted	Both acquitted	Judge acquitted; jury convicted	Overall
Judge thinks case clear	75.9% (101)	9.8% (13)	9.8% (13)	4.5% (6)	100% (133)
Judge thinks case clear					
Fairness of the law**	6.03	5.60	5.26	5.30	5.88
Fairness of legally correct outcome*	5.70	5.02	5.38	5.10	5.57
Consequences of conviction harsh*	4.34	3.95	4.07	4.51	4.28
Sympathy for the defendant	3.10	2.78	2.54	2.71	3.00
Trust in police*	5.32	4.76	4.95	5.50	5.23

* $p < .05$; ** $p < .01$
Note: Number of cases is given in parentheses.

TABLE 4.5

Means of Jury Sentiment by Outcome: Juries' View of Closeness of Case

Descriptor	Both convicted	Judge convicted; jury acquitted	Both acquitted	Judge acquitted; jury convicted	Overall
Closeness**					
Jury thinks case close	39.7% (52)	30.5% (40)	22.1% (29)	7.6% (10)	100% (131)
Jury Sentiment					
Jury thinks case close					
Fairness of the law	5.50	5.35	5.46	5.42	5.44
Fairness of legally correct outcome	5.25	4.89	5.25	4.96	5.12
Consequences of conviction harsh	4.26	4.28	4.17	4.37	4.26
Sympathy for the defendant	2.97	2.76	2.74	3.07	2.87
Trust in police*	5.08	4.81	5.27	4.89	5.04

Descriptor	Both convicted	Judge convicted; jury acquitted	Both acquitted	Judge acquitted; jury convicted	Overall
Jury thinks case clear	88.2% (120)	3.7% (5)	3.7% (5)	4.4% (6)	100% (136)
Jury thinks case clear					
Fairness of the law**	6.14	4.98	5.11	5.30	6.02
Fairness of legally correct outcome	5.77	5.96	5.93	5.44	5.77
Consequences of conviction harsh*	4.29	3.83	3.85	4.60	4.27
Sympathy for the defendant	3.13	2.80	2.43	2.53	3.06
Trust in police*	5.33	4.44	4.55	5.00	5.25

* p < .05; ** p < .01
Note: Number of cases is given in parentheses.

correct outcome, and the level of trust in the police) vary significantly across judge-jury agreement on case outcomes. Juries were least likely to find the law or the legally correct outcomes fair in liberation cases and least likely to trust the police in reverse liberation cases. The values for each of these sentiments were higher when judges and juries agree than they are when judges and juries disagree.

Sentiment was at work to an even greater extent when, in the judges' view, the cases were clear on the evidence. When judges were clear as to guilt or innocence, four jury sentiments varied significantly across case outcomes. These include the harshness of the consequences of a conviction, fairness of the law, fairness of legally correct outcomes, and trust in the police. Juries were least likely to think legally correct outcomes were fair in liberation cases regardless of whether the judge thought the case was clear or close. Juries were least trusting in the police in liberation cases. Sentiment about the fairness of the law behaved quite differently; juries were least confident about the fairness of the law when both they and the judges acquitted. Indeed, jury sentiment had as much, if not more, explanatory power in clear cases as in close ones. Although disagreements were more frequent in cases that judges considered close than in those they considered clear, disagreements were related to jury sentiment in both situations.

The Jury's Evaluation of Whether the Case Is Close

Table 4.5 indicates that when juries considered cases to be close, the only sentiment significantly associated with outcomes was whether the juries trusted the police. They were least trusting in liberation cases. No other sentiment was significantly related to outcomes. When juries considered cases clear on the evidence, beliefs about the fairness of the law, the harshness of the consequences of convictions, and trust in the police all had significant relationships to outcomes. Juries were least likely to think the law was fair, least likely to be concerned about the consequences of convictions, and least likely to trust the police when they acquitted in cases in which the judges would convict in clear cases.

Jurors, then, were least likely to be affected by sentiment in the very cases in which the liberation hypothesis suggests that sentiment should flower, those cases that juries believe to be close on the evidence. They were most likely to be influenced by sentiment when judges considered the cases to be clear. Juries arrived at conclusions contrary to the judge in clear cases in about 6 percent of all the cases in the Kalven and Zeisel surveyed and in about 7 percent of the cases in the NCSC data.[61] Juries seemed about equally likely to be affected by sentiment in cases that the judges considered close as in cases that the juries considered clear.

Although sentiment was related to case outcomes, it had a larger role in explaining disagreements when the cases were assessed as clear on guilt or innocence than when the cases were assessed as close on this question. This was true whether we used the judges' or juries' assessments of closeness. Although this result seems logical—sentiment should be a factor in explaining why judges and juries disagree when either considers cases to be clear—it does not provide support for the theory that evidentiary uncertainty may trigger juries to retreat to sentiment. Even when we restricted consideration of the role of sentiment to just those cases that were close, we found very little evidence of its operation in cases in which the theory indicated it should occur (i.e., when juries think cases are close on the evidence). Sentiment had a greater effect in cases that judges considered close on the evidence. To say the least, it is not obvious that judges possessed a better sense of when juries would consider cases to be close than did the juries themselves.

These results should not be surprising. There should be some reason that a jury refuses to decide a case in the way that the judge considers to be clear on the evidence. It is interesting, but ultimately unsatisfying, to speculate on the reasons Kalven and Zeisel did not discuss disagreements in "values only" or clear cases as separate categories. Although they explicitly eschewed the role of advocate for or against the jury system, their work has remained a powerful and reassuring testament to the justice of the jury system, as the many judicial citations to it show.[62] Perhaps they considered that an extensive treatment of cases in which juries' decisions flew in the face of the evidence would undercut their message. Whatever the reason, the NCSC data revealed, as did Kalven and Zeisel's survey forty years earlier, that there is a small but persistent fraction of jury trials that result in verdicts the judges consider to be counterfactual.

Conclusion

We began this chapter with newspaper reports about two men accused of participating in the same homicide—a Brooklyn baker (Fortunato) who chose to have his fate decided by a judge and was convicted and a Brooklyn pizza maker (Polito) who chose a jury and was acquitted. Notwithstanding the surprise at the outcome expressed by the judge, the data we have reviewed in this chapter indicates that there is nothing aberrational about the conflicting views of the Brooklyn jury and the Brooklyn judge as to guilt. Like Judge Goldberg of the Brooklyn Supreme Court, most of the judges responding to the NCSC survey would have convicted the defendants whom the jury acquitted. The same was true of the judges responding to Kalven and Zeisel's questionnaire a half-century ago.

Kalven and Zeisel explained disagreements in part through the liberation hypothesis, which posited that juries, in close cases, resorted to sentiment in deciding whether the defendants were guilty. To see whether we could find evidence of this phenomenon at work, we looked at the data from a four-jurisdiction survey of criminal trials undertaken for the explicit purpose of analyzing hung juries but employing survey instruments and techniques that enable researchers to inquire into a broader set of questions. Analyzing this data set, Eisenberg et al.[63] found that contemporary juries, like those studied by Kalven and Zeisel, were more likely to acquit than judges. Our analysis indicates that sentiments, as measured by the NCSC study, may provide a meaningful partial explanation of the tendency of juries to acquit when judges would convict but that this phenomenon is not limited to close cases. Indeed, sentiment was least likely to have a role in the very situation in which the theory suggests it should have the greatest effect, when the jury finds the case close on the evidence. Such was the case for Fortunato and Polito. The judge who convicted Fortunato believed the evidence against both defendants was clear and suggested that the evidence against Polito, who was acquitted by a jury, was even more striking than that against Fortunato. We cannot know what factors specifically motivated jurors to acquit in the Polito case or the degree to which sentiment played a role in their decision, but the case illustrates both the conundrum of judge and jury disagreements and the limits of the liberation hypothesis as an explanation of these disagreements.

This conclusion requires a number of qualifications. First, because in the NCSC study judges were not asked to identify the reasons juries disagreed with them as to guilt, we do not know whether contemporary judges would offer the same explanations of disagreements that their counterparts offered in the 1950s. If the NCSC researchers had asked the same questions as Kalven and Zeisel, perhaps they would have received the same answers. Even if the NCSC study had asked the same questions, however, the data would still provide no support for the view that it is particularly when juries consider cases close that they turn to sentiment to decide the cases.

It is possible, of course, that sentiment has a significant role in leading jurors to consider cases as close on the evidence; but the jurors who responded to the NCSC study were unaware of this subtle influence on their perceptions. They answered in light of the votes they had just cast, and they understood their votes in terms of resolving factual disputes rather than of permitting sentiment to outweigh the conclusions indicated by the facts. One might imagine that jurors may be more aware of the role of sentiment when they choose to acquit despite clear evidence of guilt. If we accept both of these premises, while the NCSC data would not fully undermine the liberation hypothesis, it fails to provide support for its central premise—that factual uncertainty opens a juror's mind to considering sentiment in determining guilt or innocence rather than the presence of sentiment leading the juror to be skeptical about the persuasiveness of the state's evidence. We cannot discount the possibility that jurors' failure to acknowledge the role of sentiment in liberation outcomes reflects their inability to understand their own emotions rather than the absence of those emotions. However, we can suggest that, if this is the case, it has yet to be demonstrated. In our view, the data rather support the less exciting possibility that, in close cases, jurors "call them as they see them" and acquit because they believe that, on the evidence presented, the state failed to persuade them of the defendants' guilt.

The liberation hypothesis suggests that when juries disagree with judges they do so out of emotion, emotion unleashed by those cases that are close on the evidence. The findings presented here suggest that when juries decide to acquit in cases in which judges would have convicted, they arrive at these decisions because they evaluate the evidence differently than judges. We should understand differences between judges and juries not as evidence of the juries' "flight from the law" but rather as an indication that judges and juries rationally evaluate similar evidence but arrive at different conclusions based on their unique vantage points.

Ultimately, it is less important to understand the reasons why judges and juries disagree than to understand who is correct in those cases in which they do disagree. Even if juries are not moved by sentiment to a greater extent than judges, it is still possible that judges do a better job of evaluating credibility and weighing the evidence than do juries. If so, it may be that the judges' conclusions as to guilt or innocence are the ones that reflect the most accurate application of law to fact. We explore this issue in the following chapters.

However, we have answered the question of whether juries arrive at conclusions different from judges in close cases because they are unusually susceptible to sentiment in such cases. The answer to that question, at least as measured by the data in the NCSC study, is no. This finding has important implications for the way we think about the meaning of acquittals. If courts and other criminal justice professionals are going to continue to treat jury acquittals as irrelevant to the question of whether the defendants committed the crimes, they are going to need a firmer base than the belief that juries are moved by sentiment and judges by fact.

5

The Defense Case

Eighteen years after he was sent to death row for the 1984 murder of hotel executive Ray Liuzza, a New Orleans man was acquitted Thursday night and will go home today.

John Thompson, 40, who has always insisted he was innocent, smiled with relief as the verdict was announced less than an hour after the jury began deliberating. His relatives seated behind him sank back into their chairs with tears.

The jury's decision Thursday caps a case that has run a tortured history through the court system, from the discovery that prosecutors hid critical evidence from Thompson's first defense attorney to the successful appeal last summer that overturned his first-degree murder conviction and paved the way for the new trial this week.

Liuzza, 34, was gunned down by a robber after midnight Dec. 6, 1984, in the 1700 block of Josephine Street, just around the corner from his apartment building. He was shot five times, including three times in his back.

Nearly two decades after his arrest for murder, Thompson, for the first time, took the witness stand and professed his innocence.

In 1985, Thompson did not take the stand because he had been convicted in an unrelated armed robbery. Convicted felons rarely take the stand in their defense, because their criminal history is open to attack by prosecutors. This week, Thompson's defense team presented a series of witnesses who had never testified before a jury. Having tracked down three people who lived near the murder scene in 1984, the attorneys presented testimony that fingered another man as Liuzza's killer: Kevin Freeman.[1]

Most studies of judge-jury agreement (as discussed in more detail in chapter 2) reflect the assumption implicit in Kalven and Zeisel: that judges make the correct judgments.[2] Yet the differences in decision making between judges and juries "tells us nothing about whether either decision maker (or group) is actually accurate; both could be wrong."[3] Both empirical and theoretical investigations suggest that juries apply "commonsense justice" as they arrive at their conclusions concerning guilt or innocence through consideration of factors beyond those that are legally relevant.[4] Jury justice results from a process of collective deliberation conducted under the veil of secrecy that may result in decisions different from those that would result from public, mechanical application of received law to the facts, however determined.[5] These studies do not indicate, however, whether, in George Fisher's[6] phrase, juries are better "lie detector[s]" than judges in routine criminal cases. We simply do not know the answer to the question of whether judges' or juries' views of guilt are more accurate. The very process that we wish to examine, the criminal trial, is treated as producing the authoritative resolution to the question.

In previous scholarship on jury decision making, MacCoun drew important distinctions between coherence and correspondence "theories of truth."[7] Our ultimate concern is with correspondence: When judges and juries disagree, which decision maker accurately determines what happened? Although the coherence of the decision is relevant to this inquiry, it cannot resolve it. Thus, although it is useful in much research to analyze the quality of the decision in terms of the degree to which the decision maker relies on bad cues or misses good cues,[8] we cannot know whether the information to which judges and juries appear to have disparate reactions (i.e., the defendants' evidence and personal backgrounds) are bad cues to which juries pay too much attention or good cues to which judges pay too little.

The studies we have discussed in earlier chapters were focused primarily upon the effect of the prosecution's evidence on the juries' decisions. Defense cases were represented only in terms of whether defendants testified and whether they had criminal records or were otherwise unattractive. Kalven and Zeisel's two other measures related to defendants' credibility (e.g., whether there were renounced confessions or accomplice testimony) were typically part of the prosecution's cases. Other studies of the effect of trial evidence on juries (Myers,[9] Visher,[10] and Heuer and Penrod[11]) either reflected the same focus or, at a minimum, did not differentiate between the prosecution and defense cases.

Defense cases should matter in criminal trials. Juries are told by judges that they must arrive at their conclusions of guilt or innocence on the basis of the evidence presented in court. A considerable body of literature suggests that decision makers resolve factual questions through creating coherent narratives into which they can place the evidence that they hear.[12] The "story model" of the way jurors process evidence suggests that jurors construct stories upon which they can decide given cases because of the interaction between the evidence formally introduced in court and the jurors' prior knowledge of similar events and generic expectations of how events unfold.[13] "If there are multiple coherent explanations for the available evidence, belief in any one of them over the others will necessarily be diminished. If there is a single coherent story, this story will be accepted as the explanation of the evidence."[14]

Criminal cases do not all involve competing stories in the sense of alternative explanations for given events (e.g., Was the defendant the man who, at gunpoint, took the money from the supermarket cashier?). Many criminal cases involve only the attempt of the prosecutor to create a satisfying account of whether a crime occurred and, if so, how it occurred:

> In these one-sided cases, jurors construct only one story, and confidence in the verdict is determined by coherence and fit of the single story to the verdict category. In this situation, a weak defense story

is worse than no story at all; in fact, a weak prosecution story is bol-stered and more guilty verdicts are rendered when a weak defense story is presented versus no defense story at all.[15]

As the case of John Thompson illustrates, a strong defense can change the outcome of a case. In the NCSC data that we analyzed, there were no defense witnesses in 25 percent of the cases; and the defendants were the sole witnesses in another 17.5 percent.

When defendants go beyond attacking the coherence and fit of the state's cases and instead offer competing stories to explain either the events in question or the reasons the defendants are on trial, the fact finders should be less likely to determine that the state's explana-tions are the only coherent and comprehensive accounts of events. The NCSC data provided a unique opportunity to examine the way judges and juries responded to defendants' evidence as they determined guilt or innocence.

Understanding the effects of defense cases has important impli-cations for any evaluation of the justice in our adjudicatory process. We purport to place a higher value on acquitting the innocent than upon convicting the guilty, yet we treat acquittals as having established nothing other than that the state cannot retry the defendant for the same crime.[16] Judges contribute to the perception that acquittals have little connection to innocence when they report that they would not have acquitted when the jury did.

Data on the Defense Case and Jury Decision Making

We suggest that the differences between judges and juries are not sim-ply explained by the notion that judges are guided by facts and juries by values. Rather, judges and juries respond to the evidence, albeit in distinctive ways. Juries attend to the defense cases whereas judges, at least in responding to questionnaires, may not.

Trial judges make far more rulings focusing upon the adequacy (sufficiency) of the state's evidence than they make rulings resolving factual conflicts between the state's evidence and that of the defense.

Determining whether to admit an accused on bond, whether to issue a warrant, whether the prosecution has provided sufficient evidence to hold the defendant pending the action of the grand jury, whether the prosecution has introduced sufficient evidence to withstand a motion to dismiss, whether a prosecution witness will be permitted to disclose certain information to the jury, whether there is sufficient evidence to permit the giving of a particular instruction—with rare exceptions, these decisions that criminal trial judges are called upon to make repeatedly rest upon the judge's evaluation of whether the prosecutor has introduced sufficient evidence to permit the action in question. Given that judges spend much of their professional energy scrutinizing whether the state's evidence, if believed, justifies a particular action, it is perhaps not surprising that judges retain this focus when asked to indicate how they would have resolved the cases in front of them if they had been bench trials.

If judges are inclined to view criminal trials in terms of the adequacy and credibility of the state's evidence, one may expect that they will form their views of guilt or innocence through the lens of the prosecution's case. Jurors are unlikely to have comparable experience or expectations and, thus, may be more likely than judges to attend to defense cases, particularly when they go beyond simple denials of guilt. We expect that judges and juries are most likely to agree when the state's evidence is unchallenged by disinterested witnesses since the question in such cases is whether the state's evidence of the defendants' guilt eliminates sufficient doubt to permit juries to find the defendants guilty. Judges and juries would be most likely to disagree when the question is one of choosing between competing versions of the events because jurors are more likely than judges to have no a priori investments, either professional or personal, in crediting the state's case.

Individual Effects of Defense Cases on Judge and Jury Outcomes

In the following analysis, we attempt to isolate the degree to which variables indicative of the strength of defense cases affect judge and jury outcomes in the NCSC data, taking into account differences in the court locations and types of criminal charges. Table 5.1 shows the descriptive statistics and bivariate analysis with judge and jury outcomes for all variables included in this study.[17]

Judges and juries in the NCSC data acquitted at roughly the same rate when the defense presented no witnesses or the defendants were the only witnesses testifying on their behalf. However, when additional witnesses testified for the defendants, juries became much more likely to acquit than judges (see table 5.1). Judges appeared to focus on the state's cases and did not appear to be as persuaded as juries by increased defense testimony or evidence. Conversely, juries tended to find for defendants when they offered more evidence in the form

TABLE 5.1
Descriptive Statistics and Bivariate Analysis: Judge and Jury Outcomes

		Outcomes			
		Judges acquitted		Juries acquitted	
		No	Yes	No	Yes
		81.5%	18.5%	74.3%	25.7%
Descriptors	Total cases	(251)	(57)	(254)	(88)
Location*					
Los Angeles	23.7% (90)	85.2%	14.8%	83.1%	16.9%
Maricopa	28.0% (106)	72.9%	27.1%	79.8%	20.2%
Bronx	25.1% (95)	81.8%	18.2%	63.4%	36.6%
Washington, DC	23.2% (88)	86.8%	13.2%	72.3%	27.7%
Crime type*					
Murder	18.8% (64)	92.5%	7.5%	79.0%	21.0%
Other violent crime	31.0% (106)	77.9%	22.1%	69.8%	30.2%
Drugs	29.6% (101)	85.1%	14.9%	77.2%	22.8%
Other nonviolent crime	20.5% (70)	71.9%	28.1%	74.3%	25.7%
Testimony type*					
No witnesses testified	25.1% (77)	87.3%	12.7%	84.0%	16.0%
Defendant testified alone	17.5% (59)	80.0%	20.0%	80.4%	19.6%
Witness other than defendant testified alone	26.1% (76)	81.8%	18.2%	69.0%	31.0%
Defendant and witness testified together	29.3% (88)	75.0%	25.0%	61.4%	38.6%
Criminal history*					
No prior record	19.9% (62)	72.4%	27.6%	57.4%	42.6%
Prior record: jury doesn't know	56.9% (177)	84.2%	15.8%	78.8%	21.2%
Prior record: jury does know	23.2% (72)	84.6%	15.4%	81.4%	18.6%
	76.0% (288)	84.5%	15.5%	80.5%	19.5%
Defendant claimed innocence*	24.0% (91)	72.4%	27.6%	55.8%	44.2%

* $p < 0.05$
Note: Number of cases is given in parentheses.

of their own or supporting witness testimonies, when they refused to plead on the grounds that they were innocent, or when they lacked prior criminal histories.

Strong Defense Testimony: The Effect of Witnesses

Why do acquittal rates differ when there is a third party witness for the defense? There are a number of possible reasons. First, the very existence of a witness for the defense makes the case closer; thus, the jury is liberated to consult values. Second, the testimony of the witness results in the case being even closer; thus, the jury, with its more exacting standard of reasonable doubt, finds for the defendant. Third, the judge's obligation to determine the sufficiency of the evidence role may result in more attention being focused on the prosecution's case than on the defense's case, making differences in defense evidence less important to judges than to juries.

If judges have information not shared with juries, typically it has to do with the defendants (e.g., criminal records, suppressed evidence, withdrawn pleas) and not the defense witnesses. If the state knows that a witness (other than the defendant) has a criminal record, its ability to impeach the witness with that record is virtually unconstrained. Thus, a logical explanation for a judge-jury disagreement (i.e., the judge knowing something the jury does not) seems particularly inapplicable here.[18] If Kalven and Zeisel are correct and the explanation for judge-jury difference is in the interaction between facts and values, it seems odd that the difference is not manifested in those instances in which either there is no defense or the defendant is the only witness. Rather, the difference between the rates at which judges and juries acquit is significantly attributable to those cases in which witnesses other than the defendants appear for the defense.

This finding is consonant with the liberation hypothesis, if we use the presence of witnesses other than the defendants as a placeholder for cases that are, in Kalven and Zeisel's terms, close on the evidence.[19] In this view, someone other than the defendant contesting the prosecution's version of events from the witness stand results in freeing the jurors from the narrow confines of the evidence to permit them to decide on the basis of sentiment. There is another, less romantic explanation for this phenomenon: the jury, having heard from someone other than the defendant, accurately determines that the defendant's version is correct and that of the prosecution is mistaken. The only liberation that occurs is that the jury may choose between two versions of the events in question rather than simply decide whether they are persuaded by the government's version. Thus, in the John Thompson case with which we began this chapter, the jury that convicted him did so based on the evidence presented to them. The jury that acquitted him at his retrial heard from defense witnesses who had not been presented to the original jury. One witness, in particular, had witnessed the killing of Liuzza from her apartment balcony and knew that John Thompson was not guilty. She explained at the second trial, "I've carried a burden for years. I just need to do the right thing."[20]

Judges, professionally habituated to decide evidentiary questions in terms of the state's showing, may conflate the question of whether there is evidence sufficient to justify a conviction with the question of whether the defendant ought to be convicted. Perhaps judges and juries disagree in these cases not because the juries are liberated but because the judges remain shackled to the belief that guilt or innocence depends upon the state's evidence, not the defendant's.

Criminal Record

Judges and juries also respond differently to defendants' lack of criminal records. Juries in the NCSC data acquitted in 43 percent of the cases in which defendants had no prior criminal histories, whereas judges would have acquitted in 28 percent of those cases. In cases in which defendants did have prior criminal histories (whether the jury knew about the history or not), juries and judges acquitted at much closer rates (see table 5.1).

The existence of criminal records may affect the kinds of evidence that defendants put forward. With rare exceptions, juries cannot learn of defendants' criminal records unless the defendants take the stand

TABLE 5.2

Relationship between Type of Defense and Past Criminal Record

Type of defense	Past criminal record			Total
	No criminal history	Criminal history; jury does not know	Criminal history; jury knows	
No witnesses*	12.8% (10)	82.1% (64)	5.1% (4)	100%
Witness(es) other than defendant testified alone*	14.3% (11)	77.9% (60)	7.8% (6)	100%
Defendant testified alone*	22.2% (14)	31.7% (20)	46.1% (29)	100%
Defendant and at least one witness testified*	34.1% (30)	32.9 % (29)	32.9% (29)	100%

* p < 0.05
Note: Number of cases is given in parentheses.

and testify in their own defense. One may expect, then, that defendants without criminal records were more likely to testify than those with such records, and table 5.2. shows that this is the case. What was a bit less predictable, however, was that defendants without criminal records were most likely to testify when there was at least one additional witness for the defense. Defendants had no criminal records in 22 percent of the cases in which they testified alone as opposed to 34 percent of the cases in which at least one other witness for the defense also testified. Defendants had criminal records that juries learned about in 46 percent of the cases in which defendants testified alone as opposed to 33 percent of the cases in which defendants testified with at least one other witness for the defense. The latter difference (whether the jury learns of the criminal record) may reflect the seriousness of the prior records, but there is no a priori reason why this should differ depending upon whether defendants can call on others to testify on their behalf. Technically, judges should balance the probative value of questioning defendants about their prior records against the unfair prejudice likely to flow from the practice. It is hardly obvious that balance should be struck in the state's favor more often when defendants are their only witnesses than when the defendants' testimonies are bolstered by at least one other witness.

When we consider the information from both tables 5.1 and 5.2, a striking fact emerges. When defendants without criminal records testified along with other witnesses, juries acquitted in 64 percent of the cases. Judges would have acquitted in only one third of the same cases (see table 5.3).[21] When defendants and other witnesses testified and the defendants had records, whether or not the juries learned of them, judge-jury differences virtually disappeared. If we assume that when the defendants with no records testified in their own behalf, juries learned of the defendants' lack of criminal records, juries appeared to treat the lack of records more positively than did judges. This was true of the Kalven and Zeisel[22] study as well.

This finding may be an artifact of the legal culture within which judges operate. Because they have been taught (and tell juries) that prior convictions may only be considered as they affect the credibility of the witnesses, they may actually believe this. The records are irrelevant in terms of telling us anything about the likelihood that the defendants committed the crimes. Jurors, unfamiliar with the governing

TABLE 5.3
Judge and Jury Outcomes: Defendant and at Least One Witness Testify Together

Defendant and at least one witness testify	Criminal history	Judge would acquit	Judge would not acquit	Jury acquitted	Jury did not acquit	Difference: jury-judge
No	No criminal history	22.6% (7)	77.4% (24)	25.0% (89)	75.0% (24)	2.4%
	Criminal history but jury does not know	13.0% (17)	87.0% (114)	19.7% (28)	80.3% (114)	6.7%
	Criminal history and jury does know	15.4% (6)	84.6% (33)	17.5% (7)	82.5% (33)	2.1%
Yes*	No criminal history	33.3% (9)	66.7% (18)	64.3% (18)	35.7% (10)	31.0%
	Criminal history but jury does not know	29.6% (8)	70.4% (19)	28.6% (8)	71.4% (20)	−1.0%
	Criminal history and jury does know	15.4% (4)	84.6% (22)	22.2% (6)	77.8% (21)	6.8%

* $p < 0.05$
Note: Number of cases in parentheses.

law, may apply common sense and treat the absence of prior records as making it less likely that the defendants committed the crimes with which they are charged.

Kalven and Zeisel reported that the "judge and jury show a systematically different evaluation" of the testifying defendant who has no criminal record and that this difference "furnishes a substantial explanation for judge-jury disagreement."[23] Indeed, they attributed one-fifth (21 percent) of all evidentiary disagreements between judges and juries to this factor.[24] The NCSC data did not confirm this observation. Indeed, in the few cases in which defendants with unblemished records testified by themselves, there was very little difference between the judges' willingness to find for the defense and the juries' acquittal rates.[25] It was the presence of additional witnesses, not the existence of testifying defendants without criminal records, that was the trigger for the judge-jury deviation.

Claims of Innocence

In the NCSC study, researchers asked both the defending and prosecuting attorneys to explain why the cases had not ended in plea bargains. Although several types of responses were given, they could be reduced to a few common reasons why plea bargaining failed: (1) defendants claimed they were innocent, (2) defendants refused to plead, (3) no offers were made, and (4) the parties could not agree on appropriate pleas. Through recoding these responses into separate categories, we were able to examine whether there was a relationship between the reason for the failure of plea bargaining and the outcome of the case. Unlike either the constellation of witnesses or the existence or nonexistence of criminal records, the reason for failed plea bargaining was a fact that the jury would not know. Indeed, unless the judge participated in the plea negotiations, the judge would not have this information either. Thus, it is intriguing that the defendants' insistence on their innocence as the reason why plea bargaining failed was significantly related to both jury acquittals and judges being prepared to find for the defense (see table 5.1). In addition, the gap between judicial and jury willingness to acquit increased significantly when defendants claimed they were innocent.

One possible explanation for both phenomena is that defendants only insist upon innocence when they have strong evidentiary bases for doing so. Defense lawyers will probably challenge more aggressively their defendants' insistence on going to trial if there is not much in the way of a defense that can be mounted. Moreover, defense lawyers with clients insisting on innocence and witnesses to help prove it may be more energized and effective lawyers than ones forced to rely solely on poking holes in the state's cases. It is also possible, of course, that defendants claim innocence and have supportive witnesses because they are, in fact, innocent.

The Combined Effect of Strong Defense Case Measures on Jury and Judge Decisions

As indicated in the previous analyses, the independent effects of defendants and witnesses testifying together, criminal histories, and defendants' claims of innocence on judge and jury outcomes were strong. When these three factors were put together as a measure of a strong defense case, however, the differences between judge and jury acquittals were quite striking. As seen in table 5.4, juries acquitted in 77 percent of the cases in which all three factors were present and in 64 percent of the cases in which two of the factors existed. Interestingly, the gap between judges and juries was actually narrowed when the claim of innocence was added to the analysis. Although the numbers of cases became quite small, the percentages were dramatic, indicating the need for analysis that can control for multiple effects together.

Examining the interactive effects of criminal records and defendants' claims of innocence on the various combinations of defense testimony while holding constant for other relevant variables helps explain why juries are more likely to acquit than judges when defendants testify with supporting witnesses.

A series of four logistic regression models predicting judge acquittal

TABLE 5.4
Strongest Cases for Innocence

	Judge would acquit	Judge would not acquit	Jury acquitted	Jury did not acquit	Difference: jury-judge
Defendant and witness testified together	25.0% (21)	75.0% (63)	38.6% (34)	61.4% (54)	13.6%
Defendant and witness testified together, and defendant had no prior record	33.3% (9)	66.7% (18)	64.3% (18)	35.7% (10)	31.0%
Defendant and witness testified together, defendant had no prior record, and defendant claimed innocence	53.8% (7)	46.2% (6)	76.9% (10)	23.1% (3)	23.1%

and jury acquittal were employed to test the relationship between the strength of the defense case and acquittal (see tables 5.5 and 5.6). For these models, the outcome variable of interest was a dichotomous measure indicating either that a judge would not acquit (coded 0) or that a judge would acquit (coded 1). The second dependent variable was the vote of the jury (coded 0 for either a hung jury or a conviction; coded 1 for acquittal).[26] Some moderate correlation exists between our control variables (location and severity of charge) and our test variables (defense testimony type, prior history, and defendant's claim of innocence; see appendix B).

Model 1 showed a weak relationship between any of the courtroom location variables or types of charges and jury or judge acquittals. Site variations or charges alone did little to explain why judges or juries vote for acquittal (none of the variables was statistically significant, with the exception of jury outcomes in Los Angeles). Model 2 indicated a strong relationship between jury acquittals and the defendants and at least one witness testifying together as compared to no witnesses testifying, defendants testifying alone, or witnesses testifying alone.[27] When court location and type of crime were held constant, the odds of defendants receiving acquittals were over three times as great when defendants and a witness testified together as when there

TABLE 5.5
Separated Logistic Regression Models for Judge Acquitting and Jury Acquitting: Models 1 and 2

| | Model 1: court and charge | | | | | | Model 2: court, charge, testimony, and prior record | | | | | |
| | Judge (r-sq. = .062) | | | Jury (r-sq. = .065) | | | Judge acquitted (r-sq. = .098) | | | Jury acquitted (r-sq. = .095) | | |
Descriptor	(B)	SE	Odds	(B)	SE	Odds	(B)	SE	Odds	(B)	SE	Odds
Los Angeles	-0.21	0.51	0.81	-0.79	0.41	0.45**	-0.22	0.54	0.8	-0.62	0.43	0.54
Maricopa	0.68	0.45	1.99	-0.6	0.39	0.55	1.04	0.49	2.83**	-0.14	0.43	0.87
Bronx[b]	0.32	0.47	1.38	0.38	0.33	1.47	0.45	0.49	1.57	0.48	0.37	1.61
Murder	-0.89	0.64	0.41	-0.58	0.45	0.56	-1.05	0.73	0.35	-0.69	0.52	0.50
Other violent crime	0.23	0.42	1.26	0.02	0.37	1.02	0.27	0.45	1.32	-0.2	0.41	0.82
Drug crime[c]	-0.14	0.47	0.86	-0.44	0.39	0.65	0.14	0.51	1.16	-0.11	0.44	0.9
Defendant + witness							0.65	0.47	1.92	1.13	0.41	3.10***
Defendant alone							0.18	0.53	1.19	0.15	0.48	1.17
Witness other than defendant[a]							0.7	0.53	2	0.8	0.44	2.22*
No prior record												
Prior record; jury doesn't know[d]												
Defendant claims innocence												
Constant	-1.74	0.5	0.17***	-0.67	0.4	0.51**	-2.29	0.68	0.10***	-1.35	0.56	0.25**

* p < 0.01; ** p < 0.05; *** p < 0.01

[a] Reference category No Witness Testifies
[b] Reference category DC
[c] Reference category other crime
[d] Reference category prior record and jury does know

TABLE 5.6
Logistic Regression Models for Judges Acquitting and Jury Acquitting: Models 3 and 4

| | Model 3: courtroom and charge | | | | | | Model 4: testimony and courtroom | | | | | |
| | Judge (r-sq. = .107) | | | Jury (r-sq. = .168) | | | Judge acquitted (r-sq. = .12) | | | Jury acquitted (r-sq. = .22) | | |
Descriptor	(B)	SE	Odds	(B)	SE	Odds	(B)	SE	Odds	(B)	SE	Odds
Los Angeles	-0.26	0.57	0.77	-0.58	0.47	0.56	-0.17	0.57	0.84	-0.45	0.48	0.63
Maricopa	0.84	0.51	2.313*	-0.37	0.46	0.69	0.8	0.5	2.22	-0.41	0.47	0.66
Bronxb	0.61	0.51	1.84	0.82	0.41	2.26**	0.53	0.52	1.7	0.7	0.42	2
Murder	-1.03	0.75	0.36	-0.97	0.56	0.378*	-1.08	0.75	0.33	-1.0	0.57	0.36*
Other violent crime	0.14	0.48	1.15	-0.47	0.44	0.63	0.03	0.48	1.03	-0.62	0.46	0.53
Drug crimec	0.14	0.53	1.15	-0.12	0.46	0.89	0.03	0.53	1.02	-0.21	0.47	0.8
Defendant + witness	0.84	0.53	2.31	1.17	0.47	3.23*	0.64	0.55	1.89	0.87	0.49	2.38*
Defendant alone	0.31	0.59	1.36	0.15	0.54	1.16	0.23	0.59	1.25	-0.02	0.55	0.97
Witness other than defendant[a]	0.67	0.55	1.96	0.62	0.46	1.85	0.5	0.56	1.64	0.37	0.47	1.44
No prior record	0.65	0.51	1.91	1.39	0.48	4.02***	0.64	0.52	1.9	1.43	0.49	4.16***
Prior record jury doesn't know[d]	0.3	0.5	1.34	0.48	0.46	1.61	0.29	0.51	1.33	0.44	0.47	1.55
Defendant claims innocence							0.63	0.38	1.87*	1.08	0.33	2.93***
Constant	-2.65	0.86	0.071***	-1.9	0.74	0.15***	-2.62	0.85	0.07***	-1.93	0.74	0.15***

$p < 0.01$; ** $p < 0.05$; *** $p < 0.01$
[a] Reference category No Witness Testifies
[b] Reference category DC
[c] Reference category other crime
[d] Reference category prior record and jury does know

were no defense witnesses presented. Interestingly, the effect of defendants and witnesses testifying together on judge outcomes, although positive (odds 1.9), was not statistically significant. The presence of witnesses other than the defendant testifying alone resulted in the odds of a judge acquitting being 2 times more likely and the odds of juries acquitting being 2.2 times more likely (although the odds were only statistically significant for juries).

The results shown in Model 3 indicate that judges remained unmoved by defendants without prior records or prior records that the juries did not know about. Yet juries were significantly more likely to acquit defendants when they did not have prior records (four times more likely). Having prior records, even when juries did not know about them, appeared to decrease the likelihood of juries acquitting. This might reflect the difference between juries hearing affirmative testimony about the lack of prior records (defendants are entitled to put their character at issue by testifying that they have no prior records) and juries receiving no information at all about defendants' prior records (as occurred when defendants did have such records but judges ruled that prosecutors could not bring this out in cross-examination).[28] The effect of defendants and other witnesses testifying on their behalf was strengthened when prior records was controlled for in Model 3: but the effect of witnesses testifying alone, although still positive, became nonsignificant.[29]

In Model 4, the effects of each of our hypothesized indicators of a strong defense case were measured. In this final model, defendants and witnesses testifying together remained positive and significantly related to jury acquittals, as did defendants having no prior criminal records. Intriguingly, the only variable that had a significant effect on both judge and jury outcomes was the defendant claiming innocence. When defendants claimed they were innocent to their defense attorneys, the odds that judges would acquit were 1.9 times more likely than when the defendant did not claim they were innocent, and jury acquittals were 2.9 times more likely. As noted, juries are extremely unlikely to know that defendants have refused to plea bargain on these grounds; and judges will only know this if the judges are actively involved in pretrial plea bargaining. This suggests that there may be something qualitatively different in either the defense presentation of the case or the prosecution response when the defendant claims innocence. Alternatively, it may be that the defendant *is* innocent and the judge and jury figure this out.

Our analysis was focused upon the effect of external factors on the jury decisions to render not guilty verdicts. By external, we mean factors other than those relating to the composition of the jury and the way in which it processes information and arrives at a result. Treating the jury as a "black box," we asked what inputs were most likely to produce the outputs of not guilty verdicts.

We identified the constellation of witnesses, the defendants' lack of criminal records, and the defendants' refusal to plead because of innocence as being significantly correlated to the jury decisions to acquit. Of these, only the claim of innocence, a fact the judges and juries in many cases are unlikely to know, is significant in explaining judicial decisions. We also showed that judges and juries will acquit at approximately the same rate when the defendants offer no witnesses or the defendants are their only witnesses; acquittal rates diverge once witnesses other than the defendants appear for the defense, with or without the defendants also testifying. The difference in acquittal rates increases when defendants and witnesses testify and the defendants have no criminal records, with juries going from being 50 percent more likely to acquit when defendants and witnesses testify to being 90 percent more likely when the defendants also have no criminal records.

One view of these findings is that they confirm Kalven and Zeisel's[30] liberation hypothesis. The existence of witnesses other than the defendants or in addition to the defendants results in cases being close on the evidence. This closeness has the effect of freeing juries to acquit for reasons unrelated to innocence. One may as easily attribute the differing reactions when outside witnesses testify for the defendants to the contrasting views of reasonable doubt: through their counterstories, defendants plant doubts in the minds of unsophisticated jurors that experienced judges know to be unreasonable. The distinction between naïve jurors and experienced judges is intensified when defendants have no prior criminal records, a factor that is beguiling to juries but does not move judges. Knowing that defendants without records and confirmed (by defense witnesses) stories of innocence have decent chances of acquittal, defense counsel present their cases with uncommon vigor and certitude, thus communicating to the juries their beliefs in their clients' innocence. The judges are, of course, not fooled. Thus, these explanations serve to preserve the narrative that juries react emotionally, even irrationally, while judges adjudicate accurately.

There is, of course, another way of viewing juries' responsiveness to defense cases and the weight they may attach to the lack of prior criminal records: the juries are correct in attending to these factors, and the judges err when (and if) they discount them. Neither the police nor the prosecutors are likely to have investigated the defendants' stories; the decisions to prosecute are made ex parte, on the basis of witnesses who present one side of these stories. There are no a priori reasons to believe that the state's witnesses never err and always tell the truth. Although courts insist that propensity evidence (e.g., once a thief, always a thief) is irrelevant, individuals not trained in the law may have some difficulty endorsing a proposition so at odds with the way they make judgments about human behavior. Finally, whether the adjudicators are aware of it or not, there is the sheer fact that many defendants refuse to plead because they insist that they are innocent; and many of them are, in fact, found innocent by juries. Were we not inclined to accept the view that to be charged is to be guilty and to be acquitted is to be given an undeserved gift, we might attend to the possibility that the very factors that appear to distinguish judge and jury decision making are factors that are fully consistent with the defendant's innocence. The NCSC data indicated that the difference between judge and jury decision making is centered on the attention paid to the defendants: whether they can produce witnesses to support their versions of the events, whether or not they have criminal records, and whether or not they refuse to plead on the grounds of innocence.

What accounts for the different reactions of judges and juries to defendants' cases? One possibility is that what is real for juries is only hypothetical for judges and that judges faced with actually deciding these cases may have acquitted more frequently. When the cases are theirs to decide alone, federal judges are currently more likely to acquit than juries;[31] state judges are at least as likely.[32] This explanation fits with what happens currently even though the data from forty years ago showed an opposite pattern of federal judges, at least, being more likely to convict than juries.[33] It may be odd, albeit not impossible, that judges who are today no more likely to convict than juries nonetheless view themselves as being much tougher than juries. If so, it may be a tribute to the power of *The American Jury* and the liberation hypothesis it generated.

A second possibility is that judges and juries are called upon to decide very different cases. It is possible that judges might have convicted at a much higher rate than juries if the trials in the NCSC study had been before the judges alone. The current acquittal rate by judges in jury-waived trials may simply reflect the choice by innocent defendants to seek accurate decision making provided by a judge rather than the less-than-accurate, sentiment-driven decision making of a jury.[34] However, this explanation does not account for the shift in judge versus jury acquittal rates over time[35] or the (often considerable) sentencing incentives to waive jury trials. Nor is there evidence that defense counsel (who advise defendants on whether to waive jury trials) believe that judges are more accurate fact finders than juries or that judges, in fact, do better jobs of fact-finding in criminal cases than do juries. Nonetheless, it represents a possible way to reconcile judges' criticism of jury verdicts with their behavior in jury-waived cases.

Another explanation for the difference may lie in the roles of judge and jury. For jurors, criminal trials are anything but routine parts of their work lives. Called together with strangers to decide the fate of yet other strangers, jurors are likely to pay considerable attention when they are told that their job is to decide whether the state has proved its case beyond a reasonable doubt. Jurors also bring with them whatever native sympathy they may have for individuals in the defendants' situations, as well as their understanding of what motivates people and how to evaluate credibility. Looking at the state's evidence with fresh eyes and listening to the defendants' explanations with fresh ears, jurors may well have doubts when judges would not. As unique experiences as trials may be for jurors, they are routine for the judges. As noted, judges naturally focus on the state's cases because that is what they are regularly called upon to consider in a very large number of rulings.

Judges are also part of work groups in which they play a central role, even though one very much constrained by the expectations of other participants in the adjudication of criminal cases.[36] Judges who are perceived to conclude *routinely* that the police are not telling the truth are judges who quickly gain notoriety and, sometimes, epithets (e.g., "Turn 'em loose Bruce"). In addition, the overwhelming number of criminal defendants who come before judges *are* guilty; and the vast majority of these admit it in open court in the form of pleas. Although it is tempting to believe that judges can identify the rare innocents, judges, like prosecutors and defense counsel, work in settings in which the only practical approach is to presume guilt, not innocence. As a matter of legal doctrine, a presumption shifts the burden of proof; and it is likely that the operative presumption of guilt works in the same way extralegally. Even though juries may believe that the state must eliminate doubt, judges sitting without juries may assume defendants are guilty unless there is something wrong with the states' cases.

Even if juries are correct and judges wrong when they disagree about acquittals, this does not mean that defendants are factually innocent. However, the factors that result in jury acquittals (i.e., defense witnesses, lack of prior criminal records, and refusal to plead on the grounds of innocence) are entirely consistent with factual innocence. That judges are less affected by these factors than juries does not prove that these defendants are guilty; it only confirms that judges are readier to convict than juries. Finally, that a refusal to plead on the grounds of innocence is a significant explanation of both judge and jury acquittals suggests that there may be considerably more to acquittals than meets the eye. It may be that we are acquitting innocents.

The case with which we began this chapter—John Thompson, who went from death row to acquittal and freedom once he presented a defense case—has a byzantine quality worthy of the Big Easy. Thompson did not take the stand at his initial trial for murder because he did not wish the jury to know that he had also been convicted of an attempted armed robbery that had occurred a few weeks after the murder. The prosecutor apparently had made the strategic decision to pursue the attempted armed robbery case before the murder case in order to secure a conviction that could then be used to impeach Thompson should he choose to take the stand at the murder trial. However, even as he pursued the attempted robbery case against Thompson, the prosecutor possessed evidence of the attempted armed robber's blood type that exonerated Thompson. This prosecutor did not disclose the evidence, Thompson was convicted, and the threat of being impeached with this conviction led Thompson's lawyer to keep him off the stand at the murder trial.

Fourteen years later, the defense discovered the blood type evidence a month before Thompson was due to be executed. It also learned that a New Orleans assistant district attorney, suffering from a fatal illness, had told a colleague some five years earlier about the blood evidence and its suppression. The state's withholding of the potentially exculpatory blood evidence led the appellate court to reverse Thompson's murder conviction on the theory that Thompson had not testified in his own behalf in the homicide trial because he was afraid the jury would learn of his attempted robbery conviction. At the retrial, Thompson testified along with three other defense witnesses; the jury took thirty-five minutes to return a verdict of not guilty.[37] The two trials illustrate the power of a strong defense case and potential of juries to evaluate evidence of innocence.

6

The Impact of Race on Judge and Jury Decision Making

After a trial with heavy racial overtones, a Rensselaer County jury acquitted a Nassau man of all charges in connection with a fight in East Greenbush last year that ended with a teen in a bonfire.

Bruce Vroman, 24, was found not guilty on first- and second-degree assault charges after a weeklong trial. He had maintained since his arrest after the Oct. 8, 2009 incident that he pushed 18-year-old Derek George off of him during a fight and George subsequently stumbled into the fire.

"It's been 13 months of hell" for Vroman since his arrest, said his attorney, David Taffany, after the verdict. "This was a long haul," he said. "We feel for (George), but the fact is Bruce Vroman did not do this. It was a terrible accident."

Special prosecutor Matthew Hug had alleged Vroman "body slammed" George into the fire after a dispute began when Vroman and a friend used racial slurs against George, who is black.

During his closing argument Friday morning, Hug suggested Vroman considered George an "ignorant n——," prompting Taffany to ask Judge Andrew Ceresia, unsuccessfully, for a mistrial.

A pair of activists who sat through the trial expressed outrage. They said they will not give up on the case and will ask for the help of the NAACP or call leaders like Al Sharpton if necessary.

"I'm going to continue fighting for Derek. If it means pro-
testing, I'll do that," said Kim Weekes, an Atlanta-based activist. Jodi Williams, an activist involved in criminal justice issues,
noted the jury was entirely white.[1]

All-white jury chosen in Pa. hate crime trial
An all-white jury has been seated in the trial of two Pennsylvania teenagers in the fatal beating of an illegal immigrant from
Mexico. Prosecutors say the attack on 25-year-old Luis Ramirez
was racially motivated. The jury was seated Wednesday and the
trial opens Monday.[2]

Jury finds immigrant's killing wasn't a hate crime
Prosecutors called the beating death of an illegal immigrant
from Mexico a hate crime, and they urged an all-white jury in
Pennsylvania coal country to punish two white teenagers for
their roles in the attack.

Instead, the jury found the teens innocent of all serious
charges, a decision that elicited cheers and claps from the
defendants' families and friends—and cries of outrage from
the victim's.

Brandon Piekarsky, 17, was acquitted of third-degree murder and ethnic intimidation, while Derrick Donchak, 19, was
acquitted of aggravated assault and ethnic intimidation. Both
were convicted of simple assault late Friday after a trial in
which jurors were left to sort out the facts of an epithet-filled
brawl that pitted popular football players against a 25-year-old
Hispanic man, Luis Ramirez, who appeared willing to fight.

A representative of Ramirez's family said the jurors got
it wrong.

"There's been a complete failure of justice," said Gladys
Limon, staff attorney for the Mexican American Legal Defense
and Education Fund, who attended the trial and informed
Ramirez's family of the verdict. "It's just outrageous and very
difficult to understand how any juror could have had reasonable doubt."

Prosecutors had cast Ramirez as the victim of a gang of drunken white teens motivated by a dislike of their small coal town's burgeoning Hispanic population. But the jury evidently sided with defense attorneys, who called Ramirez the aggressor and characterized the brawl as a street fight that ended tragically.

Jury foreman Eric Macklin said he sympathized with Ramirez's loved ones but that the evidence pointed to an acquittal. "I feel bad for Luis' friends and family. I know they feel they haven't gotten justice," he said.[3]

New research . . . from Shamena Anwar, Patrick Bayer, and Randi Hjalmarsson uses data from criminal trials and finds "strong evidence that all-white juries acquit whites more often and are less favorable to black versus white defendants when compared to juries with at least one black member." While perhaps not shocking, their research has meaningful implications: "Our findings speak to the substantial impact that variation in the composition of the jury pool can have on trial outcomes. If, for example, the jury pool in Sarasota County was 10 or 20 percent black instead of the 3 percent observed in the data, conviction rates for black defendants would be much lower and those for white defendants much higher than those observed in the data."[4]

Race permeates the discussion—private, public, and scholarly—of criminal justice issues. The news stories introducing this chapter identified the race of the defendants, jurors, and victim as important in explaining the verdicts of juries. Those disappointed in the verdict saw racial bias at work. Had the verdict come out the other way, the news coverage probably would have again emphasized race although now the story would have focused on how the jury rose above racial solidarity with the accused to return a just verdict. Regardless of how individual cases are resolved, the problem of race and the potential for racial bias in jury decision making requires attention. In this chapter, we explore the role played by race in the criminal trials in the NCSC study.

The role of defendant race in criminal case adjudication is strongly contested. Since the early twentieth century, criminologists have debated the existence of racially discriminatory case processing practices and the potential for differential criminal penalties to be imposed on racial and ethnic minorities. Numerous empirical studies suggest that a defendant's race does affect the types of legal outcomes he or she receives. For example, research on sentencing indicates that black, male offenders are disproportionately likely to be convicted and to receive lengthy prison terms.[5] Other studies suggest that when relevant legal factors are taken into account, a defendant's race does not matter.[6] Researchers have also looked at the interactive role of defendant and victim race suggesting that when defendants of color commit crimes against White victims, they are punished more harshly. One of the more famous studies on race and sentencing, conducted by David Baldus and colleagues in 1983, found that prosecutors in Georgia sought the death penalty in over 70 percent of cases involving a Black defendant and a White victim and only 34 percent of cases involving a Black victim. Defendants charged with killing a White victim were over 4 times more likely to receive a death sentence than those charged with killing a Black victim.[7] Researchers have also explored the effect of juror and judge race on the dispositional decisions for defendants of different races, with mixed results.[8] The NCSC data provides a new opportunity to examine the role of race in the decision making of jurors and judges.

Kalven and Zeisel reported their findings regarding the role of defendant race solely in terms of whether the defendant was White or Black. In their study, nearly three-quarters (73 percent) of all defendants were identified as White, with the remaining quarter identified as Black (27 percent). According to the 1960 census, 87 percent of all Americans were identified as White and 12 percent as Black.[9] The racial demographic of defendants and society has changed substantially since Kalven and Zeisel's original analysis. For example, in the NCSC study, in more than half of the cases the defendant was Black, the defendant was Hispanic in about a quarter of cases, and defendants were Whites in only 10 percent of all cases.[10] Unlike Kalven and Zeisel, who attempted to provide a national picture of criminal jury trials by surveying judges throughout the country, the NCSC data were drawn from four large metropolitan areas with populations, according to the 2000 census, that were 47.1 percent White and 30.4 percent Black.[11] Thus, as was true of the Kalven and Zeisel survey, Black defendants in the NCSC survey were present at roughly twice the rate at which they appeared in the overall population.[12]

The racial composition of juries has also changed since the 1950s. Fifty years ago when the Kalven and Zeisel data were collected, the all-White jury was the subject of intense scrutiny and distress.[13] In the NCSC data, the all-White jury was rare; only 27 out of 362 juries were all-White. Of these, only eight (2.2 percent of the total number of cases) sat in judgment of Black defendants.[14] Thus, very few of the cases in the sample involved what has been viewed traditionally as the breeding ground of racist outcomes, the all-White jury determining the fate of a Black defendant. Black defendants were twice as likely to have their cases adjudicated by juries with no White members as they were to confront all-White juries. Indeed, there were more juries (thirty-four) with no White members than there were juries that had no Black members. Overall, fewer than four out of ten juries (37 percent) were more than half-White. However, these data did not mean that Black defendants fared as well as defendants of other races in the criminal justice system overall, only that the outcomes in their cases could not be laid at the doors of all-White juries.

Applying Kalven and Zeisel's hypothesis that close cases result in juries being liberated to embrace values, some commentators have found that race (an extralegal factor if ever there was one) has its greatest role in those cases that are close on evidence.[15] The NCSC data indicated no support for this proposition as an explanation of jury behavior. When judges believed that the evidence was evenly balanced, juries were as likely to acquit as to convict. Their inclination to do so did not vary with the race of the defendants. When the defendants were Black and the judges viewed the evidence as evenly balanced, juries acquitted in 52 percent of the cases. When the defendants were of other races and the evidence was in equipoise, juries acquitted in 50 percent of the cases. If cases that the judges considered close resulted in releasing juries to consider values (a proposition we doubt), juries did not consider the race of the defendants as a value affecting the outcome of their deliberations.[16]

Jury verdicts overall did not vary significantly with the race of the defendants in the NCSC study. Juries acquitted 29 percent of Black defendants as opposed to 32 percent of all other defendants. Judges were a different story. They would have acquitted only 14 percent of all Black defendants as opposed to slightly more than a quarter (26 percent) of all other defendants. Juries were more than twice as likely (2 to 1) as judges to find Black defendants not guilty while slightly less than 25 percent more likely (1.25 to 1) to find other defendants not guilty. To judges, at least, it appears that race did matter.

Judges were, on average, more satisfied with jury convictions than they were with jury acquittals. They were considerably more satisfied with convictions and less satisfied with acquittals when the defendants were Black than when defendants were of any other race. Even more, judges believed that juries had better understanding of the cases when they convicted Black defendants than when they returned verdicts of not guilty. Jurors' satisfaction with their decisions, measured on a scale of 1–7, where lower scores represent less satisfaction, was quite positive (5.80 when defendant Black and 6.06 when defendant another race) regardless of the decisions or the race of the defendants. Understandably, the jurors who rendered the decisions were consistently more satisfied with their verdicts than were the judges. In addition, the jurors varied little in terms of their satisfaction with acquittals as opposed to convictions regardless of the race of the defendants (see table 6.1). The jurors' views are neither surprising nor alarming. The same cannot be said for the views of the judges.

The NCSC data also provide a unique window into the perceptions of attorneys as to case verdicts. Defense counsel was pleased with acquittals (6.43) and displeased with convictions (3.22 on a 7-point scale)

TABLE 6.1
*Average Rating: Jury Understanding and Satisfaction with Verdict
by Type of Defendant and Case Outcome (Scale 1–7)*

Defendant/case outcome	Jury's understanding of case	Judge's satisfaction with jury verdict	Jury satisfaction with verdict
Black defendant conviction (*n* = 107)	6.2	5.5	5.7
Black defendant acquittal (*n* = 44)	5.8	4.2	5.9
Other defendant conviction (*n* = 91)	6.2	5.7	5.9
Other defendant acquittal (*n* = 43)	6.0	5.2	6.3
All convictions	6.2	5.5	5.8
All acquittals	5.9	4.7	6.1

if the defendants were Black, with the numbers being 6.90 and 3.49 if the defendants were of another race. Like defense counsel, prosecutors were satisfied when they achieved the results they sought and unhappy when the juries acquitted. However, their unhappiness was particularly severe when Black defendants were acquitted: their satisfaction with the verdicts was 2.50 on a 7-point scale. When the acquitted persons were of other races, their satisfaction was 2.90 on the same scale. Like judges, they found the acquittal of Black defendants particularly unsatisfactory.

In terms of the judges' evaluations of the juries' verdicts, judges agreed with jury verdicts 76 percent of the time when the defendants were Black and 78 percent of the time when the defendants were of another race. However, this apparent agreement masks very different reactions to acquittals and convictions. When juries convicted Black defendants, judges agreed 94 percent of the time. When juries convicted defendants of another race, judges agreed 88 percent of the time. Acquittals were different. When the defendants were Black, judges agreed with jury verdicts of not guilty 30 percent of the time. When the defendants were not Black, judges agreed with acquittals at nearly twice this rate, 56 percent of the time (see table 6.2). Unless prosecutors for obscure reasons initiated proceedings against more innocent Whites and Hispanics than they did against innocent Blacks or brought weaker cases against Whites and Hispanics than they did against Blacks, it is hard to square these data with the ideal of color-blind judges administering a color-blind criminal justice system. These findings call into question the practice of treating the judges' views of the correct outcomes of criminal trials as the gold standard.

The factors associated with jury acquittals (i.e., claims of innocence, lack of prior criminal records, and testimony of the defendants combined with that of at least one witness) also affected judges. With respect to the most significant of these factors, the defendant's refusal to plead on the grounds of innocence, judges were more likely to indicate that they would have acquitted in its presence when the defendants were not Black. The judges indicated that they would have acquitted in approximately 30 percent of all cases in which the defendants refused to plead on the grounds of innocence; they would have done so in 38 percent of the cases in which the defendants were not Black in contrast to 22 percent of the cases in which the defendants were Black. This was in stark contrast with the actual decisions of juries. The race of the defendants did not affect jury acquittal rates: whether Black or not, defendants who refused to plead on the grounds of innocence were acquitted about 50 percent of the time.

In terms of other factors that affect acquittals, when the defendants did not have criminal records, judges indicated that they would have acquitted 34 percent of the cases of White and Hispanic defendants in contrast to 24 percent of cases with Black defendants. Again, in these cases, juries acquitted slightly fewer than half the defendants regardless of race (48 percent of Black defendants and 46 percent of other defendants). Finally, we noted that juries acquitted at higher rates when the defendants testified along with at least one other witness than

TABLE 6.2
Judge and Jury Agreement on Case Outcome by Defendant Race

	Defendant Black	Defendant other race
Jury convicts: judge agrees	68.1% (98)	59.5% (72)
Jury acquits: judge agrees	8.4% (12)	18.2% (22)
Jury convicts: judge disagrees	4.2% (6)	8.3% (10)
Jury acquits: judge disagrees	19.5% (28)	14.1% (17)
Total	100% (144)	100% (121)

Note: Number of cases is given in parentheses.

otherwise. Judges would have acquitted 27 percent of the White and Hispanic defendants presenting this kind of evidence in contrast to 24 percent of Black defendants. Juries acquitted in more than one-half (53 percent) of these cases when the defendants were not Black as opposed to four out of ten cases when the defendants were Black (39 percent).

Why were the judges readier to convict Black defendants than others? The first and most reassuring possibility is what we noted earlier: the judges were answering a hypothetical question whereas the jurors were struggling with decisions fraught with immense real-world consequences. In this view, judges' decisions may be reflexive rather than thoughtful. If the judges were forced to decide the cases in actuality, perhaps they would have considered the evidence in more depth and arrived at conclusions similar to those of the juries. Although it is troubling that judges instinctively assumed that Blacks were more likely to be guilty than others, training and professional discipline should counteract these instinctive beliefs when judges must actually decide cases.

A second possibility is that these decisions were not affected by race at all. They were entirely responsive to the evidence the judges perceived as more powerful than did the juries. This explanation does not reject the possibility that race affected the perceptions of the strength of the cases but rather posits that the judges were consciously reacting to their perceptions of what the evidence showed rather than to the race of the accused when the judges indicated how they would have ruled from the bench. However, the data did not reveal support for this possibility.

The Judge's View of the Evidence

In the NCSC data, judges who assessed the strength of the prosecution's cases comparably came to very different conclusions as to guilt depending upon the race of the defendants. Judges did not differ in terms of the verdicts they would render when they believed that the evidence was strongly in favor of the prosecution. Regardless of the race of the defendants, judges would find the defendants guilty in overwhelming numbers.

Distinctions did arise when the judges considered the evidence to be in equipoise or in favor of the defendants. As shown in table 6.3, judges considered the evidence to be in equipoise or in favor of the defendants in 43 percent of the cases with White or Hispanic defendants (30 in equipoise and 25 in favor of defendant out of 128 cases) and in 39 percent of the cases involving Black defendants (42 in equipoise and 21 in favor of defendant out of 161 total cases). Overall, judges evaluated cases as in equipoise or favoring the defendant in four out of ten (41 percent) cases. However, in the cases that the judges evaluated as being in equipoise or in favor of the defendant, they would have convicted 65 percent of the Black defendants as opposed to 46 percent of the White and Hispanic defendants. When cases were evenly balanced (4 on a 7-point scale), judges would have convicted Black defendants 74 percent of the time; if the defendants were of a different race, the conviction rate decreased to 57 percent.

Table 6.4 shows that the judges' assessment of the weight of the evidence was shared by the juries. Juries convicted overwhelmingly when judges viewed the cases as strong for the prosecution, split between

TABLE 6.3
Judge Conviction Rate: Judge's Evaluation of Evidence

Race of defendant	Strong for prosecution	Equipoise	Strong for defense
White, Hispanic, or Asian	95.9% (70/73)	56.7% (17/30)	32% (8/25)
Black	99% (97/98)	73.8% (31/42)	47.7% (10/21)
Total	97.7% (167/171)	66.7% (48/72)	39.1% (18/46)

Note: Number of cases is given in parentheses.

TABLE 6.4
Jury Conviction Rate: Judge's Evaluation of Evidence

Race of defendant	Strong for prosecution	Equipoise	Strong for defense
White, Hispanic, or Asian	81.7% (41/60)	50% (15/30)	57.7% (15/26)
Black	84.9% (67/79)	47.7% (20/42)	53% (9/17)
Total	83.5% (116/139)	48.7% (35/72)	55.8% (24/43)

Note: Number of cases is given in parentheses.

convictions and acquittals when the judges assessed the cases as even, and acquitted in more than half the cases when the judges thought the cases were strong for the defendant. Unlike the judges, however, the jury rates did not vary significantly by the race of the defendants. The contrast with the actual jury verdicts is instructive. Holding constant the strength of the cases as assessed by the judges, juries convicted at virtually the same rate regardless of whether the defendants were Black or not.

The Jury's View of the Evidence

When we used the juries' assessment of the closeness of the cases rather than those of the judges, jury verdicts did not vary by race except with respect to cases that the juries considered strong for the defendants. In those situations, Black defendants were convicted at a lower rate than other defendants (see table 6.5).

When we reversed our approach and examined the verdicts the judges would have returned using the juries' assessments of the relative strength of the cases, a different picture emerged (see table 6.6).

TABLE 6.5
Jury Conviction Rate: Jury's Evaluation of Evidence

Race of defendant	Strong for prosecution	Equipoise	Strong for defense
White, Hispanic, or Asian	94.9% (92/97)	38.9% (7/18)	22.2% (8/36)
Black	96.3% (77/80)	40.9% (9/22)	15.6% (5/32)
Total	95.5% (169/177)	42.1% (16/38)	19.2% (13/68)

Note: Number of cases is given in parentheses.

TABLE 6.6
Judge Conviction Rate: Jury's Evaluation of Evidence

Race of defendant	Strong for prosecution	Equipoise	Strong for defense
White, Hispanic, or Asian	88.6% (70/79)	52.4% (11/21)	50% (14/28)
Black	93.5% (100/107)	61.9% (13/21)	75.8% (25/33)
Total	91.4% (170/186)	57.2% (24/42)	64% (39/61)

Note: Number of cases is given in parentheses.

For any given assessment of the evidence by the juries, judges would have convicted Black defendants at a higher rate than those of other races. This was manifested particularly when juries believed the evidence was strong for the defendant. In these cases, judges would have entered guilty verdicts in slightly more than three-quarters of the cases involving Black defendants but in only half of the cases involving defendants of other races.

The difference between judge and jury responses to cases that juries viewed as strong for the defense is both impressive and depressing. If we consider tables 6.5 and 6.6 together, when juries considered the case strong for the defense, judges would nonetheless convict Black defendants at five times the rate that juries in fact convicted them. Judges would find them guilty 76 percent of the time, while juries found these defendants guilty only 16 percent of the time. This difference was manifest in every jurisdiction but was most dramatic in the District of Columbia. When the defendants were Black and the juries believed the cases were strong for the defendants, juries convicted only 10 percent of the time. In the same cases, the judges would have convicted 82 percent of the defendants. A difference this extreme cannot be bridged by the liberation hypothesis or any other reasonably comforting explanation. If the judges were correct, the juries were engaging in widespread nullification. If the juries were correct, the judges might be prepared to convict people on the basis of their race.

This sample consisted of cases in which informed observers (the defense counsel in consultation with the defendants) chose a jury trial rather than a plea or a trial to a judge alone. The risk in jury trials is that defendants will receive longer sentences if convicted than they would have received had they pled or waived jury trial and agreed to trial in front of the judge. It makes sense, then, that the cases tried in front of juries are cases in which the defendants are likely to fare better than if the same cases were to be decided by judges. We have seen that the defendants in the data analyzed here were acquitted at a higher rate by juries than they would have been by the judges. Black defendants, in particular, were beneficiaries of this phenomenon. Although this may be the reason why defendants chose jury trials, it is not an explanation for the judges being more likely to find Black defendants guilty than others.

Typically, judges know more about the defendants and the details of the cases than do juries. The defendants' criminal records are the most prominent example. There are many cases, including a strong majority of the NCSC data sample, in which juries never learn of the defendants' criminal records either because the defendants do not testify or the judges otherwise prohibit it. Judges, of course, know what juries do not. Does the judges' private knowledge of defendants' criminal records account for the judges' greater willingness to find Black defendants guilty? The answer is again no. With respect to those defendants who had criminal records known to the judges but not to the juries, judges would have acquitted 12 percent of the Black defendants and 23 percent of the other defendants.[17] Although judges may have had other information not available to the juries (e.g., illegally seized evidence, tips from confidential informers), it seems highly improbable that this information constitutes a nonracial explanation for the difference in the judges' acquittal rate when the defendants' prior records do not.

Crimes can be divided into those involving identifiable victims and those in which we are all victimized, the manufacture, transfer, or possession of illegal drugs being the most prominent example. Juries convicted those charged with harming individuals at a higher rate than those who perpetrated victimless crimes. Judges treated the two groups virtually identically, indicating that they would have convicted four out of five defendants regardless of whether the crimes involved victims (80 percent convictions) or not (81 percent convictions).

Juries were more likely to convict those charged with crimes involving victims (73 percent) than those charged with other kinds of crimes (65 percent). If we add the race of the defendants to the existence of victims, the judges reacted quite differently than the juries. Although jury verdicts were narrow in range (73 percent convictions if the defendants were Black; 71 percent otherwise), the judges would have convicted 87 percent of Black defendants if the crimes involved victims compared with 71 percent if the defendants were of another race. Juries convicted at a higher rate and the judges indicated they would have convicted at a higher rate when both defendants and victims were Black than otherwise (judges, 89 percent; juries, 79 percent). Although judges indicated they were also more likely to convict Black defendants charged with victimless crimes than they were other defendants, the differences were considerably narrower.

Race of the Jury

The racial composition of juries has long been suggested as a potential explanation of jury verdicts. A good deal of social science research has been devoted to understanding how individual and group demographic characteristics of jurors and juries, such as race, gender, and age composition, affect jury decision making. While racial groups appear to differ in their assessment of the criminal justice system, empirical research finds individual juror demographic characteristics to be only weakly associated with criminal jury verdicts,[18] though there is a consistent line of research suggesting an interaction between juror and defendant race with juror leniency toward defendants with similar characteristics as jury members.[19]Additionally, the composition of more racially mixed juries has been found to alter juror interactions and decision making, mainly in the direction of increased leniency for Black defendants.[20] Despite a relatively large body of research on the effect of racial compositions of juries, few studies have directly examined the relationship between judge and jury agreement across juries with variable levels of non-White group representation.[21]

In terms of the judges' responses to the racial composition of the juries, in the NCSC data race and agreement appear related. Judges were more likely to agree with the verdicts of juries with no Black members than they were with juries with substantial Black representation. When there were no Black jurors, juries would have arrived at the same verdicts as the judges in five out of six cases (84 percent). When juries had substantial numbers of Black members (i.e., four or more), the overall level of agreement decreased to 65 percent.[22]

Judges concurred with jury verdicts of guilt in nine out of ten cases regardless of the racial composition of the juries. However, judges had decidedly different reactions to acquittals depending upon the composition of the juries. When juries without Black members acquitted, the judges agreed in more than two-thirds of the cases (68 percent). However, when the juries were at least one-third Black and acquitted, the judges agreed in only 23 percent of the cases. *Judges were three times as likely to agree with acquittals when the juries had no Black members as when the juries were at least one-third Black.*

Judges were asked whether they were satisfied with jury verdicts. The results displayed in table 6.7 are disquieting. Judges were most satisfied with jury verdicts when all-White juries acquitted defendants (6.25 on a 7-point scale). Judges were most dissatisfied with jury verdicts when mixed-race juries returned not guilty verdicts. In terms of the percentage of Black jurors (as opposed to simply jurors who are not White), judges were most satisfied with the outcomes when juries without any Black members acquitted defendants. They were least satisfied with the outcomes when juries that were at least one-third Black acquitted defendants. These findings have important implications for our assessments of who is correct in cases of judge and jury disagreements.

To what extent were these results reactions to the race of the defendants rather than the race of the jurors? In examining data from those

TABLE 6.7
Average Judge Satisfaction and Perception of Jury Understanding by Racial Compositions of Jury (Scale 1–7)

Jury composition	Judges' satisfaction		Judges' perception of juries' understanding	
	Conviction	Acquittal	Conviction	Acquittal
All White jurors (n = 22)	6.08	6.25	6.33	6.50
No Black jurors (n = 80)	5.59	5.87	6.41	6.46
Half or more White jurors (n = 132)	5.77	5.03	6.30	5.86
Fewer than half White jurors (n = 152)	5.46	4.46	6.06	5.69
One-third Black jurors (n = 100)	5.35	4.21	6.01	5.73
Half or more Black jurors (n = 64)	5.02	4.25	6.02	5.46
No White jurors (n = 31)	5.28	4.50	5.65	5.20

Note: Racial composition categories are not mutually exclusive.

cases involving Black defendants, when the juries were at least one-third Black, the judges *never* disagreed with jury findings of guilt. On the other hand, judges disagreed with jury acquittals and would have convicted in three-quarters of the cases when at least one-third of the jury was Black. Overall, there was a nearly 70 percent level of agreement about outcomes (see appendix C).

Judges and juries without Black representation had a high level of agreement (83 percent) concerning Black defendants. Juries agreed with judges' conclusions that Black defendants were guilty 88 percent of the time and with the judges' findings of not guilty in two-thirds of the cases. Judges agreed with jury verdicts at virtually identical rates (88 percent when the juries convicted; 73 percent when the juries acquitted).

Juries that were at least one-third Black had a much lower level of agreement with judges. Both the juries and the judges contributed to this difference. Juries without Black members convicted in 72 percent of all cases; the rate was slightly higher when the defendants were Black (77 percent). Juries that were one-third Black convicted 60 percent of the time. The rate was virtually identical when the defendants were Black (59 percent) for those juries in which one-third of the members were Black.

Judges moved in the other direction. Their conviction rate was virtually identical to that of the juries when the juries lacked any Black members (74 percent vs. 72 percent) and was quite comparable to such juries when the defendants were Black (80 percent vs. 77 percent). When juries had substantial Black representation, however, judges and juries had widely divergent views of guilt. Juries that were one-third Black convicted 60 percent of all defendants, while judges in these cases would have convicted 86 percent of all the defendants and nearly 90 percent of the defendants who were Black.

These differences are not easily reconciled. The jury results can (and perhaps should) be viewed as a reflection of the successful struggle to integrate juries. That jury results *did not vary* with the race of the defendants or the race of the victims represents a genuine achievement of the Supreme Court's massive effort to remove overt racism from the operation of the criminal justice system. On the other hand, it is more than a bit disconcerting to see that racial disparities once associated with jury verdicts emerged vigorously in the judges' hypothetical verdicts. Judges both shape the rules regulating criminal trials and evaluate the results of those trials. Even when they do not decide guilt or innocence, judges make the decisions—from setting the conditions of pretrial releases to ruling upon the admissibility of evidence to determining the sentences after convictions—that are significant determinants of the quality of criminal justice. To an unknowable but potentially significant extent, judges' views that juries acquit those whom judges would convict is a contributing factor in the belief that juries acquit the guilty routinely. That judges express particular displeasure with acquittals by juries with substantial Black representation and with acquittals of Black defendants suggests that their views may be neither color-blind nor accurate. To the extent that judges assume, even unconsciously, that race is related to guilt, the accuracy and justice of our system are compromised.

7

Conclusion

We began with the question of whether those acquitted of crimes are innocent in fact as well as in law. Like the comedian Rodney Dangerfield, acquittals "get no respect." They are treated (and therefore discounted) as the products of jury nullification, or the inability of the state to find or prepare important witnesses for trial, or the defendant's chicanery in dissuading witnesses from appearing, or the jury's failure to understand or evaluate the evidence—anything, that is, but the state's prosecution of an innocent person. These claims cannot be disproved for the very reason that gives wing to them in the first place: in law, an acquittal represents a failure of the state's proof, not an affirmative declaration of the defendant's innocence.

Absent definitive answers about whether or not acquittals are correct, empirical research affords a useful vehicle to determine the degree to which acquittals correspond to factors that are consistent with actual innocence. Looking at data on jury decision making in four U.S. cities, we find that jury acquittals reflect the quantity and quality (in terms of credibility) of the evidence presented. Juries appear to acquit in the face of unpersuasive presentations by the prosecution, persuasive presentations by the defense, or both. We do not suggest that juries never err in assessing either the credibility of the witnesses or the importance of their testimony. However, we find no convincing theoretical or empirical support for the proposition that jurors (as opposed to judges) always err or that, when they do so, they invariably err on the side of leniency. Nor do the data we have analyzed indicate support for the claim that juries differ from judges in that jurors make decisions in which they allow values to overwhelm objective assessments of the evidence whereas judges do not.

Lacking any information not available to juries other than the defendants' reasons for refusing to plead, we cannot be certain that even acquittals that are entirely responsive to the evidence betoken actual innocence. Apparently the judges do not think so. As was true fifty years ago, judges were ready to convict more than half of those the juries acquitted. Judges reported that they were surprised and dissatisfied when juries acquitted individuals the judges would have convicted. Given the chance, perhaps judges would have explained jury verdicts in terms that resonate with the liberation hypothesis. Instead, when asked, jurors gave responses that suggest that it was their views of the evidence rather than any discernible embrace of values that was the explanation for their decisions.

In summary, judges and juries agreed about the strength of the cases against the defendants in about six out of ten cases.[1] They agreed that the defense cases were strong in nearly 6 percent of the cases. The juries acquitted in five out of six of these cases (83 percent).[2] They agreed that the prosecution cases were strong in 47 percent of the cases, and the juries convicted an overwhelming majority (97 percent) of the time. Both agreed the evidence was in equipoise in 7 percent of the cases, and the juries acquitted in 58 percent of those cases. In about 40 percent of the cases, the judges and juries could not agree about the strength of the cases. The juries acquitted in 45 percent of those cases.[3]

The difference between judge and jury assessments may reflect something more troubling than disagreement concerning which witnesses to credit or which inferences to draw. Kalven and Zeisel thought that the jury deviation from the judges' views should be explained. One may suggest—and we do—that judges' deviations from jury verdicts are equally in need of exploration. We know that judges were much more likely than jurors to find defendants guilty. Unfortunately, in the data collected by the NCSC and analyzed here, there was a distinct racial cast to these disagreements. Judges indicated that, had the decisions been theirs, they would have convicted Black defendants at a higher rate than defendants of other races. Also, judges were much more satisfied with jury verdicts of guilt when the defendants were Black than when they were White or Hispanic. Judges were considerably more likely to agree with jury verdicts of acquittal when the defendants were White or Hispanic than when the defendants were Black.

The NCSC juries were more likely to render race-neutral verdicts than judges. This does not establish that these verdicts are accurate. However, it does eliminate a difficulty presented when we treat the judges' hypothetical views as accurate: if the judges correctly assessed the evidence considered by the juries, prosecutors were necessarily bringing stronger criminal cases against Black defendants than they were against defendants of other races. To say the least, it is unclear why prosecutors would do this. At a minimum, it would contradict a great deal of evidence that Blacks are treated disadvantageously within the criminal justice system.

We cannot compare today's judges' reactions to the race of the defendants with those sitting fifty years ago. Race had a surprisingly small role in the analysis presented in *The American Jury*, published in 1966. Kalven and Zeisel stated that they had expected to provide data as to whether juries were color-blind but found that they were unable to do so. They did not explain why. Instead, they presented a brief discussion of whether juries were prone to be less condemning of Black-on-Black crimes than they were of White-on-White crimes (the answer was no)[4] and reported that jury leniency relative to the judges did not vary with the race of the defendants once one controlled for the juries' sympathy for the defendants.[5] Their presentation did make it possible to infer that judges thought juries were more sympathetic to White defendants than to Blacks defendants and, from this, to speculate that juries acquitted White defendants at a higher rate than Black defendants; but speculation it is.[6]

Judges may have special insight into whether those who are acquitted are actually innocent, but no data show support for this conclusion. Kalven and Zeisel employed the judge as a benchmark because they were exploring whether juries made a *distinctive* contribution to the administration of criminal justice. But, if the concern is accuracy rather than distinctiveness, there is no reason to privilege the conclusions of judges over those of juries. Given that judges were twice as likely to acquit defendants who were not Black as those who were and that judges were much more likely to agree with the results of juries with no Black members than with juries with substantial Black representation, using the judges' hypothetical decisions of guilt or innocence as a measure of jury accuracy seems inappropriate. It seems that it is the jury, not the judge, that has the greatest success in treating defendants of all races comparably.

Jury verdicts are likely to provide a more accurate reflection of the lay of the evidence than those of the judges. Jurors attend to the evidence presented knowing that they are going to be required to decide the case. Jurors discuss the evidence with one another before arriving at their verdicts. Judges need to evaluate the sufficiency of the evidence (i.e., Is there enough to justify a guilty verdict?), but they are not necessarily listening to it with an ear toward resolving credibility disputes to decide guilt or innocence. According to experimental studies, groups do a better job than individuals at lie detection.[7] These studies cannot replicate trials in which all credibility evaluations are made by those who have observed a number of witnesses whose testimony has been tested through cross-examination and elaborated or denigrated through closing arguments. Perhaps judges are better lie detectors than jurors in these situations; but, if so, the point has yet to be demonstrated.

Legal scholar George Fisher argued that the jury emerged as the preferred mechanism for resolving factual disputes in criminal cases because of the inadequacy of other techniques.[8] Its attractiveness, he asserted, rests in its very opacity: like sausages that are often more palatable the less we know of how they are made, our inability to know how juries arrive at their decisions enhances the acceptability of their verdicts. This is hardly a ringing endorsement of the accuracy of jury verdicts, but it does reveal the essential problem that juries solve: we have no way of making consequential and nuanced determinations of disputed historical fact that is superior to the jury. Unless one agrees that it is literally impossible ever to determine accurately the truth behind the state's claim that a particular individual acted in a particular way with a particular state of mind, the jury's conclusion as to these points is likely to be at least as accurate as any other mechanism we may employ. We then confront the difficulty that, unless we employ the judge's assessment of the case, we lack any decision against which to measure the jury's result.

There appear to be two approaches to identifying actual innocence under these circumstances. One is to treat the judge-jury agreement that the defendant is not guilty as an indication that the defendant may be actually innocent. Although there are reasons other than actual innocence why juries or judges may acquit someone who is actually guilty, this is less likely to be the case when they agree that the state has failed to prove guilt than when they disagree. In the NCSC data analyzed here, judges and juries agreed on not guilty verdicts in only 11 percent of the cases. Were these defendants actually innocent?

This approach confronts the immediate difficulty that the rate of agreement depends upon the race of the defendants. Judges and juries agreed that Hispanic, White, and Asian defendants were not guilty 18 percent of the time. When the defendants were Black, judges and juries agreed that acquittals were appropriate less than half as often, in only 8 percent of the cases. If these figures reflect the reality of who is actually innocent, as noted, we have the curious result that prosecutors proceed only against the most obviously guilty Black defendants while requiring less certainty of guilt when they bring felony charges against defendants of other races. For this to be true, Black criminal behavior must be so pervasive that prosecutors can only proceed against its most obvious manifestations while criminal behavior by those of other races is sufficiently rare that prosecutors proceed against Whites and Hispanics on considerably less compelling evidence. These differences in guilt by race are both unrelated to the apparent strength of the evidence presented in court (as evaluated by judges) and invisible to the juries that acquit all races at about the same rate. The other, more likely, explanation is that judges are readier to believe that Black defendants are guilty than they are to believe this of defendants of other races.

A second approach is to examine how frequently cases involve those features that are consistent with innocence. Defendants refused to plead on the grounds of innocence in 42 percent of the cases for which we have this information. These defendants were acquitted half of the time. This suggests that approximately one in five of the defendants in the NCSC study both refused to plead on the grounds of innocence and was acquitted by the jury. Defendants who insisted on trials because they were innocent were equally likely to be acquitted whether they testified or not.[9] That juries acquitted in only one-half of these cases appears inconsistent with the claim that the presence of these factors betokens actual innocence. At least, if these factors are signals of actual innocence, juries have not always been quick on the uptake.

Unfortunately, there is no magic bullet to solve this problem. Neither the NCSC data nor any other conceivable source of trial data enables us to identify with precision the percentage of criminal trials that end in the acquittal of someone who is innocent of the crime charged. On the other hand, there are no data that indicate any justification for embracing as an empirical matter the assumption underlying current evidentiary and sentencing practices that *all* those who are acquitted of crimes are in fact guilty, the acquittals being simply artifacts of the burden of proof. We cannot take the matter further than to suggest that when juries acquit those who refuse to plead because they insist they are innocent, these defendants are likely to be individuals who did not commit the crimes with which they were charged. If we use both measures, the defendant's reason for going to trial and the jury's decision, we arrive at an estimate of actual innocence in about one in five of those individuals who go to trial.

Understanding the challenges of measuring acquittals, some may be tempted to ask, "Does it really matter whether the acquitted are innocent?" We suggest that it does, both for pragmatic and for principled reasons. As a matter of principle, as we have noted, our practice of treating those who are acquitted strictly as beneficiaries of jury largesse can result in the profound injustice of punishing individuals for crimes they did not commit. Only the belief that acquittals have little to do with actual innocence justifies the practice of using prior criminal charges of which the defendant has been acquitted as proof that the person has committed a subsequent crime or as a justification for an enhanced sentence for that subsequent crime. If the assumption underlying this practice, that the defendant is guilty despite the acquittal, is counterfactual in a very large number of cases, the practice falls short of determining guilt through previous association with the criminal justice system.

Treating acquittals as unrelated to innocence means that neither the prosecutor nor the judge receives any meaningful feedback concerning the justice of the charging decision. Judges and prosecutors have no exposure to the acquitted who never again become embroiled in the criminal justice system. The previously acquitted who have no further involvement with the criminal justice system are "out of sight and out of mind." If an acquittal can be discounted as factually inaccurate even if legally permissible, prosecutors, being human, can and will continue to believe that they have made the correct decisions in charging particular defendants with particular crimes. Acquittals may be signals indicating a need to change tactics or to rethink criteria, and this pragmatic response may have the benefit of reducing the likelihood that the innocent will be charged and brought to trial. Perhaps it may make little practical difference if the reason for rethinking charging criteria is pragmatic (i.e., the need to select more carefully those among the guilty who should be prosecuted to increase the likelihood of convictions) rather than idealistic (i.e., the need to ensure that we do not run the risk of convicting the innocent). But as long as prosecutors and judges can hold to the belief that the difference between the convicted and the acquitted lies in trial technique, witness availability, and jury responsiveness rather than in guilt versus innocence, the danger that we will prosecute and occasionally convict the innocent remains both present and unacknowledged.

In the end, we cannot establish through empirical research with certainty that many (or indeed most) of the acquitted are innocent. We can only point out that the data are entirely consistent with this possibility. Overall, jury acquittals appear to be rational responses to the evidence presented at trial; and the most logical explanation for the state not providing more persuasive evidence of guilt is that the defendant is not guilty. Prosecutors and judges notwithstanding, the innocent are prosecuted and acquitted. The jury does its job.

Though long ignored by scholars, judges, lawyers, and policy makers, the process by which jurors arrive at acquittals and the meanings that we as a society attach to the status of an acquitted person merit continued inquiry and scrutiny. The research presented in the preceding chapters challenges commonly held assumptions that jury decisions to acquit, particularly in the face of judicial preference to convict, are attributable to emotional responses reflecting the sentiment of a community, rather than rational responses to the evidence presented. These findings challenge the traditional understanding about the relationship between the results of the criminal trial process and objective truth. While it is comforting to believe that innocent people are never brought to trial and those who are acquitted represent the fortunate guilty, acquittals represent a more complex and troubling phenomenon. These findings question the appropriateness of the negative consequences that flow from the belief that the acquitted are actually guilty: public censure and restrictions on obtaining or retaining employment due to a criminal history marked by an arrest and prosecution. We cannot ignore acquittals by resorting to the comfortable belief that acquitted persons are probably guilty of something. Understanding the relationship between acquittals and innocence necessitates increased dialogue, scholarship, and data about the trial process. Ultimately, if we are to take seriously the question of what acquittals mean, we must be ready to confront the challenge of rectifying the way communities and social institutions treat acquitted persons. Fairness requires moving acquittals out of the shadows and into the forefront of our conversations about the justice of our criminal justice system.

Appendix A

In the NCSC study, researchers collected information about individual case characteristics from court records and surveys of judges and attorneys.[1] They also surveyed individual jurors in each case about their opinions of the cases and the factors that went into their decision-making process. To keep all data at the case level for the present multivariate analysis, we aggregated multiple juror responses from each case to represent the average responses of the jury as a whole for each case. Because multinomial regression models are predictive of a set of coefficients for each of the outcome groups compared to a reference category, we used judge and jury agreement on conviction as the reference category.

Three models were employed to measure the independent effect of jury sentiment on case outcomes. In all models, the comparison category for the dependent variable was judge-jury agreement on conviction, meaning that the coefficients for agreement on acquittal and disagreement on conviction or acquittal were measured against agreement on conviction. Three models were designed to test additively the effects of (1) relevant court, case strength, and demographic information; (2) measures of jury sentiment; and (3) judge and jury perceptions of case closeness. The results from the multinomial models have been given in table A1.

Model 1 indicated some difference in judge-jury agreement between study sites, with Maricopa County showing significant differences from Washington, DC (the reference category) with respect to the infrequency with which juries acquitted defendants the judges would have convicted. As shown in previous research, when defendants had no criminal records, juries were more likely to acquit when judges

TABLE A.1
Multinomial Regression Models for Predicting Judge and Jury Agreement on Case Outcome

Descriptor	Model 1: courtroom and charge			Model 2: judge-jury perceptions			Model 3: full		
	Judge convicted; jury acquitted	Judge acquitted; jury acquitted (r-sq. = .15)	Judge acquitted; jury convicted	Judge convicted; jury acquitted	Judge acquitted; jury acquitted (r-sq. = .37)	Judge acquitted; jury convicted	Judge convicted; jury acquitted	Judge acquitted; jury acquitted (r-sq. = .46)	Judge acquitted; jury convicted
	B/(SE)	B/(SE)	B/(SE)	B/(SE)	B/(SE)	B/(SE)	B/(SE)	B/(SE)	B/(SE)
Los Angeles	-.99 (.86)	.50 (.86)	-.58 (1.69)	-.39 (1.09)	-.11 (1.08)	2.70 (2.61)	-.11 (1.36)	-.40 (1.20)	2.37 (2.35)
Maricopa	-2.08* (1.04)	.82 (.90)	-.20 (1.60)	-2.71* (1.31)	-.21 (1.11)	2.21 (2.43)	-2.67* (1.46)	-.55 (1.21)	1.49 (2.52)
Bronx[a]	.66 (.62)	1.11 (.74)	1.23 (1.29)	.60 (.74)	.59 (.90)	1.61 (1.53)	.17 (.87)	.47 (.98)	1.43 (1.64)
Black	-.23 (.55)	.12 (.52)	-1.43 (.95)	-.10 (.66)	-.01 (.63)	-1.32 (1.20)	.17 (.78)	.33 (.70)	-.95 (1.19)
Defendant and witness testified	.14 (.53)	.83* (.49)	.18 (.83)	-.67 (.66)	.82 (.64)	.61 (1.10)	-1.26 (.81)	.37 (.71)	-.06 (1.07)
Prior criminal history	-1.17 (.58)	-.65 (.56)	-1.17 (.87)	-2.34* (.85)	-.67 (.73)	-1.87 (1.23)	-2.80** (1.04)	-.89 (.83)	-2.34 (1.21)
Defendant claimed innocence	.86 (.54)	1.28* (.54)	.15 (.76)	.64 (.66)	1.43* (.66)	-.85 (1.14)	.46 (.76)	1.50* (.73)	-1.10 (1.16)
Jury: % black	.00 (.01)	.00 (.01)	.01 (.02)	-.007 (.02)	-.004 (.02)	.07 (.05)	-.02 (.02)	-.02 (.02)	.02 (.02)
Judge: prosecutor skillful				.38 (.22)	-.04 (.19)	.16 (.34)	.42* (.24)	-.04 (.22)	.08 (.32)
Judge: importance of testimony				-.28 (.31)	-.80* (.31)	-.41 (.52)	-.48 (.36)	-.84** (.32)	-.35 (.54)

Jury: prosecutor skillful				-.60* (.30)	-.80* (.29)	-.40 (.44)	-.45 (.34)	-.67** (.32)	-.32 (.45)
Jury: fairness of law				-.64 (.51)	-.97* (.45)	-1.07 (.75)	-.23 (.59)	-.62 (.48)	-.94 (.79)
Jury: sympathy for defendant				-1.10* (.39)	-.94* (.37)	.61 (.62)	-1.30** (.43)	-.93** (.40)	.68 (.61)
Jury: correct legal outcome				-.62 (.50)	.21 (.44)	-1.38 (.86)	-.34 (.59)	.60 (.53)	-1.31 (.80)
Jury: consequences harsh				1.19* (.62)	-.25 (.59)	-.45 (1.01)	1.25** (.69)	-.16 (.58)	-.25 (.96)
Trust in police				-.98* (.57)	-.10 (.48)	-.72 (.95)	-1.51** (.62)	-.61 (.54)	-1.55* (1.02)
Judge: case closeness							.89 (.74)	.53 (.72)	.85 (1.09)
Jury: case closeness							3.26** (.98)	2.97** (.92)	1.21 (1.10)
Intercept	-3.46* (1.76)	.29 (1.68)	-2.22 (3.27)	7.35 (4.82)	11.82** (4.70)	18.15** (8.22)	1.59 (5.35)	7.88 (4.82)	14.51** (7.31)

* p < .05; ** p < .01
[a] Reference category D.C.

would convict as compared to agreement on convictions.[2] Judges and juries were significantly more likely to agree on acquittal when defendants and supporting witnesses testified and when defendants claimed they were innocent.

The second model was a measure of judge-jury agreement when jury assessments of the evidence in the cases and jury sentiment toward the defendants were added to the models. We hypothesized that jury sentiment distinguishes cases in which judges and juries disagree on the outcomes and has the strongest effect on judge-jury disagreement in cases that are close on the evidence. Model 2 indicated that jury assessment of either the fairness of the law or the correct legal outcome had no significant effect on case outcomes. Jury sympathy for defendants, however, decreased the likelihood of juries acquitting when the judges would convict compared to agreement on conviction. Interestingly, the likelihood of agreement about acquittal also decreased as juries expressed sympathy for defendants. That may be the case because judges and juries feel less sympathy for defendants who are acquitted.

Two sentiment variables did have interesting effects on judge-jury agreements. As juries thought the consequences of conviction were too harsh, they were more likely to acquit when judges would convict. Similarly, as trust for the police decreased, juries were more likely to acquit when judges would convict.

By adding judge and jury perceptions of case closeness into the third model, we were able to identify the effects of both case closeness and jury sentiment on judge-jury agreement. Indeed, the amount of variance explained in the model increased when we added judge and jury perceptions of closeness (from .37 to .46). However, it was the *juries'* perceptions of closeness, not the *judges'*, that had significant effects on differential case outcomes. As juries thought the evidence was in favor of the defense, they were significantly more likely to acquit when the judges would have convicted or to acquit in agreement with the judges compared with those cases in which judges and juries agreed on conviction.

Despite the effect of jury perceptions of case closeness on outcomes, the relationships between jury sentiment and outcomes remained little changed in Model 3. The significant effects of jury perceptions about the consequences of conviction and trust of the police remained in the same direction but were strengthened slightly after controlling for judge and jury perceptions of the closeness of the case. Additionally, when defendants did not have criminal histories, juries were significantly more likely to acquit when the judges would have convicted than to agree with the judges that the defendants were guilty. This relationship was strengthened through all three models, suggesting that jurors were strongly moved by defendants without criminal histories.

Although with multinomial regression, we could examine the independent effects of evidentiary and nonevidentiary variables on judge-jury agreement while controlling for important factors such as whether cases were close or clear on the evidence, such analysis was not helpful in understanding the importance of jury sentiment in these two case types. The liberation hypothesis suggests that, when cases present evidentiary concerns, juries who disagree with judges by acquitting when the judges would have convicted are more likely than juries in other cases to be persuaded by sentiment. To test this contention directly, we constructed dichotomous measures of judges' perceptions of closeness and juries' perceptions of closeness. As explained earlier, judges and juries were each asked to rate on a 7-point scale the degree to which the evidence was in favor of the prosecution or the defense. The responses were recoded into categories of not close (coded 0 when judges or juries indicated answers at the ends of the scale, that is, 1–2 or 6–7) and close (coded 1 when judges or juries indicated answers in the middle of the scale, that is, 3, 4, or 5).

Judges and juries agreed on the outcomes much more frequently when either viewed the cases as clear as when either viewed the cases as close. When judges believed cases were clear on the evidence, juries and judges agreed on the verdicts more than 85 percent of the time. When judges viewed cases as close, agreement decreased to 69.2 percent. When we looked at juries' assessments of the evidence, the differences were even starker. Judges and juries agreed 92 percent of the time when juries believed cases were clear but agreed only 62 percent of the time when they viewed cases as close. Clear cases resulted in agreement and close cases in disagreement. This does not necessarily mean that sentiment has more effect in close cases than in clear cases. Indeed, the NCSC data revealed that sentiment affects jury decision making in different ways in close and clear cases and its most prominent role may be as explanation for disagreements when judges and juries come to different verdicts in clear cases. Kalven and Zeisel did not analyze clear cases separately, even though nearly one-quarter of all instances of normal judge-jury disagreements occurred in cases that judges believed to be clear on the evidence.[3]

Appendix B

Correlation Matrix

Descriptor		x_1	x_2	x_3	x_4	x_5	x_6	x_7	x_8	x_9	x_{10}	x_{11}
Defendant and at least one witness	x_1											
Defendant alone	x_2	−0.27**										
Only witness	x_3	−.39**	−.30**									
Los Angeles	x_4	−0.02	−.01	.06								
Maricopa	x_5	−0.03	.20**	−.23**	−.35**							
Bronx	x_6	−0.06	−.10	.07	−.32**	−.36**						
Murder	x_7	−0.09	−.15**	.28**	.06	.17**	.06					
Other violent	x_8	0.19**	−.05	−.05	.01	−.01	−.00	−.33**				
Drugs	x_9	−0.09	.05	−.09	.05	−.18**	.03	−.31**	−.44**			
No prior	x_{10}	0.21**	.01	−.09	−.18**	.23**	−.09	−0.06	.11	−.06		
Prior jury doesn't know	x_{11}	−0.3**	−.25**	.25**	.06	−.11*	−.02	.13*	−.10	.00	−.58**	
Defendant claims innocence	x_{12}	0.22**	−.04	.02	−.14**	−.06	.1*	−.07	.11*	−.02	.07	−.11

Appendix C

These tables show the breakdown of case outcomes according to the different racial composition of the juries.

TABLE C.1
Jury without Black Members: All Defendants

| Judge's verdicts | Jury's verdicts | | Total |
	Guilty	Not guilty	
Guilty	64.6% (51)	8.9% (7)	73.5% (58)
Not guilty	7.6% (6)	19.0% (15)	26.6% (21)
Total	72.2% (57)	27.9% (22)	100.0% (79)

Note: Number of cases is given in parentheses.

TABLE C.2
No Black Jurors; Black Defendants

| Judge's verdicts | Jury's verdicts | | Total |
	Guilty	Not guilty	
Guilty	70.0% (21)	10.0% (3)	80.0% (24)
Not guilty	6.7% (2)	13.4% (4)	20.0% (6)
Total	76.7% (23)	23.4% (7)	100.0% (30)

Note: Number of cases is given in parentheses.

TABLE C.3
Juries One-Third Black; Black Defendants

| Judge's verdicts | Jury's verdicts | | Total |
	Guilty	Not guilty	
Guilty	59.3% (35)	30.5% (18)	89.8% (53)
Not guilty	0% (0)	10.2% (6)	10.2% (6)
Total	59.3% (35)	40.7% (24)	100.0% (59)

Note: Number of cases is given in parentheses.

Notes

NOTES TO THE PREFACE

1. Scheck, Neufeld, and Dwyer, *Actual Innocence*; Bakken, "Truth and Innocence Procedures to Free Innocent Persons: Beyond the Adversarial System"; Gross et al., "Exonerations in the United States, 1989 through 2003"; Leo and Gould, "Studying Wrongful Convictions"; Risinger, "Unsafe Verdicts: The Need for Reformed Standards for the Trial and Review of Factual Innocence Claims."

2. http://www.innocenceproject.org/about/Other-Projects.php (accessed January 27, 2011).

3. Hannaford-Agor et al., *Are Hung Juries a Problem?*

NOTES TO CHAPTER 1

1. Dolan and Liu, "Acquitted but Not Declared Innocent."

2. "Reagan Seeks Judges," *U.S. News and World Report.*

3. Only a small fraction of criminal cases are resolved through a trial. The overwhelming majority of cases are disposed of through guilty pleas or dismissals. Out of a hundred individuals charged with a crime, only about five will go to trial. Of those five, between one and two will be acquitted (Kyckelhahn and Cohen, *Felony Defendants*).

4. Kalven and Zeisel, *The American Jury*, table 12, 58; Schwartz, "Innocence."

5. Stith, "The Risk of Legal Error."

6. Ayres, "Civil Jury Finds Simpson Liable."

7. Freiss, "After Apologies." Simpson was sentenced to between nine and thirty-three years for an armed robbery he committed in Las Vegas in 2008.

8. Kyckelhahn and Cohen, *Felony Defendants*.

9. Schwartz, "Innocence."

10. Kalven and Zeisel, *The American Jury*.

11. Hannaford-Agor et al., *Are Hung Juries a Problem?*

12. Blackstone, *Commentaries on the Laws of England*, 358.

13. Kalven and Zeisel, *The American Jury*, 165.

14. Ibid., 165, note 4.

15. Hans and Vidmar, "'The American Jury' at Twenty Five Years."

16. Surette, *Media, Crime, and Criminal Justice*. One study using interviews with over four hundred jurors about their experiences serving as jurors and their impressions of courts revealed that jurors who frequently watched courtroom dramas were more influenced by the shows than by their direct experiences as jurors in real courts (Podlas 2006).

17. Papke, "Conventional Wisdom"; Rafter, *Shots in the Mirror*.

18. Rafter, *Shots in the Mirror*.

19. Dershowitz, *The Best Defense*, 117–18.

20. Erdmann's views did not go unnoticed. His expression of his views, particularly as they related to judges, resulted in his censure for violating his ethical responsibilities as a lawyer (see *Matter of Erdmann*, 33 A.D. 2d 223, 1972). His censure was overturned by the New York Court of Appeals by a 3–2 vote the following year (33 N.Y.2d 559, 301 N.E.2d 426, 347 N.Y.S.2d 441, 1972). Erdmann did not mince words. Justice Burke, in dissent, quoted from the article:

> The charge was based on statements and language used in an article entitled "I Have Nothing to Do with Justice," which appeared in the March 12, 1971 issue of Life magazine. Lawyer Erdmann said of and concerning the courts within the First Judicial Department: "There are so few trial judges who just judge, who rule on questions of law, and leave guilt or innocence to the jury. And Appellate Division judges aren't any better. They're the whores who became madams. I would like to [be a judge] just to see if I could be the kind of judge I think a judge should be. But the only way you can get it is to be in politics or buy it —and I don't even know the going price" (James Mills, "I Have Nothing to Do with Justice," *Life*, March 12, 1971, 61–62).

The *Life* article stated,

> He defends killers, burglars, rapists, robbers—the men people mean when they talk about crime in the streets. Martin Erdmann's clients are crime in the streets. In 25 years, Martin Erdmann has defended more than 100,000 criminals. He has saved them tens of thousands of years in prison and in those years they have robbed, raped, burglarized and murdered tens upon tens of thousands of people. The idea of having

had a very personal and direct hand in all that mayhem strikes him as boring and irrelevant. "I have nothing to do with justice," he says. "Justice is not even part of the equation. If you say I have no moral reaction to what I do, you are right."

21. "No Apology for Robert Blake Jury." Los Angeles County District Attorney Steve Cooley said jurors who acquitted actor Robert Blake of the murder of his wife were "incredibly stupid" and insisted his office put on a good case: "Quite frankly, based on my review of the evidence, he is as guilty as sin. He is a miserable human being," he said.

22. Lynch, "Our Administrative System."

23. Kyckelhah and Cohen, *Felony Defendants.*

24. Ibid.

25. Ibid.

26. Rosen, "After 'One Angry Womanн ';"Uviller, "Acquitting the Guilty."

27. See Justice McCormick's dissenting opinion in *Ex parte Brandley* (1989), 896, objecting to the majority decision to uphold a lower court's grant of relief based upon (a) suppression of exculpatory evidence, (b) encouragement of false testimony, and (c) refusal to conduct simple forensic tests. In Justice McCormick's view, "There is absolutely no evidence which remotely tends to exculpate applicant or show that he is not guilty."

28. Fisher, "Convictions of Innocent Persons." A "factually innocent" person is one who did not commit the actus reus of the crime, either himself or through another for whose conduct he was responsible as an accomplice. Thus, the category "wrongfully convicted" excludes a convicted person who was "legally" innocent because he lacked the required mens rea, had a good defense of excuse (e.g., insanity, duress) or justification (e.g., self-defense, necessity), was denied a fair trial, or was convicted in violation of some other specific substantive or procedural right

29. Gross et al., "Exonerations in the United States, 1989 through 2003." Making creative use of DNA exoneration data, Michael Risinger has argued that between 3 and 5 percent of rape murder convictions between 1982 and 1989 may be factually erroneous. He arrives at this figure by dividing the number of DNA capital rape murder exonerations by the number of rape murder cases in which there was biological material suitable for DNA testing. He notes that there is no substantial reason to believe that the error rate in murder cases generally would be lower than in the capital rape murder cases he examined in detail. Risinger, "Innocents Convicted."

30. Assuming that we can accurately distinguish between acts that are

justified (e.g., self-defense) and those that are excused (e.g., insanity, duress), the latter group falls into a netherworld between the innocent and the guilty. The excused commit forbidden acts with a prohibited mental state, but their cases present extenuating circumstances that preclude judgments of guilt. These verdicts are not factually inaccurate in the same sense as a not guilty verdict of a defendant who committed the crime and has no relevant legal defense, but they are not factually innocent as that term is discussed here.

31. Innocence Project.

32. *Brewer v. Williams* (1977).

33. Chief Justice Burger also took the unusual step of commenting on the majority opinion in *Brewer* directly from the bench, describing it as "weird" and as an "error." He stated that the majority "regresses to playing the grisly game of hide and seek." See Oelsner, "Justices Spurn States' Plea."

34. *Dowling v. United States*, 493 U.S. 342 (1990).

35. Packer, *The Limits of the Criminal Sanction*.

36. "Reagan Seeks Judges."

37. Packer, *The Limits of the Criminal Sanction*.

38. Eisenstein and Jacob, *Felony Justice*.

39. See Gross, "Loss of Innocence," for a sophisticated presentation of this viewpoint as a possible explanation for what is explicitly assumed to be a low rate of false convictions flowing from eyewitness misidentification.

40. Ibid.

41. Eisenstein and Jacob, *Felony Justice*, 274. Little sympathy for the unconvicted but punished defendant existed in the courtroom workgroups (prosecutor, defense lawyer, judge, court officers) because of the widespread belief that all defendants brought to court were guilty of something. Most courtroom regulars believed that the unconvicted were lucky to escape with such mild punishment; they grumbled about the technicalities and other circumstances that led to the release of these defendants.

42. Ponser, *The Problems of Jurisprudence*, 216. This approach rationalizes the existing criminal justice system. If all defendants who stand trial are guilty and efforts are directed at establishing legal innocence, even when the facts are known otherwise, then it is entirely legitimate to turn a deaf ear toward defendants who insist that their legal guilt is erroneous on the ground that they are factually innocent. How much screening is done by prosecutors probably depends to a large extent on their resources relative to the amount of crime. The lower this ratio, the more carefully prosecutors will screen, and the ratio is extremely low in this country today. The implication, which is counterintuitive,

is that fewer innocent people will be convicted in a society with a high (and, especially, a rising) crime rate than in one with a low crime rate. Prosecutorial screening leaves untouched, however—indeed exacerbates—the problem of the acquittal of the guilty. The more screening there is, the fewer guilty people are convicted; the screening gives them an additional chance to beat the rap. In general, unless the resources devoted to determining guilt and innocence are increased, the only way to reduce the probability of convicting the innocent is to reduce the probability of convicting the guilty as well.

43. Damaska, "Evidentiary Barriers to Conviction."

44. Posner, *The Problem of Moral and Legal Theory*, 163–64. Posner's claim that the lawyers are good enough to protect the innocent is highly debatable. See Stuntz, "The Pathological Politics," disagreeing with Posner's claim that the lawyers are good enough to protect the innocent and arguing that criminal trials provide a poor check on whether a prosecutor will sort cases in a way to ensure that only the guilty are charged: more precisely, the interaction of criminal procedure and legislative funding of appointed defense counsel has this effect. The law of criminal procedure creates a range of claims defendants can raise at various points in the process, and those claims tend to be cheaper to investigate and litigate than claims bearing on defendants' factual guilt. Legislatures, meanwhile, fund appointed defense counsel at levels that require an enormous amount of selectivity—counsel can contest only a very small fraction of the cases on their dockets, and can investigate only a small fraction of the claims their clients might have. This effect applies to the mass of criminal litigation, since roughly 80 percent of criminal defendants receive appointed counsel. The consequence is to steer criminal litigation away from the facts, and toward more cheaply raised constitutional claims. Those claims tend not to correlate with innocence; or if they do, the correlation may be perverse (note 242). This argument is further elaborated in Stuntz, "The Uneasy Relationship," arguing that the criminal process with its focus on constitutional claims has reduced the difference in the likelihood that an innocent will be acquitted as opposed to a guilty person being acquitted.

45. Dershowitz, *The Best Defense*.

46. Freedman, "Professional Responsibility of the Defense Lawyer: The Three Hardest Questions."

47. Smith, "Defending the Innocent," 512.

48. Kyckelhahn and Cohen, *Felony Defendants*.

49. Kassin, "Human Judges of Truth." Studies show that in terms of assessing accuracy of statements,

college students had a 52.8 percent accuracy rate, which is pretty typical. Police detectives were only slightly higher, at 55.8 percent; CIA, FBI, and military polygraph examiners were at 55.7 percent, trial judges were at 56.7 percent, and psychiatrists were at 57.6 percent. U.S. Secret Service Agents won the prize, exhibiting a 64 percent accuracy rate, the highest of all groups. As in other research, then, performance was modest, to say the least.

Posner (*Frontiers of Legal Theory*) has also suggested that "two heads are better than one—and six, eight or twelve inexperienced heads may be better than the one experienced head when they pool their recollections and deliberate an outcome" (352).

50. If all of those who go to trial are guilty of more serious crimes than witness intimidation, perhaps each of them has an incentive to commit the crime of obstructing justice to avoid conviction of a more serious offense. But those who are guilty of no crime lack that incentive, and there is no basis for the belief that the only reason individuals are acquitted is that they have intimidated the witnesses against them.

51. Givelber, "Punishing Protestations of Innocence."

52. Hannaford-Agor et al., *Are Hung Juries a Problem?*

53. Justice Scalia may be an exception. Gross, "Souter Passant, Scalia Rampant: Combat in the Marsh."

54. Hannaford-Agor et al., *Are Hung Juries a Problem?* note 53.

NOTES TO CHAPTER 2

1. U.S. Congress, Senate, Subcommittee on Internal Security, *Recording of Jury Deliberations*, 1.

2. Kalven and Zeisel, *The American Jury* (1971), vii.

3. Dean Levi, as quoted in U.S. Congress, Senate, Subcommittee on Internal Security, *Recording of Jury Deliberations*, 8

4. Corbin, "The Jury on Trial"; Hall, "The Present-Day Jury."

5. Curtis, "The Trial Judge"; Pound, "Law in Books."

6. Wigmore, "A Program for the Trial."

7. Corbin, "The Jury on Trial"; Tocqueville, *Democracy in America.*

8. Sunderland, "The Inefficiency of the American Jury."

9. Frank, *Courts on Trial*; Green, "Jury Injustice"; Perkins, "Proposed Jury Changes."

10. U.S. Congress, Senate, Subcommittee on Internal Security, *Recording*

of Jury Deliberations, 5. The Ford Foundation grant was used to support two other behavioral studies of the law unrelated to the study of juries. One project dealt with the commercial arbitration process. The second was to be a public opinion survey about federal income taxation, but it was never completed.

11. A number of smaller studies were conducted in tandem with the four main methodologies. For example, smaller studies were conducted to understand how lawyers involved in the voir dire make decisions about selecting jurors and the degree to which they conduct pre–voir dire screening of potential jurors (see Broeder, "The University of Chicago Jury Project," for additional details).

12. Hans and Vidmar, *Judging the Jury*. Some concern was raised following the publication of *The American Jury* that data from judges did not represent a random sample of decisions made throughout the country. In fact, over half of the cases analyzed came from only 15 percent of the judges who originally agreed to participate in the study, each of whom provided information on over ten cases. Kalven, "The Dignity of the Civil Jury Trial." Although the main focus of the analyses in *The American Jury* was on judge-jury outcomes in criminal cases, some discussion of civil cases was included in the book (63–65); and one article using the jury data was published.

13. U.S. Congress, Senate, Subcommittee on Internal Security, *Recording of Jury Deliberations*, 214. Judges were given five options: (a) the composition of the jury, (b) crucial events during the trial, (c) personalities in the case (defendant, witness, attorneys), (d) peculiarities of the case, or (e) other reasons.

14. Ibid., 41. Material quoted from research note prepared by Hans Zeisel for submission to the subcommittee.

15. Ibid., 199.

16. See Broeder, "The Negro in Court"; Broeder, "Occupational Expertise"; Broeder, "Plaintiff's Family Status"; Broeder "Previous Jury Trial Service."

17. U.S. Congress, Senate, Subcommittee on Internal Security, *Recording of Jury Deliberations*, 42.

18. See Strodtbeck and Mann, "Sex Role Differentiation"; Strodtbeck and Hook, "Social Dimensions"; Strodtbeck, James, and Hawkins, "Social Status."

19. The researchers sought permission from Judge Phillips, the chief judge of the U.S. Court of Appeals in Denver, Colorado. Judge Phillips agreed to allow the taping of jury deliberations but insisted that the juries be notified that their deliberations were tape recorded and informed of the safeguards that were being taken by the research team to protect the confidentiality of the information. Judge Phillips expressed two main concerns about the covert

recording of jury deliberations: first, that the recordings might eventually become public and future jurors would be concerned that their deliberations were being recorded, which might "inhibit full and frank discussion in the jury room" (Letter from Judge Phillips in U.S. Congress, Senate, Subcommittee on Internal Security, *Recording of Jury Deliberations*, 191); second, that it was only fair and decent to let jurors know that their discussions were being taped for the purposes of research.

20. Kalven and Zeisel, *The American Jury*, vii.

21. Recordings were made in two automobile damage suites, two government land condemnation suits, one breach of promise to marry, and one civil damage suit concerning the alleged underground seepage of water from a private water reservoir (Letter from Judge Hill to Judge Phillips regarding the jury taping procedures in U.S. Congress, Senate, Subcommittee on Internal Security, *Recording of Jury Deliberations*, 192).

22. U.S. Congress, Senate, Subcommittee on Internal Security, *Recording of Jury Deliberations*, 135–43.

23. There are only a handful of jury deliberations that have ever been taped since the Wichita, Kansas, tapings. In 1986, a Wisconsin law professor worked with a public broadcast show, *Frontline*, to secure permission from all parties, including the jurors, to tape a jury deliberation. Portions of the deliberation along with comments from law professor Steven Hertzberg aired on the April 8, 1986, episode entitled "Inside the Jury Room." In the mid-1990s, the Arizona Supreme Court authorized the placement of video cameras in several jury rooms during deliberations. In the case of the Arizona taping, jurors were told in advance, and cameras were unobtrusively located in the deliberation room. The taping of the jury deliberations in Arizona resulted in a television broadcast to publicize many concerns about the jury system, but no empirical research was conducted using the taped deliberations (Kressel and Kressel, *Stack and Sway*).

24. Kalven and Zeisel, *The American Jury*, 111.

25. Ibid., 115.

26. For purposes of demonstrating the interplay between the evidence and other factors in accounting for judge-jury disagreement, Kalven and Zeisel treated all factors not related to the evidence offered at trial (i.e., sentiments about the defendant, sentiments about the law, disparity of counsel, and facts only the judge knew) as values. Perhaps to guard against the possibility that their characterization of repugnant explanations (e.g., those relying on gross racial stereotypes [Kalven and Zeisel, *The American Jury*, 339–44]) as values

might suggest approval, they specifically used the term "sentiment" in the text to refer to all explanations not based in the evidence, the superiority of counsel, or facts that only the judge knew.

27. Kalven and Zeisel, *The American Jury*, 115–16.

28. By "close" in this context, they apparently meant that the judge identified both value-based and evidence-based reasons to explain why the jury acquitted when the judge would have convicted (Kalven and Zeisel, *The American Jury*, 165). Although they did ask expressly about whether the case was "close" in their second survey (Question 12) involving 1,191 responses, they did not ask this question in the initial survey involving 2,385 trials (47). Perhaps for this reason, although they employed the closeness variable from the second survey to provide a map of the evidence and to demonstrate that jury verdicts follow the evidence (134, 159), they did not make substantial use of that variable in their development of disagreement cases and the relative roles of values and evidence (163–64). In a footnote, they presented an apparently mislabeled table (they titled it "Normal Disagreements" when the table only makes sense if it included both "normal" and "cross-over" disagreements), indicating the percentage of disagreements between judges and juries in clear and close cases. They did so, as indicated in the footnote, to show that disagreement occurs in clear cases as well as close cases. This was not a point they developed at any length in the text (164, note 2).

29. Kalven and Zeisel, *The American Jury*, 165.

30. Ibid.

31. Ibid., 499.

32. Ibid., 495.

33. Ibid., 494.

34. Ibid., 495.

35. Ibid.

36. Ibid., 219.

37. Ibid., 195.

38. Kyckelhal and Cohen, *Felony Defendants*.

39. Ibid.

40. William Stuntz has argued that the criminal procedure revolution has been of little aid to the innocent. The factors affecting the extent to which the innocent go to trial and are acquitted extend beyond either the formal law or the race and gender of the participants to include, for example, the crime rate, the definition of the substantive law, and relative funding levels for prosecution and defense service (Stuntz, "The Uneasy Relationship").

41. *Duncan v. Louisiana*, 391 U.S. 145 (1968).

42. Ibid., 156–57.

43. Ibid., 156.

44. Ibid.

45. The Supreme Court has disapproved of the practice of permitting judges to sentence defendants to more than the statutory maximum for the crime that the jury has determined that the defendant committed. See *Apprendi v. New Jersey*, 530 U.S. 466 (2000); *Blakely v. Washington*, 542 U.S. 296 (2004); and *U.S. v. Booker*, 543 U.S. 220 (2005). As Justice Stevens concluded in *U.S. v. Booker* (2005),

> The new sentencing practice [sentencing guidelines] forced the Court to address the question how the right of jury trial could be preserved, in a meaningful way guaranteeing that the jury would still stand between the individual and the power of the government under the new sentencing regime. And it is the new circumstances, not a tradition or practice that the new circumstances have superseded, that have led us to the answer first considered in *Jones* and developed in *Apprendi* and subsequent cases culminating with this one. It is an answer not motivated by Sixth Amendment formalism, but by the need to preserve Sixth Amendment substance. (*Booker* at 232)

46. *McCleskey v. Kemp* (1987).

47. Ibid., 311, quoting Kalven and Zeisel, *The American Jury*, 488.

48. Ibid., 325, note 4.

49. *Roper v. Simmons* (2005), 620.

50. Cases such as *Gideon v. Wainwright* (1963; right to counsel at trial), *Pointer v. Texas* (1965; right to confront witnesses), *Batson v. Kentucky* (1986; illegality of race-based jury challenges), *Taylor v. Louisiana* (1975; jury must reflect cross-section of community; cannot exclude women as a class), *In re Winship* (1970; requirement of proof beyond a reasonable doubt), *Brady v. Maryland* (1963; prosecution must disclose exculpatory evidence), and *Duncan v. Louisiana* (1968) were all decided after the Kalven and Zeisel survey.

51. Robbenolt, "Evaluating Juries."

52. Vidmar, "Making Inferences."

53. Bornstein and McCabe, "Jurors of the Absurd?"

54. Robbenolt, "Evaluating Juries."

55. Heuer and Penrod, "Trial Complexity"; Robbenolt, "Evaluating Juries."

56. Diamond, "Order in the Court."

57. Robbenolt, "Evaluating Juries," 479.

58. Reskin and Visher, "The Impacts of Evidence."

59. Visher, "Juror Decision Making."

60. Measured as use of a weapon, physical evidence, evidence of force, eyewitness evidence, other victims' testimonies, defendant's relatives' testimonies, and defense claimed victim's story was implausible (Visher, "Juror Decision Making," 11).

61. Visher, "Juror Decision Making."

62. Gastwirth and Sinclair, "A Re-examination of the 1966 Kavel and Zeisel Study of Judge-Jury Agreement s and Disagreements and their Causes."

63. Black, *Social Justice*. Data from the Capital Jury Project, a national study of capital jurors' decision making using interviews with more than one thousand actual jurors from trials in fourteen states, indicated there were significant differences between Black and White jurors in terms of their degree of doubt about guilt, perceptions of defendant remorse, and beliefs about the future dangerousness of the defendant (see Bowers, Steiner, and Sandys, "Death Sentencing").

64. Ugwuegbu, "Racial and Evidential Factors"; Johnson, "Black Innocence"; Sommers, "On Racial Diversity."

65. Hans and Vidmar, *Judging the Jury*; MacCoun and Kerr, "Asymmetric Influence."

66. Pennington and Hastie, "Evidence Evaluation."

67. Devine et al., "Strength of Evidence."

68. Keil and Vito, "Race, Homicide Severity." The authors found no support for the liberation hypothesis in their study of prosecutors' decisions to request the death penalty in Kentucky. They suggested that considerations of defendant and victim race were not confined to legally ambiguous cases. Baumer, Messner, and Felson, "The Role of Victim Characteristics." The authors found only mixed support for the liberation hypothesis in the disposition of murder cases at various stages of the criminal justice process. They concluded that although victim characteristics affect the processing of murder cases, the effects are not clearly limited to a particular level of case severity.

69. Spohn and Cederblom, "Race and Disparities."

70. Baumer, Messner, and Felson, "The Role of Victim Characteristics."

71. Barnett, "Some Distribution Patterns."

72. Baldus, Pulaski, and Woodworth, "Comparative Review of Death Sentences."

73. Robbenolt, "Evaluating Juries," 471.

74. Galanter, "Why the Haves Come Out Ahead."

75. Some psychological studies have shown a relationship between non-verbal judge cues about evidence or proceedings and jury decision making (Blanck, "What Empirical Research Tells Us"; Burnett and Badzinski, "Judge Nonverbal Communciation").

76. Robbenolt, "Evaluating Juries," 502.

77. Alschuler and Rodriguez, "Jury Nullification."

78. The question specifically asked judges whether they had seen verdicts over the prior year that were "the product of jury nullification." Jury nullification was defined as "a jury's power to ignore the law and acquit despite clear evidence of guilt" (Alschuler and Rodriguez, "Jury Nullification," survey instrument question 4, 1).

79. A full acquittal means not guilty on all charges. The judges were also asked to report instances of nullification resulting in either partial acquittals or deadlocked juries. Overall, judges believed that they had seen jury nullification occur in 224 out of 2,273 cases, or 10 percent of all cases. The 137 cases not involving full acquittals involved either partial acquittals or hung juries.

80. American studies of jury accuracy have traditionally relied upon judges to assess whether juries are correct. Those who have employed this approach have conceded its problematic nature but note that there appears to be no alternative (Kalven and Zeisel, *The American Jury*).

81. Eisenberg et al., "Judge-Jury Agreement"; Hannaford-Agor and Hans, "Nullification at Work?"

82. The NCSC data have also been used in other scholarship to measure the probability that jury decision making may be prone to either type I (jury incorrectly convicts the innocent) or type II error (jury acquits the guilty) (Spencer, "Estimating the Accuracy of Jury Verdicts").

83. McCabe and Purves, *The Jury at Work*.

84. Ibid., 38, table 3.

85. This is based on tables 113 and 114 in *The American Jury* (Kalven and Zeisel). Table 113 reveals that 34 percent (77) of the cases in which the jury and judge disagreed about guilt (226 cases from the second survey) were viewed by the judge as "without merit." This is 7 percent of all the cases in the second survey.

86. Baldwin and McConville, *Jury Trials*.

87. Ibid., 46.

88. Ibid.

89. Ibid., 54.

90. Alshuler and Rodriguez, "Jury Nullification."

91. Ibid., 41. The judge and one other observer questioned an acquittal in forty-one cases representing 11 percent of the total cases (indicating 370 total trials in Birmingham).

92. This analysis rests on an assumption that lacks any empirical support: that judges are correct and juries in error when judges would convict although the juries have acquitted. To the extent that the outcomes of criminal trials turn on questions of credibility, there is no reason to expect that judges will do better jobs than juries in determining who is telling the truth. Although judges have far more experience than jurors in trying to answer that question, judges lacks any system for evaluating whether their conclusions were accurate. In the absence of any kind of reliable feedback as to the accuracy of one's judgment, experience may result in consistency but it does not necessarily result in accuracy. Professionals called upon to determine whether someone is telling the truth tend to arrive at consistent results: role does matter. But consistency is very different from accuracy, and there is no evidence that judges are more likely than jurors to draw the correct conclusions about the accuracy of testimony that they have heard.

93. Sites were chosen on the basis of a convenience sample with some attention to sites with concerns about the problem of hung juries. Jurors in Los Angles, the Bronx, and D.C. were twelve-person juries. In Maricopa County approximately two-thirds of the cases were heard by eight-person juries. For a detailed description of the study design, sampling, and response rates, see Hannaford-Agor et al., *Are Hung Juries a Problem?*

94. Kalven and Zeisel, *The American Jury*, 339–402.

95. The response rates for juries across all four sites was 80 percent (see Hannaford-Agor et al., *Are Hung Juries a Problem?*).

NOTES TO CHAPTER 3

1. Mills, "I Have Nothing to Do with Justice," 59, 62.

2. Those concerned with measuring and analyzing the extent to which the innocent are falsely convicted have focused upon the adjudicatory process and how that can be improved. This concern embraces the quality of the evidence relied upon as well as the procedures for assessing the meaning of that evidence. It touches on police investigation to the extent that the investigation is likely to produce unreliable evidence of guilt or to obfuscate or ignore exculpatory evidence. Those proposing remedies for dealing with false convictions have tried to address those investigatory techniques that

result in unreliable evidence as well as a broad range of adjudicatory failures. They have not addressed the broader question of the extent to which pretrial screening effectively results in the removal of the innocent from the risks associated with trial.

3. Kyckelhal and Cohen, *Felony Defendants*.

4. In Chicago in 1972, the police made 35,000 felony arrests; but fewer than 2,500 were convicted of felonies in that same year (Eisenstein and Jacob, *Felony Justice*). In a large-scale effort to track offenders from arrest to adjudication, in 1990, the Bureau of Justice Statistics collected data on persons arrested for felonies in six states (Alaska, California, Minnesota, Missouri, New Jersey, and New York). Of the 524,223 persons arrested for felonies in these six study states, 70 percent were convicted. Of the remaining arrestees whose case went to trial, 23 percent were dismissed by the courts, 6 percent resulted in a judgment other than acquittal or conviction, and 1 percent were acquitted (Perez, "Tracking Offenders, 1990").

5. Kyckelhal and Cohen, *Felony Defendants*.

6. Reaves, *Felony Defendants*; Boland, Mahanna, and Sones, *The Prosecution of Felony Arrests*.

7. Ibid.

8. National Center for State Courts, *Caseload Highlights*.

9. Wright and Miller, "The Screening/Bargaining Tradeoff."

10. Boland, Mahanna, and Sones, *The Prosecution of Felony Arrests*.

11. Ibid.

12. Ibid., 40. The authors noted that this was true in seven of the nine jurisdictions (Denver; Los Angeles; Manhattan County; Portland, Oregon; St. Louis, Missouri; Seattle, Washington and San Diego, California); that in Brighton County, Colorado, and the District of Columbia, dismissals attributable to "witness" outnumbered those attributable to "evidence"; and that as a percentage of all dismissals, "witness" accounted for between 6 percent (San Diego) and 21 percent (D.C.) of all cases. All of the felony cases examined in the Boland, Mahanna, and Sones study were prosecuted in 1988.

13. The one exception was Brighton, Colorado, a jurisdiction with many fewer dismissals than the other eight areas.

14. Boland, Mahanna, and Sones, *The Prosecution of Felony Arrests*.

15. Zeisel, *The Limits of Law Enforcement*.

16. Ibid., 112. For example, interviewees described reasons for dismissal, including the failure of the complaining witness to come forward, "[p]ersonal considerations (in conjunction with evidential reasons)," and specific evidentiary concerns.

17. Ibid., 111–12. Zeisel explained that one-fifth of the dismissals involved assaults against women that were not treated as mandating prosecution for reasons including the complaining witness lacked credibility because the victim was a prostitute, the complaining witness lacked credibility because the victim had given "consent to rape," and the crime was a domestic dispute.

18. Ibid., 111. Six cases involved the delayed return of a rental car, six involved cases in which possession or ownership was difficult to prove, two involved prosecutorial acceptance of the idea that the defendant acted in self-defense, one involved a defendant with a bill of sale, one involved "consent to rape," eight involved the complaining witness's lack of credibility, one involved a codefendant acquitted at trial, and one involved the codefendant assuming responsibility.

19. Boland, Mahanna, and Sones, *The Prosecution of Felony Arrests.*

20. Ibid., 40–48; Zeisel, *The Limits of Law Enforcement*, 111. Boland, Mahanna, and Sones found that, based on thousands of cases, concerns about the witnesses accounted for, on average, 12 percent of dismissals, whereas Zeisel found that concerns about witnesses accounted for 62 percent of the dismissals.

21. Zeisel, *The Limits of Law Enforcement.*

22. Ibid., 25.

23. Givelber, "Meaningless Acquittals"; Weinreb, *Denial of Justice.*

24. Latin for "guilty mind," mens rea represents the mental state necessary to commit a crime.

25. Lynch, "Our Administrative System."

26. U.S. Department of Justice, *Felony Sentences.*

27. *North Carolina v. Alford*, 400 U.S. 25 (1970).

28. As stated by Josh Bowers in "Punishing the Innocent,"
For the typical innocent defendant in the typical case—which I will demonstrate is a recidivist facing petty charges—the best resolution is generally a quick plea in exchange for a light, bargained-for sentence. And such a plea is frequently available because prosecutors do not try to maximize sentence length in low-stakes cases. Moreover, defendants possess certain underappreciated bargaining advantages in these cases. Finally, even for innocent defendants facing more serious charges, plea bargaining may be, at a minimum, the manifestly least-bad option. (1120)

29. Givelber, "Punishing Protestations of Innocence."

30. *North Carolina v. Alford* (1970).

31. Innocence Project.

32. Shellem, "Jailed Man Set Free after False Confession."

33. Sourcebook of Criminal Justice Statistics Online, table 5.24: Criminal Defendants Disposed of in U.S. District Courts.

34. Juries convicted 2,328 federal defendants; judges convicted 279. The data reported for state courts did not reveal how often judges acquitted as opposed to juries. What they did show was that of those found guilty in state courts following trial (as opposed to the 95 percent whose conviction resulted from a plea), the majority (3 percent out of the remaining 5 percent) had their guilt determined by judges sitting without juries; whereas 2 percent out of the remaining 5 percent were found guilty by juries, See Sourcebook of Criminal Justice Statistics Online, table: 5.46: Percent Distribution of Felony Convictions in State Courts, by Offense and Method of Conviction, United States, 2004.

The relatively greater prominence of bench as opposed to jury trials in the state systems may reflect the substitution of relatively rapid bench trials for negotiated pleas as the dominant mode of resolving criminal cases in some jurisdictions (Wright and Miller, "The Screening/Bargaining Tradeoff").

35. This point may appear too cute by half. After all, the argument goes, most of these trials may be nothing more than face-saving methods for prosecutors to dismiss cases that should have never been brought in the first instance. Assuming that this, in fact, is the explanation for the 35 percent acquittal rate, it means that 5 percent of the cases that the government insists upon taking to trial are baseless. This is derived by dividing the acquittals from judge-only trials (137) by the cases that were taken to trial (Maguire and Pastore, *Sourcebook for Criminal Justice Statistics*). It requires a bit of a leap of faith to treat as omniscient prosecuting authorities who bring this many baseless prosecutions.

36. Posner, "An Economic Approach."

37. *Federal Rules of Criminal Procedure.* Rule 23(a) provides that "cases required to be tried by jury shall be so tried unless the defendant waives a jury trial in writing with the approval of the court and the consent of the government."

38. Malamud, *The Fixer.*

39. Kyckelhal and Cohen, *Felony Defendants.*

40. Many scholars treat plea bargaining as just another case of bargaining in the shadow of expected trial outcomes. They endorse plea bargaining because they presume that bargains largely reflect the substantive outcomes that would have occurred at trial anyway, minus some fixed discount. Trials are not perfect, of

course, but these scholars contend that plea bargains result in outcomes roughly as fair as trial outcomes. In short, the classic shadow-of-trial model predicts that the likelihood of conviction at trial and the likely post-trial sentence largely determine plea bargains. (Bibas, "Plea Bargaining," 2465)

41. Hannaford-Agor et al., *Are Hung Juries a Problem?*

42. It may be that prosecutors typically view claims that defendants are innocent as negotiating ploys rather than serious factual assertions or that defense counsel report the claims of innocence without endorsing them. Or it may be the prosecutors' beliefs that there are no innocents among those who go to trial that result in the disparity in prosecutor and defense explanations of why pleas failed.

43. Brown, "Jury Nullification"; Hannaford-Agar and Hans, "Nullification at Work?"; Rosen, "After 'One Angry Woman.'"

44. This analysis rests on an assumption that lacks any empirical support: that judges are correct and juries in error when the judges would convict although the juries acquitted. To the extent that the outcomes of criminal trials turn on questions of credibility, there is no reason to expect that judges will do a better job than juries in determining who is telling the truth. Although judges have far more experience than jurors in trying to answer that question, judges lack any system for evaluating whether their conclusions were accurate. In the absence of any kind of reliable feedback as to the accuracy of one's judgment, experience may result in consistency; but it does not necessarily result in accuracy. Professionals called upon to determine whether someone is telling the truth tend to arrive at consistent results: role does matter. But consistency is very different from accuracy, and there is no evidence that judges are more likely than jurors to draw the correct conclusions about the accuracy of testimony that they have heard. We explore these issues in greater depth in chapter 5.

45. Leipold, "The Problem of the Innocent." The view that acquittals were the product of withholding relevant evidence from juries achieved its apogee in a California law that addressed the concern by authorizing an acquitted person to return to court for a judicial declaration of actual innocence. West's Ann. Cal. Penal Code 851.8 (2011). The law states that it "shall be repealed on the effective date of a final judgment based on a claim under the California or United States Constitution holding that evidence which is relevant, reliable, and material may not be considered for purposes of a judicial determination of factual innocence under this section."

46. Kalven and Zeisel identified two additional explanations for juries acquitting when judges would convict: a different view of credibility, particularly when the defendant takes the stand, and a different understanding of reasonable doubt. They concluded, "If a society wishes to be serious about convicting only when the state has been put to proof beyond a reasonable doubt, it would be well advised to have a jury system" (189–90).

47. Focusing upon this difficulty, Tim Bakken has urged the recognition of a plea of innocent (as opposed to "not guilty"), which would trigger a search for the truth on behalf of both the prosecution and the defense. Thus, a defendant seeking a jury declaration of innocence would, among other things, have to waive his right to silence. In return, the prosecution would have to undertake a vigorous and thorough investigation of the defendant's possible innocence. See Bakken, "Truth and Innocence Procedures to Free Innocent Persons."

48. In arguing that we need to provide opportunities for those who have been acquitted to demonstrate that they are in fact innocent, law professor Andrew Leipold used a figure of 5 percent of all acquittals and dismissals involving innocents ("The Problem of the Innocent"). Leipold indicated that a figure this low encompasses a great number of people and providing redress to them is a worthy undertaking. It is instructive to note that even a sympathetic observer feels compelled to concede that nineteen out of every twenty acquittals and dismissals are historically inaccurate in order to argue that we should worry about what happens to the one out of twenty acquittals that is accurate.

49. According to the American Bar Association, *Standards for Criminal Justice*, prosecutors may not ethically bring charges against suspects unless they believe that the suspects are factually guilty of the crimes charged (1980: 3.9); *The U.S. Attorneys' Manual* (2005) indicates that the threshold requirement for commencing prosecution is the prosecutor believing that the suspect's conduct constitutes a federal offense.

50. Hannaford-Agor, et al., *Are Hung Juries a Problem?*

51. Eisenberg et al., "Judge-Jury Agreement." The judge would have acquitted in 29 percent of the cases in which the defendants had no records, 15.4 percent of the cases in which the defendants had criminal records of which the juries were unaware, and 16.7 percent of the cases in which the judges and juries both knew of the defendants' criminal records.

52. Special Committee on Criminal Justice in a Free Society, *Criminal Justice in Crisis*.

53. This is a weighted average: "The cases often center on such legal cir-

cumstances as the administration of blood tests, the withdrawal of guilty pleas, prior arrests for the same offense, acquittals for the same offense, and finally, as the most frequent circumstance, a prior record, usually for the same crime" (124). Table 31 lists the "facts that only the judge knew" (131).

54. Kalven and Zeisel, *The American Jury*, 114–15, table 29.

55. The one area in which a shift may have occurred is in the category of defendant with a prior criminal record. Kalven and Zeisel (*The American Jury*) reported slightly more than half (53 percent) of all defendants had no prior criminal records (145, table 42). In 1998, only 34 percent of those convicted of felonies in the seventy-five largest urban counties had no prior records, and about half had prior felony convictions (Reaves, *Felony Defendants*, 35). The National Center for State Courts study suggested an even greater imbalance: more than 80 percent of those on trial had criminal records, whether the juries learned of them or not.

56. Juries acquitted in 30.3 percent of the cases in *The American Jury* study (Kalven and Zeisel, 56, table 11).The Bureau of Justice Statistic report "Felony Defendants in Large Urban Counties" in 1988 indicated a 23 percent overall acquittal rate and a 28 percent acquittal rate for juries alone (Reaves, *Felony Defendants*, 26). The NCSC data (Eisenberg et al., "Judge-Jury Agreement") revealed virtually the identical percentage of jury acquittals, 27.6 percent. Kalven and Zeisel did not attempt to separate the data from federal and state judges, possibly because the distinction was not as significant then as it is now. However, as noted, although the federal acquittal rate was lower than that reported from the seventy-five largest urban counties, federal judges were more likely to acquit than federal juries were, a reversal of the situation that pertained in the states.

57. Reaves, *Felony Defendants*, 27, table 8.

58. Judges acquitted in 17 percent of the bench trials in large urban counties (Reaves, *Felony Defendants*).

59. This point might be overstated. Perhaps the acquittals in bench trials represent cases in which the prosecutor had no beliefs about guilt and for that reason agreed that the cases could be tried before judges alone.

60. Givelber, "Lost Innocence," 1184–85.

61. Kalven and Zeisel, *The American Jury*.

62. Ibid., 56, table 11.

63. Ibid., 115, table 29.

64. Ibid., 432, table 115.

65. Ibid., 115, table 29.

66. Ibid., 137, table 35.

67. Studies from the United Kingdom indicated that 70 percent to 74 percent of defendants testify, and anecdotal evidence suggested that virtually all defendants testify in magistrate's courts (see Bucke, Street, and Brown, *The Right of Silence*, quoting the findings from Zander and Henderson's 1993 study of the Crown Courts).

68. Justice White identified this as a problem in his dissent in *Miranda v. Arizona* (1966).

69. McConville, *The Case for the Prosecution.*

70. As Saul Kassin ("Human Judges of Truth") noted, "Investigators should first conduct an information-gathering interview during which they make a preliminary judgment of the witness or suspect based on his verbal and non-verbal behavior" (814–15).

71. When these and other variables were combined in a regression analysis (measuring the effect of each variable while holding the others constant; Appendix A), the three variables (a claim of innocence, no prior record, and both the defendant and a witness testifying) retained their importance. The first table reveals that based on regression analysis of the variables of no prior record and of a defendant and witness testifying, both of these variables were significant at the .02 level or better. The second table reveals that when the defendant's claim of innocence is added to the regression, the no prior record variable remains highly significant (less than .01) while a claim of innocence is significant at the .001 level. The combination of a defendant and witness testifying retained significance but at a less impressive level (.074). This suggests that some of the effect on acquittals of the defendant and a witness testifying can be better understood as attributable to defendants' insistence to their attorneys that they did not commit the crimes. Stated differently, the claim of innocence may result in a more vigorous defense (both the defendant and a witness testify) than would otherwise be the case. Or, finally, because defendants are innocent of the crimes charged, they both refuse to plead and are able to mount credible defense cases.

72. Heber Smith and Ehrmann, "The Criminal Courts," 112.

73. Assuming that we can accurately distinguish between acts that are justified and those that are excused, the latter group falls into a netherworld between the innocent and the guilty. The excused commit forbidden acts with a prohibited mental state but their cases present extenuating circumstances that preclude judgments of guilt. These verdicts are not factually inaccurate in the same sense as not guilty verdicts of defendants who committed the crimes

and have no relevant legal defense, but they are not factually innocent as that term is discussed here.

NOTES TO CHAPTER 4

1. Brick, "Jury Rules One Way, Judge Another in Mob Killing."
2. Shifrel, "Judge Gives Baker Minimum after Slamming Jury for Clearing Co-Defendant."
3. Shifrel, "Brooklyn Baker's Mob Hit Sentence Overturned—for Second Time." The decision is reported at 70 A.D. 2d 851, 894 N.Y.S. 2d 152 (2nd Dept. 2010).
4. *Duncan v. Louisiana*, 391 U.S. 145 (1968), 156–67.
5. This is the result of a search of Westlaw on November 6, 2011, employing the inquiry "Kalven w/3 of Zeisel."
6. As cited in Kalven and Zeisel, *The American Jury*, 488.
7. Kalven and Zeisel, *The American Jury*.
8. Ibid.
9. Cases such as *Gideon v. Wainwright*, 372 U.S. 335 (1963; right to counsel at trial); *Pointer v. Texas*, 380 U.S. 400 (1965; right to confront witnesses); *Batson v. Kentucky*, 476 U.S. 479 (1986; illegality of race-based jury challenges); *Taylor v. Louisiana*, 419 U.S. 522 (1975; jury must reflect cross-section of community; cannot exclude women as a class); *In re Winship*, 397 U.S. 358 (1970; requirement of proof beyond a reasonable doubt); *Brady v. Maryland* (1963; prosecution must disclose exculpatory evidence); and *Duncan v. Louisiana*, 391 U.S. 145 (1968) were all decided after the Kalven and Zeisel survey.
10. Kalven and Zeisel, *The American Jury*. In the cases examined by Kalven and Zeisel, 73 percent of all defendants were White and the remaining 27 percent were Black (195). As of 2002, felony defendants in the seventy-five largest counties in the United States were 31 percent White, 43 percent Black, 24 percent Hispanic, and 2 percent other (Bureau of Justice Statistics, *Sourcebook of Criminal Justice Statistics*, table 5.52). The percentage of defendants who were female doubled from 7 percent in the Kalven and Zeisel study in the 1950s to 18 percent in 2002. Defendants under the age of twenty also increased from 9 percent in the 1950s to 18 percent in 2002 (Bureau of Justice Statistics, *Sourcebook of Criminal Justice Statistics*).
11. Kalven and Zeisel, *The American Jury*.
12. Visher, "Jury Decision Making."
13. Devine et al., "Strength of Evidence."

14. Barnett, "Some Distribution Patterns"; Baldus, Pulaski, and Woodworth, "Comparative Review of Death Sentences"; Baldus et al., "Racial Discrimination and the Death Penalty in the Post-Furman Era."

15. Black, *Social Justice*; Kerr et al., "Defendant-Juror Similarity."

16. Ugwuegbu, "Racial and Evidential Factors"; Johnson, "Black Innocence"; Sommers, "On Racial Diversity."

17. Hans and Vidmar, "The American Jury"; MacCoun and Kerr, "Asymmetric Influence."

18. Pennington and Hastie, "Evidence Evaluation."

19. Keil and Vito, "Race, Homicide Severity."

20. Baumer et al., "The Role of Victim Characteristics."

21. Spohn and Cederblom, "Race and Disparities."

22. Gastwirth and Sinclair, "A Re-examination of the 1966 Kalven and Zeisel Study."

23. Ibid.

24. For an in-depth discussion of this problem, see Bornstein and McCabe, "Jurors of the Absurd?"

25. Heuer and Penrod, "Trial Complexity." In their study of judge/jury agreement in sixty-seven civil cases, the investigators found virtually no difference in the rate at which judges would find for the plaintiff (64.2 percent) as contrasted to the rate at which juries found for plaintiffs (62.7 percent). Overall, judges and juries came to the same result in a given case 62.7 percent of the time (table 12, p. 48).

26. Robbenolt, "Evaluating Juries," 502.

27. Kalven and Zeisel, *The American Jury*.

28. Eisenberg et al., "Judge-Jury Agreement"; Hannaford-Agor and Hans, "Nullification at Work?"

29. Kalven and Zeisel, *The American Jury*.

30. Hannaford-Agor and Hans, "Nullification at Work?"

31. Hannaford-Agor et al., *Are Hung Juries a Problem?*

32. Eisenberg et al., "Judge-Jury Agreement."

33. The difference is even more pronounced if we treat the cases of hung juries as instances in which the jury disagreed with the judge rather than dividing them evenly between acquittals and convictions per Kalven and Zeisel (*The American Jury*). Using this approach, we see that the Kalven and Zeisel juries agreed with the judges on acquittal four out of five times (80.2 percent), whereas the NCSC juries agreed with the judges on acquittal only slightly more than three out of five times (62.7 percent).

TABLE 4.6
Judge-Jury Agreement, including Hung Jury Cases

Data source	Jury acquits	Jury convicts	Jury hangs
NCSC			
Judge acquits	62.7%	27.0%	10.2%
Judge convicts	19.7%	71.9%	8.5%
Kalven and Zeisel			
Judge acquits	80.2%	13.2%	6.6%
Judge convicts	20.3%	74.4%	5.3%

34. Because we are testing the liberation hypothesis, we use, as did Kalven and Zeisel, the *judge's* view as our measure of the closeness of a case.

35. Kalven and Zeisel, *The American Jury*, 134, table 32.

36. Judges were asked to evaluate the closeness of the case on a 7-point scale, ranging from 1 (*evidence strongly favored the prosecution*) to 7 (*evidence strongly favored the defense*). We treated responses of 1 and 2 as indicating clear cases for conviction; 6 and 7 as indicating clear cases for acquittal; and 3, 4, and 5 as close. Kalven and Zeisel used a different measure: They asked judges whether, from the evidence, the defendants' guilt or innocence was either "very clear" or "a close question of whether or not he was guilty beyond a reasonable doubt" (*The American Jury*, question 12, Questionnaire for Sample 2). They then used the judges' responses as to how they would have decided had they been sitting without juries to divide the 57 percent of cases in which the judges indicated that the outcomes were clear on the evidence between clear for acquittal (5 percent) and clear for conviction (52 percent). Despite the different approaches to this question, it seems reasonable to conclude that the NCSC judges considered there to be a higher percentage of close cases than did the Kalven and Zeisel judges. This may reflect the diminishing rate at which criminal responsibility is determined by a jury. Kalven and Zeisel noted that, in 1945, 15 percent of all criminal prosecutions for major crimes were resolved through jury trials and another 10 percent through bench trials. As of 2006, in felony cases in the seventy-five largest jurisdictions, 4 percent of all cases went to trial and, of these, three out of four were convicted. (See Cohen and Kyckelhahn, *Felony Defendants*.)

37. Kalven and Zeisel, *The American Jury*, 94–97.

38.

TABLE 4.7

	Judge predicts jury: guilty	Judge predicts jury: not guilty
Judge would find guilty	189 (68.2 %)	36 (13%)
Judge would find not guilty	9 (3.2%)	43 (15.5%)

39. Despite this advantage, the four courts analyzed here are all in urban areas, limiting our ability to draw conclusions concerning judge and jury disagreements in suburban or rural areas.

40. Hannaford-Agor et al., *Are Hung Juries a Problem?*

41. The dataset originally included 401 cases. Cases with no case disposition information and cases in which juries hung on all charges were removed for the present analysis. Consistent with the approach of Kalven and Zeisel (*The American Jury*, 60), our analysis was focused on the cases in which juries either acquitted the defendants of all charges or convicted them of at least one charge. If judges were correct that jurors were driven by sentiment when they disagreed with the judges about guilt in close cases, we should expect to find confirmation of this explanation in those cases in which the disagreement is starkest: when judge and jury come to opposite conclusions as to whether the defendant engaged in any criminal behavior. It is possible that those who are convicted of some but not all charges were benefiting from jury sentiment, but the data do not include any way to characterize which mixed verdicts should be treated as counterfactual wins for the defense and which should not. We eschewed attempting to characterize some mixed verdicts as defendant wins and others as prosecution wins and instead treated all cases in which defendants were convicted of any counts as convictions. For the same reason, we omitted cases in which juries hung on all counts. Kalven and Zeisel treated disagreements between judges and juries with respect to guilt on various charges or penalties as agreements to convict. Thus, their famous table 11 setting forth the basic pattern of judge-jury agreement showed every case in which the jury convicted on any count as representing a case in which the jury agreed with the judge that the defendant should be convicted (*The American Jury*, 60).

42. We utilized multinomial logistic regression, an extension for binary logistic regression, because our outcome was categorical and had more than two levels (see description below).

43. Researchers in the original NCSC data collected case-level information from court records, judges, and attorneys and individual-level juror information from each juror participating in a case. Because multiple juror responses were nested in the case-level data in the original NCSC data, we aggregated all juror responses to represent the average juror response for each case to facilitate the use of multinomial regression modeling at the case level.

44. Each outcome was coded as a dummy variable where 1 represented the specified outcome and 0 represented all other types of outcomes.

45. Kalven and Zeisel, *The American Jury.*

46. In Kalven and Zeisel's study, sentiments about the defendant included reasons for disagreement that were attributable to the personal characteristics of the defendant while sentiments about the law referred to "particular instances of 'jury equity,' reasons for disagreement that imply criticism of either the law or legal result" (*The American Jury*, 107).

47. Givelber and Farrell, "Judges and Juries."

48. Farrell and Swigert, "Prior Offense Record."

49. Givelber and Farrell, "Judges and Juries."

50. The defense offered testimony (either that of the defendant or a witness) in 85 percent of the cases in which the defendant had no criminal record; the defendant testified in 68 percent of all such cases. Because defendants are entitled to put their character in issue, juries would have learned of the lack of criminal records in all cases in which the defendants testified and would have probably learned of it in the remaining cases in which witnesses other than the defendants testified.

51. Kalven and Zeisel, *The American Jury.*

52. Questions about the fairness of the law and the legal outcome were originally coded in the opposite direction, where 1 indicated *the least fair* and 7 indicated *the most fair*. To provide consistency across the sentiment measures, we reverse coded the fairness measures so the highest scores indicated feeling that the law was the most unfair, a parallel concept to feelings that the defendant was treated too harshly or the jury felt sympathy for the defendant.

53. Kalven and Zeisel, *The American Jury.*

54. Charge severity was coded as 1 = *murder, manslaughter, and attempted murder*; 2 = *rape and robbery*; 3 = *aggravated assault, weapons offense, and child abuse*; 4 = *burglary*; 5 = *drug distribution or sales*; 6 = *drug possession*; 7 = *larceny and theft*; and 8 = *other crimes.*

55. Eisenberg et al., "Judge-Jury Agreement."

56. Black defendants were coded 0 for another race and 1 for Black non-Hispanic, Hispanic defendants were coded 0 for another race and 1 for White or Black Hispanic, and other race defendants were coded 0 for another race and 1 for White non-Hispanic, Asian, and other races.

57. It was difficult to determine the causality direction of the relationship between judge assessment of prosecutorial skill and case outcomes. It is quite possible that judges perceive prosecutors to be more skillful in those cases in which the judges are more predisposed to convict.

58. Eisenberg et al., "Judge-Jury Agreement."

59. Pair-wise tests of means for all five jury sentiment variables were conducted for each case outcome within each of the partitioned groups

60. Researchers in the NCSC study did not ask judges to explain why they thought that jurors disagreed with their views of the evidence. Thus, it was not possible to determine whether contemporary judges, like those surveyed by Kalven and Zeisel, would attribute a significant part of disagreements about guilt to juror sentiment.

61. Putting aside the 101 disagreement cases for which the judges assigned no reason, Kalven and Zeisel found that values alone was the explanation for 202 out of 962 disagreements, or about 5.8 percent of the 3,475 cases remaining. The NCSC survey revealed that juries arrived at contrary verdicts in cases that the judges considered clear in 6.8 percent of all the trials. If the jury view of when a case was clear on the evidence was used, the figure decreased to 4.1 percent of all trials.

62. Kalven and Zeisel, *The American Jury*, 499.

63. Eisenberg et al., "Judge-Jury Agreement."

NOTES TO CHAPTER 5

1. Filosa, "N.O. Man Cleared in '84 Murder."

2. Robbenolt, "Evaluating Juries," 502.

3. MacCoun, "Epistemological Dilemmas," 726.

4. Finkel, *Commonsense Justice*.

5. Abramson, *We, the Jury*.

6. Fisher, "The Jury's Rise as Lie Detector," 575.

7. MacCoun, "Epistemological Dilemmas," 725.

8. Hastie and Rasinski, "The Concept of Accuracy," 193.

9. Myers, "Rule Departures and Making Law."

10. Visher, "Juror Decision Making."

11. Heuer and Penrod, "Trial Complexity."

12. Burns, *A Theory of the Trial*; Hastie and Pennington, "The O. J. Simpson Stories"; Wagenaar, *Anchored Narratives*.

13. Finkel, *Commonsense Justice*, 75.

14. Hastie and Pennington, "The O. J. Simpson Stories," 961.

15. Hastie, "The Role of 'Stories,ʜ' "32.

16. Givelber, "Lost Innocence."

17. Weapons offense ($n = 20$) cases were removed from the present analysis due to problems that skewed distribution of these offenses.

18. Facts that only the judge knew played a very small role in explaining

differences in *The American Jury* study as well: only 2 percent of the disagreement (Kalven and Zeisel, *The American Jury*, 115).

19. Kalven and Zeisel, *The American Jury*, 77. The NCSC questionnaires to both judges and juries asked the question, "All things considered, how close was the case?" However, the response categories did not include any opportunity for the respondents to indicate whether they felt the cases were close. Instead, the respondents were given a 7-point scale, ranging from *evidence strongly favored the prosecution* to *evidence strongly favored the defense*. The responses to such a scale did not indicate whether the respondents arrived at the point at which the evidence was sufficiently in equipoise so that, in Kalven and Zeisel's terms, the juries or judges were liberated to consider values in deciding the cases and sentiment could have a role.

20. Filosa, "N.O. Man Cleared in '84 Murder."

21. What is perhaps even more striking is the parallel between this finding and that of Kalven and Zeisel (*The American Jury*). They indicated that juries acquitted in 65 percent of the cases in which the evidentiary strength was normal; the balance of contradictions was in favor of the defendant, especially if the defendant testified and had no criminal record (160, table 52). Judges, on the other hand, indicated that they would have acquitted in only 29 percent of cases sharing these characteristics (162, note 19). (For an unexplained reason, in the jury table, the authors distinguished between defendants without records who took the stand and those with records who did not, yet in the judge table they made no reference to whether the defendants took the stand.)

22. Kalven and Zeisel, *The American Jury*.

23. Ibid., 180.

24. Ibid., 188.

25. Although the total number is quite small, juries acquitted in 25 percent of such cases while judges would have found for the defense in 19 percent.

26. Separate analyses for judge outcomes and jury outcomes have been utilized in this article because we are interested in specifically examining the effect of different variables and judge acquittals compared to jury acquittals, rather than seeing whether or not certain variables result in both convicting, both acquitting, or either or both hanging. Pseudo R-Square statistics are provided for each model. In logistic regression models estimates are arrived at through iterative processes rather than being calculated to minimize variance as area traditional ordinary least square (OLS) regression models. There is not a specific calculation similar to the OLS approaches to calculating the goodness-of-fit (R-square) of the models for logistic regression. Instead,

pseudo R-square measures approximate the degree to which variance is explained by predictors but should be interpreted more cautiously than traditional R-square measures.

27. Logistic regression models have binary outcomes (in this case voting for guilt versus voting for acquittal). When a binary outcome is modeled using logistic regression, it is difficult to interpret the regression coefficients (B) because it is assumed that the logic transformation of the outcome variable has a linear relationship with the predictor variables. Odds ratios can be more useful in understanding the magnitude of the effect of each variable on the dependent variable. An odds ratio in a logistic regression model provides the odds of something occurring measured as the number of times something for one group occurs divided by the number of times it does not occur. A ratio of odds compares the odds of something occurring for one group compared to another group. In table 5.5, for example, the coefficient for defendant testifying with another witness = 1.13 with a standard error of .41 for juries, and the odds ratio is 3.10. While it is difficult to compare coefficients with one another in unstandardized models, it is meaningful to know that in this model, the odds of defendants receiving acquittals were over three times as great when defendants and a witness testified together as when there were no defense witnesses presented.

28. Typically, under the rules of evidence applicable in criminal cases, defendants are entitled to put their character in issue by, for instance, testifying that they have no prior criminal records. If they do so, they can be impeached with evidence of prior bad acts, including criminal convictions. However, if defendants who testify do not put their character in issue, then the state's ability to reveal the existence of their prior criminal records to the jury is constrained by a "balancing test" in which prejudice is weighed against probative value. If judges decide that revealing the defendants' prior records is unduly prejudicial, then the defendants may testify without the juries learning of their prior records. In such situations, typically, the defendants will be careful to make no claims about their prior records because doing so would permit the prosecutors to present those records to the juries. Thus, when the defendants have no records, the juries are likely to hear this fact. When the defendants have criminal records that the judges determine the state cannot use against them, the juries will hear nothing one way or the other about the defendants' prior criminal conduct.

29. Although not impossible, it is quite unlikely that nondefendant witnesses will be testifying about the defendants' lack of criminal records.

30. Kalven and Zeisel, *The American Jury.*

31. Leipold, "Why Are Federal Judges."

32. Rainville and Reaves, *Felony Defendants*; Levine, "Jury Toughness."

33. Leipold, "Why Are Federal Judges."

34. Posner, "An Economic Approach," 1501.

35. Leipold, "Why Are Federal Judges."

36. Eisenstein and Jacob, *Felony Justice.*

37. These facts are set forth in the 2008 decision of the United States Court of Appeals for the Fifth Circuit. *Thompson v. Connick,* 553 F.3d 836, C.A.5 (La.), 2008. The decision affirmed the verdict of $14 million that the jury awarded to Thompson in his suit against the New Orleans District Attorney's Office. The verdict was appealed to the entire Fifth Circuit, which divided 8–8 on the question of whether these damages were appropriate on the facts of Thompson's case (The issue was not whether evidence had been suppressed but whether the suppression was part of a pattern of such behavior in the District Attorney's Office.). Since the consequence of an evenly divided appellate court is that the lower court ruling stands, the District Attorney's Office sought review, which was granted by the United States Supreme Court. That Court heard arguments in the case on January 8, 2011. The Supreme Court reversed by a vote of 5–4, the majority taking the view that the evidence did not establish a sufficient pattern of prosecutorial misbehavior to constitute a violation of the United States Constitution. *Connick v. Thompson,* 131 S.Ct. 1350 (2011). See Savage, "Supreme Court Takes Dim View."

NOTES TO CHAPTER 6

1. Canfield, "Bruce Vroman Acquitted of All Assault Charges in East Greenbush Fight."

2. "All-White Jury Chosen in PA Hate Crime Trial."

3. "Jury Finds Immigrant's Killing Wasn't a Hate Crime."

4. Freakonomics, "Innocent until Proven Guilty."

5. Steffensmeier and Demuth, "Ethnicity and Sentencing Outcomes in the U.S. Federal Courts"; Mustard, "Racial, Ethnic, and Gender Disparities in Sentencing." See also Levine, "The Impact of Racial Demography." For more comprehensive reviews of the literature on race and dispositional decisions in the criminal justice system, see Walker, Spohn, and DeLone, *The Color of Justice*; Zatz, "The Changing Forms"; Cole, "No Equal Justice."

6. Devine et al., "Strength of Evidence"; Myers and Talarico, "The Social

Context of Racial Discrimination in Sentencing"; and Wilbanks, "The Myth of a Racist Criminal Justice System."

7. Baldus, Pulaski, and Woodworth, "Comparative Review of Death Sentence." See also Feild, "Rape Trials and Jurors' Decisions," which found that jurors are more likely to convict Black defendants in rape cases involving White victims, and Lynch and Haney, "Discrimination and Instructional Comprehension," which found in mock jury trials that White jurors were more likely to sentence Black defendants to death compared to White defendants.

8. Uhlman, *Racial Justice*, concluded that Black trial court judges were not notably distinct in their decision making and sentencing patterns. Subsequent studies introducing better controls for legal and contextual factors revealed conflicting results. Some find that minority judges do not treat defendants differently than White judges (Walker and Barrow, "The Diversification of the Federal Bench"), and some find evidence that minority and White judges *both* sentence minority defendants more severely than White defendants (Spohn, "Sentencing Decisions of Black and White Judges"). Others do find race-related judicial decision-making differences, such as evidence that non-White judges sentence non-White defendants more leniently than White defendants (Welch, Combs, and Gruhl, "Do Black Judges Make a Difference?"), sentence non-White defendants more harshly than White defendants (Steffensmeier and Britt, "Judge's Race and Judicial Decision Making"), and sentence all defendants more consistently than White judges (Holmes et al., "Judges' Ethnicity and Minority Sentencing"). Some find that Black and Hispanic judges generally favor the defense at higher rates than White judges (Gottschall, "Carter's Judicial Appointments"), whereas others report that non-White judges are distinctly sensitive to specific defendant claims of procedural misconduct, such as the use of inappropriate police procedures (Scherer, "Blacks on the Bench"). Recent research suggests that the racial demographics of court workgroups may also impact racial disparities in sentence outcomes, with decreased disparities found in courts with more racially balanced work forces; see Ward, Farrell, and Rousseau, "Does Racial Balance in Workforce Representation Yield Equal Justice?" For a comprehensive review of the vast empirical literature on juror race and racial bias in decision making, see Bowers, Steiner, and Sandys, "Death Sentencing in Black and White."

9. For information on the demographic characteristics reported in the U.S. census see http://www.census.gov/population/www/documentation/twps0056/twps0056.html.

10. In the NCSC data, 1.6 percent of defendants were of unknown race, 10.3 percent were White non-Hispanic, 24. 5 percent were White Hispanic, 54.2 percent were Black non-Hispanic, 3.9 percent were Black Hispanic, .6 percent were Asian, and 4.8 percent were other races. The NCSC jurisdictions were not entirely representative of the races of defendants in large urban areas. As of 2004, the distribution by race of criminal defendants in the seventy-five largest urban areas was White non-Hispanic 29 percent, Hispanic (any race) 28 percent, Black (non-Hispanic) 42 percent, and other 2 percent. For information on the demographic breakdown of defendants in large urban courts, see Kykelhal and Cohen, *Felony Defendants*. The NCSC jurisdictions had higher percentages of Black defendants and considerably lower percentages of White defendants than in large urban areas nationally.

11. See table 4, http://www.census.gov/population/www/cen2000/briefs/phc-t6/index.html. In the NCSC survey, researchers divided race into six categories, distinguishing between White–not Hispanic and White Hispanic as well as between Black–not Hispanic and Black Hispanic. The census data did not indicate distinctions between Hispanic White and non-White. In the text, for purposes of comparison with the overall population (and with Kalven and Zeisel), we reported the presence in the sample of defendants identified in the NCSC study as White or Black–not Hispanic.

12. The ratio has actually improved slightly over the years. In the NCSC survey, Black defendants were present at a rate less than twice their presence in the overall population; whereas in Kalven and Zeisel's survey, they were present at a rate 2.25 times their presence in the national population.

13. The Supreme Court of the United States has struggled with the issue of how to assure nondiscrimination in the selection of jurors. Complicating the problem is the widespread availability of entirely discretionary jury strikes, or peremptory challenges in the language of the law. In 1965, in a case involving an all-White jury in an Alabama death case involving a Black defendant, the Court ruled that the prosecution's use of peremptory challenges to eliminate all Blacks from a jury *did not* violate the United States Constitution unless the defendant could prove that the strikes were the result of a consistent policy applied across a broad number of cases. *Swain v. Alabama*, 380 U.S. 202 (1965). Twenty-one years later, in 1986, in *Batson v. Kentucky*, 476 U.S. 79 (1986), another case involving an all-White jury, the Court effectively overruled *Swain* by holding that defendants did not have to show that the jury strikes in their cases were the product of a policy broadly applied to many cases. The Constitution was violated whenever defendants could show that prosecutors

exercised their discretionary challenges to eliminate Black jurors in their particular cases and the prosecutors could not produce race-neutral justification for these actions. Although the shift from *Swain* to *Batson* appears significant, the ease with which prosecutors can articulate nonracial reasons for the exercise of peremptory challenges has forestalled any dramatic breakthrough in judicial willingness to consider the possibility of racial bias in the selection of jurors. The Court returned again to the topic in 2005 in *Miller-El v. Dretke*, 545 U.S. 231 (2005), and companion cases and again ruled that some states were still making it too difficult for those challenging racial discrimination in the selection of juries to establish violations of the Constitution.

14. The eight juries acquitted in two cases and convicted in the other six. Only one case, a conviction, involved a Black defendant and a White victim.

15. Baldus et al., "Racial Discrimination and the Death Penalty."

16. The same is true if we accept the *jury's* assessment of the weight of the evidence. When the juries considered the cases in equipoise, Black defendants were acquitted 61 percent of the time (11/18), other defendants 59 percent of the time (13/22).

17. The juries acquitted 23.9 percent (21/88) of the Black defendants with records who did not testify as contrasted to 29.3 percent (19/65) of the non-Black defendants in this category. Thus, among the group of defendants with records that were not known to the juries, the judges were 100 percent (23/11.6) more likely to acquit defendants who were not Black while the juries acquitted defendants of other races at a rate 22 percent (29.3/23.9) greater than the rate at which they acquitted Black defendants.

18. King, "Postconviction Review of Jury Discrimination," and Bonazalli. "Jury Selection and Bias."

19. Chadee, "Race, Trial Evidence, and Jury Decision Making."

20. Sommers, "On Racial Diversity and Group Decision Making," found that experimental jurors deliberating on a case involving a Black defendant shared more information and were more lenient toward Black defendants than all-White juries.

21. Using the same data analyzed here, Eisenberg et al. (2005) examined the relationship between racial composition of juries and judge-and-jury conviction levels, finding weak but significant relationships between the percentage of the jury that is Black and judge convictions in cases where juries would acquit, though these findings did not consistently survive more sophisticated multivariate analyses.

22. If we look at guilty verdicts specifically, when juries had no Black

members, they agreed with the judges' verdicts of guilt 88 percent (51/58) of the time. When juries were at least one-third Black, they agreed with the judges' findings of guilty in 64.5 percent (49/76) of the cases. When the *judges* would have acquitted, juries agreed at approximately the same rate regardless of their racial composition. When the judges would have found the defendants not guilty, juries with no Blacks agreed 71.5 percent of the time (15/21), while juries that were at least one-third Black agreed 67 percent of the time (8/12).

NOTES TO CHAPTER 7

1. The judges responding to the Kalven and Zeisel survey viewed 5 percent of all cases as clear for acquittal, 43 percent as close, and 52 percent as clear for conviction. Fifty years later, the judges responding to the NCSC survey viewed nearly 60 percent of the cases as strong for the prosecution but divided the remaining cases differently, viewing 15 percent as strong for the defense and slightly more than 25 percent as in equipoise

2. The lawyers agreed with one another that the defense had strong cases in 9 percent of the cases and the juries acquitted more than eight times out of ten (81 percent). The prosecutors and judges agreed that the defense cases were strong in 7.3 percent of the cases, but the juries acquitted in only a little more than two-thirds of the cases (11/16 = 69 percent). The judges and defense counsel, on the other hand, went to the head of the class: they assessed 8 percent of the cases as strong for the defense, and the juries acquitted more than nine times out of ten (15/16 = 94 percent).

3. The judges and the lawyers did not do better in terms of assessing the strength of the cases: they agreed on the thrust of the evidence (i.e., for the defendant, for the prosecution, or in equipoise) in slightly more than one-half of the cases. The judges and prosecutors agreed that the cases were strong for the prosecution or strong for the defense or in equipoise in 127 out of 233 cases, or 57 percent; the judges and defense counsel agreed in 53.3 percent of the cases.

4. Kalven and Zeisel, *The American Jury*, 342, note 8.

5. Ibid., 212, table 66.

6. Kalven and Zeisel's table 66 shows the analysis of cases in which the juries *disagreed* with the judges. From this table it is possible to calculate that, in disagreement cases, juries were more likely to have sympathy for White defendants than Black defendants and less likely to find White defendants

unsympathetic than Black defendants. Because jury sympathy is a factor that results in juries acquitting when judges would convict, we can speculate that Kalven and Zeisel's data probably revealed a higher acquittal rate for Whites than for Blacks. They never said so explicitly, and we can only speculate as to why they did not

7. Frank et al., "Individual and Small-Group Accuracy," found that when students were assigned to detect lies either individually or as part of a small group that deliberated and came to a group consensus, students in the small groups were more accurate in their judgments than those attempting to detect lies individually. Small-group participants also reported greater confidence in their decisions than did individual decision makers. Individuals—even if trained—rarely do better than chance in determining whether someone is not telling the truth. Kassin, "Human Judges of Truth, Deception, and Credibility."

8. Fisher, "The Jury's Rise as Lie Detector."

9. Defendants who refused to plead on the grounds of innocence but did not testify at trial were acquitted 51.7 percent (16/31) of the time; those who refused to plead on the grounds of innocence and did testify at trial were acquitted 50 percent (24/48) of the time. Further, the defendants both refused to plead on the grounds of innocence and testified along with at least one witness in 17.2 percent of the cases (36/209). The juries acquitted in 19 of the 36 (52.8 percent) cases in this category.

NOTES TO APPENDIX A

1. Eisenberg et al., "Judge-Jury Agreement." The NCSC data included information from four sources: (1) case data, including the type of charge, sentence range, jury decision, and demographic information about the defendant(s) and the victim(s), voir dire, trial evidence and procedures, and jury deliberations; (2) judge questionnaires, including in part 1 (before jury verdict) information about the verdicts judges would have reached in bench trials, evaluation of the evidence, case complexity, attorney skill, and likelihood that the jury would hang and in part 2 (after jury verdict) reaction to the verdict and experience on the bench; (3) attorney questionnaires, including assessment of voir dire, case complexity, attorney skill, evaluation of the evidence, reaction to the verdict, and experience in legal practice; and (4) juror questionnaires, including individual juror responses about case complexity, attorney skill, evaluation of the evidence, formation of opinion, the dynamics

of the deliberations including the first and final votes, juror participation, conflict, reaction to verdict, opinion about applicable law, assessment of criminal justice in the community, and demographic information.

2. Givelber and Farrell, "Judges and Juries."

3. Because the second survey was the one in which judges were asked whether the cases were close or clear, it seems likely that the figures about disagreement in clear cases were based on that survey. Kalven and Zeisel (*The American Jury*) did not discuss disagreements in clear cases as a distinct category, although they noted that as a matter of theory, disagreements in clear cases should be disagreements based exclusively on values, a phenomenon that they identified as occurring in 24 percent of all cases in both surveys. They noted that the second survey indicated that disagreements occurred in 25 percent of all cases that judges designated as clear (164, note 2). The figure for all disagreements (both normal and cross-over) in Kalven and Zeisel was 22 percent (58).

Bibliography

Abramson, Jeffrey. *We, the Jury.* New York: Basic Books, 1994.

"All-White Jury Chosen in PA Hate Crime Trial." *The Guardian*, AP Foreign, April 22, 2009.

Alschuler, Albert, and J. R. Rodriguez. "Jury Nullification." MS. University of Chicago, 1998.

American Bar Association. *Standards for Criminal Justice*, 3rd ed.: *Prosecution Function and Defense Function.* Chicago: American Bar Association, 1993.

Ayres, B. Drummond. "Civil Jury Finds Simpson Liable in Pair of Killings." *New York Times*, February 5, 1997.

Bakken, Tim. "Truth and Innocence Procedures to Free Innocent Persons: Beyond the Adversarial System." *U. Michigan J. Law Reform* 41 (2008): 547–83.

Baldus, David, C. Pulaski, and G. Woodworth. "Comparative Review of Death Sentences: An Empirical Study of the Georgia Experience." *Journal of Criminal Law and Criminology* 74 (1983): 661–753.

Baldus, David, George Woodworth, David Neil Zuckerman, Alan Weiner, and Barbara Broffitt. "Racial Discrimination and the Death Penalty in the Post-Furman Era: An Empirical and Legal Overview with Recent Findings from Philadelphia." *Cornell Law Review* 83 (1999): 1638–1770.

Baldwin, John, and Michael McConville. *Jury Trials.* Gloucestershire, UK: Clarendon, 1979.

Barnett, Arnold. "Some Distribution Patterns for the Georgia Death Sentence." *University of California Davis Law Review* 18 (1985): 1327–74.

Baumer, Eric, Steven Messner, and Richard Felson. "The Role of Victim Characteristics in the Disposition of Murder Cases." *Justice Quarterly* 17 (2000): 281–308.

Berman, Douglas. "Now That O. J. Simpson Has Been Found Guilty, Should His Sentence Be Enhanced Based on His (Acquitted) Prior Killings?" *Sentencing Law and Policy* (October 2008), http://sentencing.typepad.com/

sentencing_law_and_policy/2008/10/now-that-oj-sim.html (accessed October 10, 2008).

Bibas, Stephanos. "Plea Bargaining outside the Shadow of the Trial." *Harvard Law Review* 117 (2004): 2465–2547.

Black, Donald. *Social Justice*. New York: Oxford University Press, 1989.

Blackstone, William. *Commentaries on the Laws of England (1765–1769)*. Book 4, *Public Wrongs*. Philadelphia: Lippincott, 1908.

Blanck, Peter David. "What Empirical Research Tells Us: Studying Judges' and Juries' Behavior." *American University Law Review* 40 (1991): 775–804.

Boland, Barbara, Paul Mahanna, and Ronald Sones. *The Prosecution of Felony Arrests*. Washington, DC: Bureau of Justice Statistics, 1992.

Bonazzoli, Juliet. "Jury Selection and Bias: Debunking Invidious Stereotypes through Science." *Quarterly Law Review* 18 (1998–1999): 247–305.

Bornstein, Brian H., and Sean G. McCabe. "Jurors of the Absurd? The Role of Consequentiality in Jury Simulation." *Florida State University Law Review* 32 (2005): 443–68.

Bowers, Josh. "Punishing the Innocent." *University of Pennsylvania Law Review* 156 (2008): 1117–80.

Bowers, William, Benjamin Steiner, and Marla Sandys. "Death Sentencing in Black and White: An Empirical Analysis of the Role of Jurors' Race and Jury Racial Composition." *Journal of Constitutional Law* 3 (2001): 171–275.

Brick, Michael. "Jury Rules One Way, Judge Another in Mob Killing." *New York Times*, December 15, 2007. http://www.nytimes.com/2007/12/15/nyregion/15mob.html?_r=1&ref=nyregion.

Broeder, David. "Occupational Expertise and Biases Affecting Jury Behavior: A Preliminary Look. *New York University Law Review* 40 (1965): 1079–1100.

——. "Plaintiff's Family Status as Affecting Juror Behavior: Some Tentative Thoughts." *Journal of Public Law* 14 (1965): 131–41.

——. "Previous Jury Trial Service Affecting Juror Behavior." *Insurance Law Journal* (1965): 138–44.

——. "The Negro in Court." *Duke Law Journal* (1965): 19–31.

——. "The University of Chicago Jury Project." *University of Nebraska Law Review* 38 (1959): 744–60.

Brown, Darryl. K. "Jury Nullification within the Rule of Law." *Minnesota Law Review* 81 (1997): 1152–1200.

Bucke, Thomas, Robert Street, and David Brown. *The Right of Silence: The Im-*

pact of the Criminal Justice and Public Order Act 1994; Research, Development, and Statistics Directorate Report. London: Home Office, 1999.

Burnett, Ann, and Diane M. Badzinski. "Judge Nonverbal Communication on Trial: Do Mock Trial Jurors Notice?" *Journal of Communication* 55 (2005): 209–24.

Burns, Robert P. *A Theory of the Trial.* Princeton, NJ: Princeton University Press, 1999.

California Penal Code. West 1985 and Supplement 2005.

Canfield, Dave. "Bruce Vroman Acquitted of All Assault Charges in East Greenbush Fight." *The Record* (Troy, NY), November 13, 2010. http://www.troyrecord.com/articles/2010/11/13/news/doc4cde334310481408058491.txt?viewmode=fullstory (accessed November 2010).

Chadee, Derek. "Race, Trial Evidence, and Jury Decision Making." *Caribbean Journal of Criminology and Social Psychology* 1 (1996): 59–86.

Cohen, Thomas, and Tracey Kyckelhahn. *Felony Defendants in Large Urban Counties, 2006.* Washington, DC: Bureau of Justice Statistics, 2010.

Cohen, Thomas H., and Brian A. Reaves. *Felony Defendants in Large Urban Counties, 2002.* Washington, DC: Bureau of Justice Statistics, 2006.

Cole, David. *No Equal Justice: Race and Class in the American Criminal Justice System.* New York: New Press, 1999.

Corbin, Harold H. "The Jury on Trial." *American Bar Association* 14 (1928): 507–12.

Curtis, Charles P. "The Trial Judge and the Jury." *Vanderbilt Law Review* 5 (1952): 150–66.

Damaska, Mirjan. "Evidentiary Barriers to Conviction and Two Models of Criminal Procedure: A Comparative Study." *University of Pennsylvania Law Review* 121 (1972): 508–89.

Dershowitz, Alan. *The Best Defense.* New York: Warner Books, 1982.

Devine, Dennis, Jennifer Buddenbaum, Stephanie Houp, Nathan Studebaker, and Dennis P. Stolle. "Strength of Evidence, Extraevidentiary Influence, and the Liberation Hypothesis: Data from the Field." *Law and Human Behavior* 33 (2009): 144–45.

Diamond, Shari Seidman. "Order in the Court: Consistency in Criminal-Court Decisions," in *The Master Lecture Series: Psychology and the Law,* ed. C. James Scheier and Barbara L. Hammonds. Washington, DC: American Psychological Association, 1983, 123–46.

Dolan, Maura, and Caitlin Liu. "Acquitted but Not Declared Innocent." *Los Angeles Times,* January 31, 2003.

Eisenberg, Theodore, Paula Hannaford-Agor, Valerie Hans, Nicole Waters, G. Thomas Munsterman, Stewart J. Schwab, and Martin T. Wells. "Judge-Jury Agreement in Criminal Cases: A Partial Replication of Kalven and Zeisel's *The American Jury.*" *Empirical Legal Studies* 2, no. 1 (2005): 171–206. http://ssrn.com/abstract=593941 (accessed September 15, 2006).

Eisenstein, James, and Herbert Jacob. *Felony Justice: An Organizational Analysis of Criminal Courts.* Boston: Little, Brown, 1977.

Farrell, Ronald A., and Victoria L. Swigert. "Prior Offense Record as a Self-Fulfilling Prophecy." *Law and Society Review* 12 (1978): 443–44.

Federal Rules of Criminal Procedure, vol. 23a.

Field, Hubert. "Rape Trials and Jurors' Decisions: A Psycholegal Analysis of the Effects of Victim, Defendant, and Case Characteristics." *Law and Human Behavior* 3 (1979): 261–84.

Filosa, Gwen. "N.O. Man Cleared in '84 Murder: New Trial in Liuzza Killing Brings an Emotional End to Epic Case." *New Orleans Times Picayune,* May 9, 2003. http://truthinjustice.org/John-Thompson.htm (accessed November 2010).

Finkel, Norman. *Commonsense Justice.* Cambridge, MA: Harvard University Press, 1995.

Fischer, George. "The Jury's Rise as Lie Detector." *Yale Law Journal* 107 (1997): 575–713.

Fisher, Stanley Z. "Convictions of Innocent Persons in Massachusetts: An Overview." *Boston University Public Interest Legal Journal* 12 (2002): 1–72.

Frank, Jerome. *Courts on Trial.* Princeton, NJ: Princeton University Press, 1949.

Frank, Mark, Thomas Hugh Feeley, Nicole Paolantonio, and Timothy Servoss. "Individual and Small Group Accuracy in Judging Deceptive and Truthful Communication." *Group Decision and Negotiation* 13 (2004): 45–59.

Freakonomics. "Innocent until Proven Guilty." http://freakonomics.blogs.nytimes.com/2010/09/22/innocent-until-proven-guilty (accessed January 15, 2011).

Freedman, Monroe H. "Professional Responsibility of the Defense Lawyer: The Three Hardest Questions." *Michigan Law Review* 64 (1966): 1469–84.

Freiss, Steve. "After Apologies, Simpson Is Sentenced to at Least 9 Years for Armed Robbery." *New York Times,* December 6, 2008.

Galanter, Marc. "Why the Haves Come Out Ahead: Speculations on the Limits of Legal Change." *Law and Society Review* 9 (1974): 95–160.

Gastwirth, J., and Michael Sinclair. "A Re-examination of the 1966 Kavel and

Zeisel Study of Judge-Jury Agreements and Disagreements and Their Cases." *Law, Probability, and Risk* 3 (2004): 169–91.

Givelber, Daniel. "Lost Innocence: Speculation and Data about Acquittals." *American Criminal Law Review* 42 (2005): 1167–99.

———. "Meaningless Acquittals, Meaningful Convictions: Do We Reliably Acquit the Innocent?" *Rutgers L. Rev.* 49 (1997): 1317–96.

———. "Punishing Protestations of Innocence." *American Criminal Law Review* 37 (2000): 1363–1408.

Givelber, Daniel, and Amy Farrell. "Judges and Juries: The Defense Case and Differences in Acquittal Rates." *Law and Social Inquiry* 33 (2008): 31–53.

Glaberson, William G. "'Lie or Die'—Aftermath of a Murder: Justice, Safety, and the System; A Witness Is Slain in Brooklyn." *New York Times*, July 6, 2003.

Gottschall, Jon. "Carter's Judicial Appointments: The Influence of Affirmative Action and Merit Selection on Voting on the U.S. Court of Appeals." *Judicature* 67, no. 4 (1983): 165–73.

Green, C. E. "Jury Injustice." *Judicial Review* 20 (1908): 132–39.

Greenberg, Jack. *Race Relations and American Law*. New York: Columbia University Press, 1959.

Gross, Samuel. "Souter Passant, Scalia Rampant: Combat in the Marsh." *Michigan L. Rev. First Impressions* (2006): 67; http://www.michiganlawreview.org/articles/souter-passant-scalia-rampant-combat-in-the-em-marsh-em.

Gross, Samuel R. "Loss of Innocence: Eyewitness Identification and Proof of Guilt." *Journal of Legal Studies* 16 (1987): 410–50.

Gross, Samuel R., Kristen Jacoby, Daniel Matheson, Nicholas Montgomery, and Sujata Patil. "Exonerations in the United States, 1989 through 2003." *Journal of Criminal Law and Criminology* 95 (2005): 523–60.

Gross, Samuel R., and Barbara O'Brien. "Frequency and Predictors of False Conviction: Why We Know So Little, and New Data on Capital Cases." *J. Empirical Legal Stud.* 5 (2008): 927–62.

Hall, Connor. "The Present-Day Jury: A Defense." *American Bar Association* 10 (1924): 111–14.

Hannaford-Agor, Paula, and Valerie Hans. "Nullification at Work? A Glimpse from the National Center for State Courts Study of Hung Juries." *Chicago Kent Law Review* 78 (2003): 1249–77.

Hannaford-Agor, Paula, Valerie Hans, Nicole Mott, and G. Thomas Munstermann. *Are Hung Juries a Problem? Evaluation of Hung Juries in Bronx County, New York, Los Angeles County, California, Maricopa County, Ari-*

zona, and Washington, D.C., 2000–2002. Ann Arbor, MI: Inter-University Consortium for Political and Social Research, 2002.

Hans, Valerie, and N. Vidmar. *Judging the Jury.* Cambridge, MA: Perseus, 1991.

———. " 'The American Jury' at Twenty-Five Years." *Law and Social Inquiry 16* (1991): 323–50.

Hastie, Reid. "The Role of 'Stories' in Civil Jury Judgments." *University of Michigan Journal of Law Reform* 32 (1999): 227–39.

Hastie, Reid, and Nancy Pennington. "The O. J. Simpson Stories: Behavioral Scientists' Reflections on *People v. Orenthal James Simpson." Colorado Law Review* 67 (1996): 957–75.

Hastie, Reid, and Kenneth Rasinksi. "The Concept of Accuracy in Social Judgment," in *The Social Psychology of Knowledge,* ed. Daniel Bar-Tal and Arie W. Kruglanski. Cambridge: Cambridge University Press, 1988, 193–208.

Heber Smith, R., and R. Erhmann. "The Criminal Courts," in *Criminal Justice in Cleveland: Reports of the Cleveland Foundation Survey of the Administration of Criminal Justice in Cleveland, Ohio,* ed. R. Round and F. Frankfurter. Cleveland, OH: Cleveland Foundation, 1923, 236–302.

Heuer, Larry, and Steven Penrod. "Trial Complexity." *Law and Human Behavior* 18 (1994): 29–51.

Holmes, Malcolm D., Harmon M. Hosch, Howard C. Daudistel, Dolores A. Perez, and Joseph B. Graves. "Judges' Ethnicity and Minority Sentencing: Evidence Concerning Hispanics." *Social Science Quarterly* 74 (1993): 496–506.

Innocence Project. Benjamin Cardozo School of Law (2008), http://www .innocenceproject.org/know (accessed December 10, 2009).

Johnson, Sheri. "Black Innocence and the White Jury." *Michigan Law Review* 83 (1985): 1611–1708.

"Jury Finds Immigrant's Killing Wasn't a Hate Crime." Telegraph Associated Press, May 9, 2009. http://www.telegram.com/article/20090503/NEWS/905030434/1052#ixzz16xfiiccz (accessed November 2010).

Kalven, Harry. "The Dignity of the Civil Jury Trial." *University of Virginia Law Review* 50 (1964): 1055–75.

Kalven, Harry Jr., and Hans Zeisel. *The American Jury.* Chicago: University of Chicago Press, 1971.

———. *The American Jury.* Boston: Little, Brown, 1966.

Kassin, Saul M. "Human Judges of Truth, Deception, and Credibility: Confident but Erroneous." *Cardozo Law Review* 23 (2001): 809, 811–20.

Keil, Thomas J., and Gennaro F. Vito. "Race, Homicide Severity, and Application of the Death Penalty: A Consideration of the Barnett Scale." *Criminology* 27 (1989): 511–36.

Kerr, Norbert L., Robert W. Hymes, Alonzo B. Anderson, and James E. Weathers. "Defendant-Juror Similarity and Mock Juror Judgments." *Law and Human Behavior* 19 (1989): 545–67.

King, Nancy. "Postconviction Review of Jury Discrimination: Measuring the Effects of Juror Race on Jury Decisions." *Michigan Law Review* 92 (1993): 63–130.

Kressel, Neil J., and Dorit F. Kressel. *Stack and Sway: The New Science of Jury Consulting*. New York: Basic Books, 2004.

Kyckelhahn, Tracey, and Thomas Cohen. *Felony Defendants in Large Urban Counties, 2004*. Washington, DC: Bureau of Justice Statistics, 2008.

Lagorio, Christine. "No Apology for Robert Blake Jury." *Los Angeles Times*, March 24, 2005.

Leipold, Andrew. "Why Are Federal Judges So Acquittal Prone?" *Washington Law Quarterly* 83 (2005): 151–227.

———. "The Problem of the Innocent, Acquitted Defendant." *Northeastern University Law Review* 94 (2000): 1324–26.

Leo, Richard, and John P. Gould. "Studying Wrongful Convictions: Learning from Social Science." *Ohio State Journal of Criminal Law* 7 (2009): 7–29.

Levine, James P. "The Impact of Racial Demography on Jury Verdicts in Routine Criminal Cases, the System," in *Black and White: Exploring the Connections between Race, Crime, and Justice*. New York: Praeger, 2000, 153–71.

———. "Jury Toughness: The Impact of Conservatism on Criminal Court Verdicts." *Crime and Delinquency* 29 (1983): 71–87.

Lynch, Gerard E. "Our Administrative System of Criminal Justice." *Fordham Law Review* 66 (1998): 2117–51.

Lynch, Mona, and Craig Haney. "Discrimination and Instructional Comprehension: Guided Discretion, Racial Bias, and the Death Penalty." *Law and Human Behavior* 24 (2000): 337–58.

MacCoun, Robert J. "Epistemological Dilemmas in the Assessment of Legal Decision Making." *Law and Human Behavior* 23 (1999): 723–30.

MacCoun, Robert J., and Norbert Kerr. "Asymmetric Influence in Mock Jury Deliberation: Jurors' Bias for Leniency." *Journal of Personality and Social Psychology* 54 (1988): 21–33.

Maguire, Kathleen, and Ann L. Pastore. *Sourcebook for Criminal Justice Statistics,* Albany, NY: Hindelang Criminal Justice Research Center, 1999.

Malamud, Bernard. *The Fixer*. New York: Dell, 1966.

McCabe, Sarah, and Robert Purves. *The Jury at Work: A Study of a Series of Jury Trials in Which the Defendant Was Acquitted*. Oxford: Blackwell, 1972.

McConville, Michael. *The Case for the Prosecution: Police Suspects and the Construction of Criminality*. New York: Routledge, 1991.

Medwed, Daniel. "Innocentrism." *University of Illinois Law Forum* 2008: 1549–72.

Mills, James. "I Have Nothing to Do with Justice." *Life*, March 12, 1971, 56–58, 61–62.

Munsterman, Thomas, Stewart J. Schwab, and Martin T. Wells. "Judge-Jury Agreement in Criminal Cases: A Partial Replication of Kalven and Zeisel's 'The American Jury.'" *Empirical Legal Studies* 2 (2005): 171–206. http:// ssrn .com/abstract=593941 (accessed September 15, 2006).

Mustard, David. "Racial, Ethnic, and Gender Disparities in Sentencing: Evidence from the U.S. Federal Courts." *Journal of Law and Economics* 44 (April 2001): 285–314.

Myers, Martha. "Rule Departures and Making Law: Juries and Their Verdicts." *Law and Society Review* 13 (1979): 781–97.

Myers, Martha, and Susette Talarico. "The Social Contexts of Racial Discrimination in Sentencing." *Social Problems* 33 (1986): 236–51.

National Center for State Courts. *Caseload Highlights*. Williamsburg, VA: National Center for State Courts, 2001.

Oelsner, Lesley. "Justices Spurn States' Plea to Void Miranda Ruling." *New York Times*, March 24, 1977.

Packer, Herbert L. *The Limits of the Criminal Sanction*. Stanford, CA: Stanford University Press, 1968.

Papke, David R. "Conventional Wisdom: The Courtroom Trial in Popular Culture." *Marquette Law Review* 82 (1999): 471–89.

Pennington, Nancy, and Reid Hastie. "Evidence Evaluation in Complex Decision Making." *Journal of Personality and Social Psychology* 51 (1986): 242–58.

Perez, Jacob. *Tracking Offenders, 1990*. Washington, DC: Bureau of Justice Statistics, 1994.

Perkins, Rollin M. "Proposed Jury Changes in Criminal Cases." *Iowa Law Review* 16 (1930): 20–52.

Podlas, Kimberlianne. "'The CSI Effect': Exposing the Media Myth." *Fordham Intellectual Property, Media & Entertainment Law Journal* 16 (2006): 429–65.

Posner, Richard. *Frontiers of Legal Theory*. Cambridge, MA: Harvard University Press. 2004.

———. "An Economic Approach to the Law of Evidence." *Stanford Law Review* 51 (1999): 1477–1546.

———. *The Problem of Moral and Legal Theory*. Cambridge, MA: Harvard University Press, 1999.

———. *The Problems of Jurisprudence*. Cambridge, MA: Harvard University Press, 1990.

Pound, Roscoe. "Law in Books and Law in Action." *American Law Review* 44 (1910): 12–36.

President's Commission on Law Enforcement. *The Challenge of Crime in a Free Society*, ACJS/Anderson Monograph Series. Washington, DC: Commission on Law Enforcement and Administration of Justice, 1967.

Rafter, Nicole. *Shots in the Mirror: Crime Films and Society*. Oxford: Oxford University Press, 2000.

Rainville, Gerald, and Brian Reaves. *Felony Defendants in Large Urban Counties, 2000*. Washington, DC: Bureau of Justice Statistics, 2003.

"Reagan Seeks Judges with 'Traditional Approach.'" *U.S. News and World Report*, October 14, 1985.

Reaves, B. *Felony Defendants in Large Urban Courts, 1998*. Washington, DC: Bureau of Justice Statistics, 2001.

Reskin, Barbara, and Christy Visher. "The Impacts of Evidence and Extralegal Factors in Jurors' Decisions." *Law and Society Review* 20 (1986): 423–38.

Risinger, Michael "Innocents Convicted: An Empirically Justified Factual Wrongful Conviction Rate." *J. Criminal Law & Criminology* 97 (2007): 761–804.

———. "Unsafe Verdicts: The Need for Reformed Standards for the Trial and Review of Factual Innocence Claims." *Houston Law Review* 41 (2004): 1281–1326.

Robbenolt, Jennifer. "Evaluating Juries by Comparisons to Judges: A Benchmark for Judging?" *Florida State University Law Review* 32 (2005): 469–510.

Rosen, Jeffery. "After 'One Angry Woman.'" *University of Chicago Legal Forum* 1998: 179–95.

Savage, David "Supreme Court Takes Dim View of Suing Prosecutors." *Los Angeles Times*, January 9, 2011.

Scheck, Barry, Peter Neufeld, and Jim Dwyer. *Actual Innocence*. New York: New American Library, 2000.

Scherer, Nancy. "Blacks on the Bench." *Political Science Quarterly* 119 (2004): 655–74.

Schwartz, Louis B. "'Innocence': A Dialogue with Professor Sundby." *Hastings Law Journal* 41 (1989): 154–60.

Shellem, Pete. "Jailed Man Set Free after False Confession." *Harrisburg* (Pa.) *Patriot News*, January 9, 1993. http://truthinjustice.org/wm-kelly.htm.

Shifrel, S. "Brooklyn Baker's Mob Hit Sentence Overturned—for Second Time." *Daily News*, February 13, 2010. http://www.nydailynews.com/news/ny_crime/2010/02/13/2010-0213_bakers_mob_hit_sentence_tossed.html (accessed January 15, 2011).

———. "Judge Gives Baker Minimum after Slamming Jury for Clearing Co-Defendant." *New York Daily News*, April 22, 2008. http://www.nydaily news.com/news/ny_crime/2008/04/21/2008-04-21_judge_gives_baker_minimum_after_slamming.html.

Smith, Abbe. "Defending the Innocent." *Connecticut Law Review* 32 (2000): 485–522.

Sommers, Samuel R. "On Racial Diversity and Group Decision Making: Identifying Multiple Effects of Racial Composition on Jury Deliberations." *Journal of Personality and Social Psychology* 90 (2006): 597–612.

Sourcebook of Criminal Justice Statistics Online. Table 5.24, Criminal Defendants Disposed of in U.S. District Courts (2009), http://www.albany.edu/sourcebook/pdf/t5242009.pdf (accessed January 15, 2011).

———. Table 5.46, Percent Distribution of Felony Convictions in State Courts (2004). http://www.albany.edu/sourcebook/pdf/t5462004.pdf.

Special Committee on Criminal Justice in a Free Society. *Criminal Justice in Crisis: A Report to the American People and the American Bar on Criminal Justice in the United States: Some Myths, Some Realities, and Some Questions for the Future.* Chicago: American Bar Association, Criminal Section, 1988.

Spencer, Bruce D. "Estimating the Accuracy of Jury Verdicts." *Journal of Empirical Legal Studies* 4 (2007): 1–31.

Spohn, Cassia. "The Sentencing Decisions of Black and White Judges: Expected and Unexpected Similarities." *Law and Society Review* 24 (1990): 1197–1216.

Spohn, Cassia, and Jerry Cederblom. "Race and Disparities in Sentencing: A Test of the Liberation Hypothesis." *Justice Quarterly* 8 (1991): 305–26.

Steffensmeier, Darrell, and Charles Britt. "Judge's Race and Judicial Decision Making: Do Black Judges Sentence Differently?" *Social Science Quarterly* 82 (2001): 749–64.

———. "Ethnicity and Sentencing Outcomes in the U.S. Federal Courts: Who Is Punished More Harshly?" *American Sociological Review* 65 (2000): 705–29.

Stith, Kate. "The Risk of Legal Error in Criminal Cases: Some Consequences in the Asymmetry in the Right to Appeal." *University of Chicago Law Review* 57 (1990): 1–61.

Strodtbeck, Fred L., and L. Harmon Hook. "The Social Dimensions of a Twelve-Man Jury Table." *Sociometry* 24 (1961): 397–415.

Strodtbeck, Fred L., Rita M. James, and Charles Hawkins. "Social Status in Jury Deliberations." *American Sociological Review* 22 (1957): 713–19.

Strodtbeck, Fred, and Richard Mann. "Sex /Role Differentiation in Jury Deliberations." *Sociometry* 19 (1956): 3–11.

Stuntz, William J. "The Pathological Politics of Criminal Law." *Michigan Law Review* 100 (2001): 505–600.

———. "The Uneasy Relationship between Criminal Procedure and Criminal Justice." *Yale Law Journal* 107 (1997): 1–76.

Sunderland, Edson R. "The Inefficiency of the American Jury." *Michigan Law Review* 13 (1915): 302–16.

Surette, Ray. *Media, Crime, and Criminal Justice: Images and Realities.* Florence, KY: Wadsworth, 1992.

Tocqueville, Alexis de. *Democracy in America.* 3rd ed. Cambridge, MA: Sever and Francis, 1863.

Ugwuegbu, Denis Chimaeze E. "Racial and Evidential Factors in Juror Attribution of Legal Responsibility." *Journal of Experimental Social Psychology* 15 (1979): 133–46.

Uhlman, Thomas. *Racial Justice: Black Judges and Defendants in an Urban Trial Court.* Lexington, MA: Lexington Books, 1979.

United States Attorneys' Manual. Washington, DC: United States Department of Justice, 2005.

United States Congress. Senate. Subcommittee on Internal Security. *Recording of Jury Deliberations*: Hearing before the Subcommittee on Internal Security. October 12, 1955, 84th Cong, 1st session, 1–258.

United States Department of Justice. *Felony Sentences in State Courts, 2000.* Washington, DC: Bureau of Justice Statistics, 2003.

Uviller, H. Richard. "Acquitting the Guilty: Two Case Studies on Jury Misgivings and the Misunderstood Standard of Proof." *Criminal Law Forum* 2 (1990): 1–43.

Vidmar, Neil. "Making Inferences about Jury Behavior from Jury Verdict

Statistics: Cautions about Lorelei Lied." *Law and Human Behavior* 18 (1994): 599–617.

Visher, Christy. "Juror Decision Making: The Importance of Evidence." *Law and Human Behavior* 11 (1987): 1–17.

Wagenaar, Willem A., Peter J. Van Koppen, and Hans F. M. Crombag. *Anchored Narratives: The Psychology of Criminal Evidence*. New York: St. Martin's, 1993.

Walker, Samuel, Cassia Spohn, and Miriam DeLone. *The Color of Justice: Race, Ethnicity, and Crime in America*. 3rd ed. Belmont, CA: Wadsworth/ Thomson Learning, 2004.

Walker, Thomas, and Deborah Barrow. "The Diversification of the Federal Bench: Policy and Process Ramifications." *Journal of Politics* 47 (1985): 596–617.

Ward, Geoff, Amy Farrell, and Danielle Rousseau. "Does Racial Balance in Workforce Representation Yield Equal Justice? Race Relations of Sentencing in Federal Court Organizations." *Law and Society Review* 43 (2009): 757–804.

Weinreb, Lloyd L. *Denial of Justice: Criminal Process in the United States*. New York: Free Press, 1977.

Welch, Susan, Michael Combs, and John Gruhl. "Do Black Judges Make a Difference?" *American Journal of Political Science* 32 (1988): 126–36.

Wigmore, John H. "A Program for the Trial of a Jury Trial." *Journal of the American Judicial Society* 12 (1929): 166–71.

Wilbanks, William. *The Myth of a Racist Criminal Justice System*. Monterey, CA: Brooks/Cole, 1987.

Wright, Ronald, and Marc Miller. "The Screening/Bargaining Tradeoff." *Stanford Law Review* 55 (2002): 29–118.

Zatz, Marjorie. "The Changing Forms of Racial/Ethnic Biases in Sentencing." *Journal of Research in Crime and Delinquency* 24 (1987): 69–92.

Zeisel, Hans. *The Limits of Law Enforcement*. Chicago: University of Chicago Press, 1982.

CASES CITED

Apprendi v. New Jersey, 530 U.S. 466 (2000)
Batson v. Kentucky, 476 U.S. 479 (1986)
Brady v. Maryland, 373 U.S. 83 (1963)
Brewer v. Williams, 430 U.S. 387 (1977)

Dowling v. United States, 493 U.S. 342 (1990)

Duncan v. Louisiana, 391 U.S. 145 (1968)

Ex Parte Brandley, 781 SW 2d 886, 896 (Tex. Cr. App. 1989)

Gideon v. Wainwright, 372 U.S. 335 (1963)

In re Winship, 397 U.S. 358 (1970)

Justices of Appellate Division, First Department v. Erdmann, 33 N.Y. 2d 559 (1973)

McClusky v. Kemp, 481 U.S. 279 (1987)

Miller-El v. Dretke, 545 U.S. 231 (2005)

Miranda v. Arizona, 384 U.S. 486, 543–44 (1966)

North Carolina v. Alford, 400 U.S. 25 (1970)

Pointer v. Texas, 380 U.S. 400 (1965)

Roper v. Simmons, 543 U.S. 551, 620 (2005)

Swain v. Alabama, 380 U.S. 202 (1965)

Taylor v. Louisiana, 419 U.S. 522 (1975)

United States v. Booker, 543 U.S. 220 (2005)

United States v. Sanges, 144 U.S. 310 (1892)

United States v. Watts, 519 U.S. 148 (1997)

Index

About the Authors

Daniel Givelber is Professor of Law and former Dean at Northeastern University School of Law. A founding member of the New England Innocence Project, he has also been involved in death-penalty litigation both through directing Northeastern's Certiorari Clinic and by the successful decade-long representation of a death row inmate.

Amy Farrell is Assistant Professor in the School of Criminology and Criminal Justice and the Associate Director of the Institute on Race and Justice at Northeastern University.